# The Death of Alex Barrack

## By Doris Barrack

Published in Great Britain in 2011 by
Doris Barrack and Ken Amphlett

ISBN 9780956335128

An environmentally friendly book printed and bound in England by
www.printondemand-worldwide.com

**Mixed Sources**
Product group from well-managed
forests, and other controlled sources
www.fsc.org Cert no. TT-COC-002641
© 1996 Forest Stewardship Council
FSC

PEFC Certified
This product is
from sustainably
managed forests
and controlled
sources
PEFC
PEFC/16-33-415
www.pefc.org

Dedicated to the memory of
Maureen Amphlett

*Of whom Alex once said*

"...Well, if she is only my cousin and not my aunt,
why is she so good to me?"

# CONTENTS

---

[1] William Cowper – Hope (1782)

# PREFACE
Justice or a can of Worms?

## OR
## INVITED TO DIE

Over fourteen years ago my son William Alexander Barrack aged twenty eight years, was unlawfully killed but his killers still go free. During all that wearisome period, I have tried so very hard to persuade the authorities be open with me about the cause and circumstances of his death, by using every legal means available to me, to obtain the fair and just hearing in a court of law to which I am entitled , but, I have failed. Instead my appeals and requests have been rejected and I have very painfully learned a very bitter truth, that all too often, it is the innocent families of murder victims who suffer the heartrending consequences of unlawful killings, forced to live with the knowledge that the named suspects are walking free and unpunished.

All too frequently the failure to prosecute arises from the reluctance of many servants of the State to admit that through carelessness and mismanagement of investigations they have made unreasonable decisions but, refuse to take the moral responsibility for their mistakes and will go to any lengths, including enlisting departmental heads, legal support and the use of Treasury funding, to wilfully block victims' families access to truth and justice.

Throughout these fourteen years I have been in the position that too many families are in today, trying to bring about a just closure to the distressing state of ambiguity raised by the recalcitrant officials of the justice system. Instead like them, I have been refused public funding, and therefore qualified legal advice, and have been forced into being my dead son's only advocate in attempting to bring the case into the courts for adjudication. Initially I acted in almost total ignorance of the relevant aspects of law as do most victims families, but learning all the way, I took on a prolonged, tenacious battle against those intractable officials who were not concerned with justice but were determined to maintain the cloak of secrecy, thrown over the cause and the sordid circumstances of my son's tragic death, for their own base ends.

This determination to maintain strict secrecy persists even today. However I have always known, even against all attempts to persuade me otherwise, that Alex's death was a criminal act, and recently there has been a somewhat tentative and probably an unintentional admission of a fact which I have known from the day of the coroner's inquest, that Alex's death was a homicide. This was confirmed in a letter to me from an MPS Information Access official, who described it as "an emotive murder needing to be conducted in strict secrecy".

That revelation has brought me no nearer to gaining access to the High Court for adjudication on my claim that my son's death was a homicide and to overturn the coroner's inappropriate verdict of "accidental death". A verdict used successfully by officials of the sources I have approached, to block the many avenues of appeal I have used in my attempt to bring closure to Alex's death. It is now obvious to me that such a closure will not come from the justice system and I have grown weary of such shenanigans. I am eighty-five years old and I want closure for my son's case, not for his sake because I am content in the certain knowledge that he now rests in the peace and tranquillity which was absent for many periods during his short life. No! I want peace of mind for myself, and only closure of my son's case will allow me to put it behind me, and have peace of mind for the remainder of my retirement years.

So, I intend in this book to reveal all that the authorities want to conceal, and allow the public to adjudicate on my case. It is based on the large volume of official and authentic documentation, from which I have compiled a comprehensive analysis of the facts, which in my opinion, prove conclusively that my son was murdered, during a lethal, sadomasochistic ritual, in which he was forced to participate. It will also provide the reason why such a veil of secrecy was laid over his death, which took place in the London flat of a Senior Crown Prosecutor who came under the protection of the DPP and the CPS.

It is also my intention to warn the public how an ordinary citizen, seeking only the justice guaranteed by the law for a unlawful killing of a loved one, can be enmeshed in a net of subterfuge and conspiracy, when officials of the Establishment are intent on interfering with the course of justice for their own reprehensible purposes, and unlawfully use public facilities and legal exemption clauses for this end.


Doris Barrack

# Justice

# A Can of Worms

Cartoon by
*Sheila Jackson*

**1968 – 1996**
**R.I.P**

# CHAPTER ONE

**Part 1 - Life in a two parent family**

William Alexander Barrack my only child who I loved dearly was homosexual and he claimed he was born to be so. I have never been absolutely convinced of that. I believe the people in and the circumstances in his life helped form his nature and his character, particularly during his childhood and adolescence, and influenced his sexual orientation into choosing the homosexual life which eventually led to his homicidal death. Hopefully I will give an insight into the detrimental effect on the emotional development of a parent's defection on a child or children. All too often in this situation very young children's emotional needs are unexpressed and overlooked in a general view that youngsters are resilient and will adapt. In my experience as with my son I have found that the deep physiological hurt such defection causes, surfaces during the sexual uncertainties of adolescence, and often results in adverse changes in character, and dire consequences on their attitude to family life.

Although I always called my son ALEC, while he lived in London he was known as ALEX, therefore, out of respect for his preference, I will refer to him as Alex throughout the book. I shall discuss in some length Alex's medical history and his childhood experiences, his physiological development and give my reasons why I think they influenced the uncertainties he had over his sexual orientation, throughout adolescence into his adult homosexuality. I believe they had great significance to the manner and the circumstance in which he died. They are also are of very great importance in supporting my interpretations of the medical and forensic evidence, police investigations and the coroner's and CPS decisions, and why I am convinced, that the police were directed by higher authorities into conducting the investigations into his death with such secrecy, that they denied Alex justice.

I think it possible that Alex's way of life began when he was dramatically and prematurely precipitated into the world at 9pm on the 23$^{rd}$ March 1968 by an emergency caesarean section in the Sorrento Pioneering Premature Baby Unit in Birmingham., His life ended dramatically when at the age of 28years, he was even more precipitously and prematurely forced to exit this world at about 1am on the 4$^{th}$ May 1996, by a sadomasochistic ritual held in the East London Flat of a Crown Senior Prosecutor. There is a cruel comparison between the two events in the nature of the actions and attitudes of the dedicated medical professionals who brought him into the world and those of the perverted individuals responsible for heedlessly sending him out of this world.

Both groups had a 'duty of care' but only the first group conscientiously carried out that duty to Alex when they strove to preserve the life of a desperately ill child in heart failure and weighing only 2lbs 4oz. This tiny baby's life hung in the balance for ten days, then his fragile hold on life suddenly weakened and he was speedily baptised by a Catholic Priest. However, after baptism to the great relief of parents and staff, Alex rallied and decided to live.

Alex's death though equally traumatic gave him no choice. It was inflicted on him. He died in a particularly horrible way struggling to breathe with a plastic head device secured over his head and he must have felt helpless and desperately afraid, when those responsible for his deadly situation ignored their "duty of care" and with callous indifference, allowed him to die of asphyxiation. However all that horror lay in the unknown future and will be described later.

The period following Alex's improvement though full of hope, was very difficult and emotional for both parents. Especially when Alex's father, then a Staff sergeant in the Army Medical Corp, was posted from Donnington Shropshire to Blacon in Cheshire which was even further away from Birmingham. When Alex was declared out of danger some days later, I left hospital to undertake the move to new army quarters, and, until he was ready to be discharged home after four more months, we saw Alex once a month. During all that time I never once held or touched Alex because, under the health rules then in operation, our visits were limited to viewing our son through the window of the premature baby unit as he lay in his incubator and later in a cot, through the glass window of the ward door.

Two days before Alex was discharged I was allowed to stay at the hospital and for the first time was allowed to nurse and feed him. He was still a little scrap of a baby weighing only five pounds when I dressed him in the doll sized clothes I had to make for him, and took him home.

Once settled at home Alex made better progress than expected. He was a contented baby but slept less than is usual. I had a problem at first because after so long in an incubator and isolation cots he did not take kindly to being held closely for feeding and it was some months before he allowed himself to be hugged. Also he was surprisingly hyperactive and did not like being restrained for too long and this created problems for me. It became obvious that his co-ordination and physical development were below normal and later on didn't match his determination to walk and climb and so led to frequent loss of balance and painful falls.   Through these experiences I learned he had a very low tolerance to pain and when he yelled the loudest he was the least hurt. With more serious injuries or painful conditions he tended to be very quiet and made little fuss.

When Alex was two years old he was still very small and unable to walk unaided and slow in talking but otherwise appeared to be in reasonably good health. I was worried though because after each of three childhood immunisations he had quite fierce reactions and required very careful nursing and observation. As I was a trained nurse I did this myself at home as I could give him the necessary care. These three reactions made me aware that he could be prone to other hypersensitive conditions and could potentially be an asthmatic.

I was right in my prognosis. When Alex was two and a half years old during a visit to the beach at Sunderland he had his first sight of the sea. His Nanna was holding him as he gazed in complete fascination at the incoming tide but as he turned his head towards me laughing with pleasure he winced and I saw he had, unbelievably quickly, developed extensive eczema around his mouth as reaction to the sea-air.  It was his first episode

17

of a skin condition which was eventually to become chronic. In the main his feet and hands were more severely affected during childhood and often with distressingly, prolonged episodes of intense itching and pain. The eczema became less severe as he left adolescence and he learned to treat the early symptoms himself.

The more serious condition of asthma occurred when he was five years old. Again we were in Sunderland where I was helping to nurse my terminally ill sister. It was a very severe attack, triggered in the doctor's opinion, by the emotional atmosphere generated by my elder sister's terminal condition. Asthma was also to become a lifelong condition for Alex and he had several very alarming episodes during his childhood. At fourteen he had a distressing and prolonged attack which brought him very near death from heart failure and it required several weeks of strict bed rest to stabilise his heart. Therefore it was quite understandable that he became moderately claustrophobic, panicking if his face was accidentally covered, or in confined conditions, for example he would not use lifts. As an adult living in London, on at least three occasions, the severity of the asthma attacks merited Alex's admission to hospital for emergency treatment.

The Sorrento medical staff had predicted incorrectly that Alex, statistically, would be a very small adult, he actually reached six feet, but he most certainly was very small and slight as a child. He was slow to walk and talk but when he did begin he advanced very quickly in both. He was obviously a very intelligent child but with a strong will and a determination do things in his own time and his own way without interference, a characteristic he never fully lost. He was artistic and imaginative and developed an almost insatiable thirst for knowledge. He never stopped asking searching questions and read avidly. Singularly though he only pursued with any depth those subjects which interested him, history old and modern, palaeontology, art and history of art and reading dictionaries. Later he was to develop into a talented, modern artist. Fiction held no interest for him but as a teenager he developed the usual liking for loud modern music and gigs.

This now brings me to just about the most difficult situation to describe which affected Alex's psychological development. I am very conscious that I do this from my own perspective but members of my family feel that my

18

observations are fair in the discussions we had on the unsatisfactory course of Alex's relations with his father.

Alex as I said was born into an army family and for the first two years his life was as normal as can be expected for a soldier's family. His father took a moderate interest in his son although he found his smallness quite off-putting at first, but became more confident in carrying him as Alex grew a little and lost his look of fragility. When Alex started to talk and walk he became his father's devoted follower. It was quite amusing to see this tiny child trotting beside his six foot two parent.

It was at this time Bill decided to leave the Army, against my wishes, and became a pharmaceutical representative in the Staffordshire area. I think that it was from this time on our family situation gradually deteriorated with an adverse effect on father and son relations and Alex's psychological development. The root cause of most of the subsequent problems arose from Bill's obsession with rugby; he was certainly built for rugby, but was also too involved with all its social aspects and enjoying his popularity within the team and the close comradeship peculiar to rugby players.

Before Alex was born Bill and I lived in Army quarters near Newport in Shropshire where Bill became an enthusiastic member of the local rugby club and because of this association, when he left the army, he decided we would live in Newport. I could see the problems this fixation on Newport rugby club would bring and was strongly against living so near, and it was certainly more practical for his work to find a house in the centre of Staffordshire. At my insistence we did look at several houses around Stafford but it was a waste of time. Bill was set on Newport and its Rugby Club and would not consider another area and so we bought a bungalow within walking distance of the club in a town and a sport I grew to dislike. This move established a pattern of life entirely suited to Alex's father but detrimental to our family life. He left for work before Alex woke and returned home late evening so spending little time with Alex during the week. Even at weekends Alex saw little of his father, as all Saturdays and Sunday mornings were devoted to rugby affairs during the winter playing season and in the summer he became a non-playing cricket club member.

Alex at quite a young age, seemed quite sensibly to accept that sport was out for him and concentrated on his mental interests and he tried to coax Bill into sharing in his childish activities. However Bill was often indifferent to Alex's interests and even derided his choice of hobbies. It did not shake Alex's attachment to Bill, even when he made it obvious to the child that he was disappointed in his inability to take part in sport.

Arguing over this was useless, Bill would rarely discuss the matter, in fact, any criticism usually led to him leaving the house taking the car and going to the club or a public house. Bill's attitude to Alex was hurtful to me and it seems I was always defending Alex against his father's disparagement of his son's preference for hobbies centred on subjects such as dinosaurs, ghosts, drawing and dictionaries. But then Bill is not an imaginative man but even so I considered he should have been proud of his son's advanced creative and artistic talents and encouraged him to improve. I know that Alex was often hurt by Bill's indifference but he never complained. I have wondered since if he considered it to be the norm for family life. It took years for him to realise that the failure in the relationship rested on Bill and not himself.

When Alex was almost five and a pupil at the Catholic Primary School, on economic grounds I went back to nursing as an industrial nurse, working the late shift and counting on Bill's promise to be home every evening with Alex. He rarely did so but I coped reasonably well with the aid of child minders, friends and family for about three years, until I was asked to work varying shifts. As this meant greater disruption in Alex's routine I left nursing and stayed home.

My being home all day was better for Alex's physical well being but I was troubled by the affect his father's absence had on him. Outside the home he was a polite boy, well liked by the neighbours and popular with his friends because of his story telling abilities and imaginative play. At home he slowly became more withdrawn and spent more time in his room than I thought was good. When his father did return home Alex continued to greet him eagerly and affectionately but generally went to his room discouraged when his affection was not returned. He still retained an undeserved devotion to his father, never criticised him but turned to our lovely natured dog Bertie, we had brought back from Army service in Malaya, to find comfort.

When Bill accepted a manager's post in Leeds I was delighted as I expected we would move to that city and looked forward to leaving Newport and its club. Unbelievably, as impractical as it was, Bill refused to move and as usual always looking to his own interests, and so set out a worse routine of work and rugby entirely suited to his own needs, not his family's. Now Alex and I hardly saw him as he was rarely home during the week, often staying nights in Leeds while Saturdays and Sundays were mainly devoted to rugby matches, social drinking and office work. When I applied pressure we three would occasionally spend a pleasant Sunday afternoon together, walking or at home listening to classical music and from this Alex developed a life long appreciation of Gregorian chants, probably I think, because it enhanced the rituals of his Catholic faith.

I do not want to create an impression that Alex's life was entirely unhappy because that would not be true. He and I had a loving relationship and he had a great deal of affection from my family especially my Mother and we shared many good times in relatives homes and often went on holiday with my niece Maureen and her husband Ken, (both before and after Bill left). However, some straight talking members of the family often made Bill feel uncomfortable by expressing their disapproval of his dedication to rugby and his lack of family commitment. Water off a duck's back really, once away from their criticism Bill reverted to type.

When Alex was nine it had become obvious to me that he was not happy at the Catholic Primary School he had attended from being four and a half. I was in the process of a change of school at his request but had to shelve this move when the biggest blow in both Alex's and my lives fell without warning. I discovered Bill was unfaithful with one of his Leeds based staff. Oddly, I suppose, until then I had trusted him implicitly, or perhaps I should say blindly and had not questioned his working arrangements and absences. When I challenged him though he denied vehemently that there was any affair, but he lied and used my so-called unfair accusations as an excuse to leave. When it was actually confirmed to be true by the woman herself, I began to realise that I should have seen the obvious signs long before I did, especially the significance of many phone calls from that particular female medical representative.

This happened in early September 1977 but Bill stayed in the home for six weeks until he had found a flat and made it comfortable for himself. A typically selfish action, without any thought of its affect on Alex who was at an age to understand something of the situation but lived in hope that his father would change his mind. It was a very difficult situation for me as Alex begged me repeatedly to get his Dad to stay but I could do nothing, even though for his sake I tried. All I could do was to comfort and support him. On the eve before his father departed Alex clung to me and literally begged "Mummy you won't leave me will you?" I promised him that as long as he needed me I would be there for him. I kept that promise even after his death. Alex was heart broken when at last his father finally moved out, not to Leeds as I expected, but only as far as the next street. This made matters much worse for both mother and son, yet looking back, I think more hurtful to Alex who felt a deeper hurt and an even more a sense of rejection knowing that his father lived so near and was happily living the life of a single man, irrespective of his responsibilities to his son and only occasionally seeking him out. He never once offered to look after Alex to help me out while I was at work.

## Part 2 - Life in a single-parent family

In fairness to Bill I have to say there were no problems over maintenance or the house, which was signed over to me when I agreed to pay half the bank loan taken out to redeem the mortgage. The financial arrangements and my having full custody of Alex were legalised without difficulties in the magistrate's court in November 1977. Bill was not really a bad man just an inadequate family man, more concerned with maintaining his public image of being a great guy than having his family's love and respect. His big fault was in not being able to admit he was in the wrong, and was skilful in transferring blame to others. To some extent Alex tried to do the same but as he was a poor liar he rarely succeeded with me.

During these early weeks of separation Alex worried me as he became so silent and withdrawn and talked little about his father except to ask "Will he come home". He drew more comfort from Bertie, now *his* dog, by commanding him to sleep in his bedroom and I suspect the reluctant Bertie compensated himself by sleeping in comfort on the bed. Yet only two months later I learned the great depth of Alex's pain. After his bath one evening as I was wrapping him in a warm, comforting towel I understood that was taking the blame for his father's defection. Alex looked up at me, his eyes brimming with tears and said "Mummy, have I been such a bad boy?" I, thinking he meant that day, told him no of course not he'd been very good. However I was stricken to the heart when Alex asked, "Then why did Daddy leave me", not us but me. I did my best to explain that his Daddy had left because he wasn't happy with me and not because of anything he had done. He said nothing more that night.

While carrying out the same routine the next night Alex turned to me again and this time, with eyes blazing with anger, said "I think adults are very selfish. You said that Daddy left because he wasn't happy. Well! I'm not happy and I can't do a thing about it." From then on there was a little belligerence in his attitude towards me and I realised that he had transferred most of the blame for the separation to me. This was hurtful but it would have been even more so for Alex if at that time I had given him the truth; he still had this great affection and trust in his father and a hope that he would come back to him. I can honestly say that at no time did I try to undermine his love for his father; indeed I did my best to sustain it. However that undeserved love, trust and hope was very gradually eroded by his father's own conduct.

I have said little about the mistakes I made during Alex's childhood but I believed at that time I was doing a fairly good job considering the circumstances. Hindsight would show me that in many areas I could have done better but I think my greatest mistakes were made during Alex's adolescence, sometimes by thoughtlessness, other times by being over protective but more seriously by a lack of understanding of Alex as a person not as just my son. Unfortunately there was more hurt for Alex a year later and a second experience of a family death and deep grief when his beloved Nan died, the grandparent whom Alex never forgot. To him she was "My Nan who loved me" and that love was always very important to him but especially so during the dark days of his adult life.

About a year before the separation I had returned to nursing when I discovered we were in debt to the Bank. Even so, during the first months of the separation it required very careful budgeting on a Staff Nurse's pay to cover the bank loan and extensive childminding fees arising from working the varying hospital shifts, sometimes not finishing until ten o'clock at night. However only through the co-operation of my very understanding colleagues was I able to have Alex with me at the hospital on late shifts. For a few weeks Alex loved the attention he had from staff and patients but I knew this situation could not go on as, sooner or later, Alex would want to be in his own home especially on winter nights. I was beginning to feel guilty about his situation and felt the strain of working the varying hours, so decided to find other work where I could be home in the evenings and weekends. Luckily, I had recently passed my driving test and for a change, fortune favoured me, when Shropshire's NHS Nurse Divisional Nursing Officer heard I was planning to leave and contacted me to offer me a District Sisters post with a bigger salary and day time hours.

I gratefully accepted her offer; it was an absolute life saver, it meant I was home early every evening and although I worked alternative weekends I could afford a child minder for the shorter working mornings and with a lighter case load could spend the rest of the Saturday and Sunday on standby at home. On the few occasions I was called out Alex went with me quite willingly because he was an understanding boy and tried to ease my situation. He did this until he was thirteen, then he rebelled against such "childish treatment". We came to a compromise he could have a friend, who lived in the same street, stay with him as long as they promised to stay indoors. The boy's mother, my friend Madge kept an eye on them and as I was never very far away I was able to call in at intervals to check on them. During this period Alex saw his father a little more frequently even though he gave me no practical assistance in looking after his son while I was working. I also managed an occasional night out when an older son of a friend of mine was willing to stay with Alex in our home.

I cannot remember exactly when Alex's newly established way of life was upset but it was because his father lost his job and although he quickly acquired a similar manager's position in Leeds, it was on condition he moved to Leeds. Initially this was very upsetting for the boy but in actual

24

fact, Alex saw more of his father after he had moved and received more presents from him than ever he had before.

After a while Alex settled down again and life was quite pleasant as having the car was a great boon to Alex. We could go where we liked and were able to visit family in various parts of the country, including his paternal grand parents in Aberdeen, and later I was a useful chauffeur when he and his teenage friends went to gigs. When he transferred to the Catholic Six Form College at eleven I was often in a position to take him to and from school. Everything went satisfactorily although Alex was showing more independence and could argue his case quite fluently. When he was thirteen and still very small for his age he again became a withdrawn, this worried me but he assured me all was well.

I was shocked when the College Principal called me in and told me that Alex had been accused of mildly bullying small children. I challenged Alex immediately about this, as I could not understand a boy who had always shown kindness to his younger friends, doing this, but he refused to say why but promised tearfully to apologise to his victims. Later the same evening I saw with distress one of the mothers heading to wards my house. I met her at the door and began quickly to assure her that the matter was sorted, but she interrupted to explain it was not about Alex's "mild harassment" of her son, she was contacting me at her sixth form daughters request, to tell me that the girl was very concerned at Alex being brutally bullied by two older boys and, although the sixth formers were aware of it, none of the teachers had apparently noticed.

Although I was very grateful to this mother for her information and her understanding of Alex's position I was incensed that Alex's milder bullying had been marked by the teachers, but not the cruel treatment that was being inflicted on him. Alex begged me not to intervene as I would make matters worse. I did nothing for three days until the afternoon a very distressed Alex came home, suffering from a severe asthma attack, bruised and dirty through the vicious bullying actions of the two older and much bigger boys. I lost no time in confronting the head and gave him the type of dressing down which he would never forget and he immediately expelled the two bullies. Incidentally, several years later this confrontation with the head unexpectedly paid off, when as a magistrate, he refused Bill's application to reduce my maintenance payments. Life continued quite pleasantly for a time

By the time Alex reached fifteen he was taller than my five foot five and revelled in the fact, becoming more independent of action and verbal expression but not always in the manner I approved of. However it is difficult to maintain adult dignity when your errant son listens patiently to your reprimands, then pats you on the head with a patronising "Little Mum" and walks away smiling. This usually left me struggling between anger and mirth at his audacity, usually though mirth won but not always.

As he approached sixteen he began to change in some respects. He was moody, rude and at times quite offensive in what he said, particularly in his remarks about the Catholic Church, towards which he grew quite hostile and refused to go to Mass. Considering his previous obedience and his love for church rituals this was wounding to me. Our very wise parish priest advised me to let Alex choose his own path, as pressure would only make our relationship difficult and perhaps alienate him altogether.

From then on I accepted his behaviour as being typical of a teenager coping with puberty and sexuality in common with many of my friends with teenage children. So during these formative years it did not occur to me that Alex's sexual struggle went much deeper. I should have been more aware of this when Alex began to ask probing questions about his father which I considered were intrusive and so refused to answer them. If I hadn't been such a prude I would have realised that he was trying to determine if his inclination towards homosexuality was inherited and inevitable, or if the feelings would pass. But I was of a very different generation, in fact old enough to be his grandmother. At that time he needed his younger father's support and guidance but as Alex explained much later he was afraid to ask him these questions because they might widen the distance in their relationship. He may have talked over these problems with his friends but I don't really know, although he had a large circle of friends both boys and girls, and I kept open house for them.

After a while he became less antagonistic and our lives continued along more agreeable lines and I thought Alex's behaviour was settling, until shortly after his sixteenth birthday, two events, occurring within months of each other, had devastating effects on him and damaged his self esteem even more.

I think that the first was the most upsetting and it arose from Alex asking to visit his paternal grandparents in Aberdeen. I made arrangements to do so, but before then I had to have medical tests, and was very surprised but touched when Bill insisted on coming down from Leeds to drive me to and back from Stafford Hospital. I should have known he had an ulterior motive, because he actually came at his parent's insistence and to do so before Alex and I were to visit Aberdeen. What he really came for was to tell me that he had a three year old son. I was furious that he had waited so long to break the news and I dreaded the effect on Alex, but I made Bill tell Alex himself.

Alex was extremely upset and I thought because of jealousy but I was wrong. When I tried to appease him by explaining the advantages of having a half brother and he should not mind so much, Alex turned on me and said "I don't mind him being born but it shows how little my father cares for me when he doesn't think I am worth telling that I have a half brother." He refused to see the child even though the mother, like me, was willing to have them meet. He said "If I am not worth telling about him I am not worthy to meet him and I won't." Regretfully Gregory and Alex never met.

The second upset was due to my thoughtlessness. I decided that enough was enough and even though I am a Catholic, I wanted to be legally free of Bill and asked for a divorce. Unfortunately I mentioned nothing to Alex until I obtained the divorce nisi, thinking to spare him more distress from the waiting period. His reaction was unexpected and extreme as he turned his fury on to me "You are", he said, "as bad as my dad, you don't think I am worth telling me something so important to me". I realised he had lost trust in me and that hurt. It was then I learned, that in divorcing Bill, I had destroyed the secret hope Alex nursed that his father would come back and that we would be a family again.

That lost hope only added to the confusion he was experiencing from his emerging sexuality and helped shape his negative view on the value of family life. Alex became very silent and withdrawn from me and many of his friends, and this continued for several months until we discovered that the fifteen year old sister of three friends, had from being nine years old, been sexually abused by her father. Alex was almost distraught as he was very fond of the family, but did his best to support and comfort the girl and her brothers against the unkind gossip of neighbours. This incident was probably the final turning point in his attitudes to sex and family life. One evening when Alex had barely spoken a word to me all day, he burst into a sudden storm of crying and told me "Mum I don't ever want to be married and have children because I don't want to make so many people as unhappy as my Dad did". Nothing I could say ever changed that opinion, and I may not be right, but it is possible that this was the time when he settled his mind to be homosexual, and put aside any thoughts of heterosexual relationships; although I do believe he didn't practice homosexuality until he was twenty and had lived away from home for a year or so.

Alex had two further setbacks before leaving home. The first was when he decided to leave school and was accepted on a two year YTS scheme to learn the art of furniture restoration. He loved the course, it fulfilled his ambition to be involved in antiques and he did so well, that he was offered a post with an antique furniture firm, to become operative when he had obtained the necessary qualification through the YTS. Happily, he had no problems with his asthma or eczema during this time, due to the very high standards of health and safety standards maintained by the YTS. Therefore I can't describe Alex's despair when the YTS department refused him the second year, because he was already eighteen, and the job offer was withdrawn. However, he went back to college to do his "A" levels but he had lost any incentive he may have had to work hard, but he did manage a B and two Cs out of the seven he took.

The final blow to Alex's esteem came from his father who had remarried and had a step son, a keen rugby player and the same age as Alex. On a visit to Newport Bill literally bragged to us about Reece's success in his "A" levels but didn't even ask about Alex's. When I reprimanded him for this neglect it was obvious he had little regard for Alex's academic skills and had just assumed he didn't do 'A' levels. When I told him Alex did have "A" levels he said to Alex "Why didn't you tell me" Alex literally hissed at him "Because you never asked" and left the room.

This was the penultimate meeting with his father; he made no attempt to see him again until he was twenty one and had been away from home for two years. For some reason Alex never explained, he visited his father in Leeds and on his way back to London, called in to see me and announced with surprising satisfaction "Mum! I have decided never to see my father again". When asked the reason all he said was that he had not realised that his father was such a 'wet'. To me it was that Alex had finally accepted that the responsibility for the failed father/son relationship rested with his father not with himself. Yet I have always regretted Alex making that decision.

At nineteen Alex had left home and settled down in Shepherds Bush, London sharing a flat at the invitation of Steve Jones an older man, who he had met at a gig in Birmingham. It was during my many visits to them and confiding talks with my son, I understood why the adolescent Alex changed his attitude to his Catholic faith. It was due to the strong homophobia he had encountered within the church, and in particular, the cruel and derisive views expressed by his catholic college friends about homosexuals, at the time when Alex was struggling to understand his own sexuality. After several visits to London, I strongly suspected the relationship between Alex and Steve was more than ordinary friendship. In the forlorn hope that I was mistaken I waited for Alex himself to tell me that this was so, but it was quite a while before he plucked enough up courage to broach the subject. Even then I had to provide him with the opportunity to 'come out'. I said to him "Alex I know you have something to tell me, don't be afraid, and go ahead, I think I know what it is". He said quite simply. 'Mum I'm homosexual" and that was it. We talked awhile about his reasons for this conviction, and when we finished, the look of relief on his face when I told him that I accepted his homosexuality unconditionally, and the hug he gave me I will treasure all my life; I then went to my room and cried.

Those tears were the only ones I ever shed over Alex's homosexuality and they weren't for me they were for him, I felt such deep compassion for my son in his homosexual state as I believed that because of it he was never to know real happiness in this life.

# CHAPTER TWO

## Part 1 – Life in London

I wish I could say that my prediction about the unhappiness my son would face as a homosexual was completely wrong, but unfortunately I can't. Obviously there are many aspects of Alex's life in London of which I knew little or nothing and I certainly can't claim, simply because he was my son, to have fully understood him or his way of life. What parent does? Alex underwent many varied experiences during his years in London, but in this chapter I concentrate on those episodes in his life which I know of, and believe affected him most, some which inflicted more pain on his fragile self-esteem, and others were more up-lifting experiences which gave him the courage to attempt to rise above his misfortunes and eventually, to consider making his life more rewarding.

I had his confidence in some areas of his life and I therefore know he certainly found a type of happiness from living in the city of London, where homophobia was less prevalent, and attitudes less hostile than in the urban areas where he lived his early years. He made many friends, men and women, gay and straight, but he had a special sympathy with those whose normal pattern of family life had been torn apart by their homosexuality and subsequent rejection by their parents and families, and he became a trusted mentor to several of them, some of whom I had the privilege of meeting before and after Alex died.

A few days after Alex had died, I met a group of Alex's friends, his peers, and was very surprised when one said to me "Mrs B., we envied Alex his mum." I asked "why?" And the same boy replied quite simply "Because you accepted him." As I looked at their faces, I was deeply moved by the sense of rejection behind those words. I began to understand the loneliness they felt from being isolated from their families, but I could not find words to comfort them.

From what I learned from his friends Alex, like his father, became animated when in Group Company and was well liked as an intelligent conversationalist with a 'wicked sense of humour'. I suppose while he was with them, he was able to suppress the deep unhappiness and the uncertainties which at times continued to overshadow his life. Alex and I were sufficiently alike for me to empathise with his deep sense of inner loneliness, which surfaced when the animation died down and he was alone, however, I had my faith to sustain me, while Alex who had set aside his Catholic faith, tried hard, but could never find an adequate substitute to replace it.

I suppose that what Alex really wanted and needed was the opportunity to share his life with an older man, in a steady and lasting relationship, and given his history, someone who would provide the affection and guidance his own father had withheld. However, that type of relationship can only be built on stability, which in general, requires an adequate income and good living conditions; Alex had neither income nor his own home and certainly would not have stability living with the volatile Steve, the friend who gave Alex the opportunity to live in London. On the whole, like so many other unemployed and unqualified homosexuals, Alex's encounters, more often than not, were transitory and unfulfilling affairs, giving only a temporary illusion of being wanted.

Although Alex had a long relationship with Steve and shared his London flat on and off for over eight years, it could never have been, in my opinion, a relationship with any real commitment. In the first few years they seemed to rub along together reasonably well and on my first visit to the flat to deliver Alex's personal possessions, Alex seemed content enough. Steve had welcomed me with warmth and friendliness dubbing me 'Mrs. B', a title which was used by all Alex's friends. I did not then see any cause for real concern even though they seemed to have little in common. They frequently went to clubs and gigs together but my impression was that, in the main, they socialised with different groups of friends.

After a while Alex told me that Steve was HIV positive and that he acted as his unofficial carer, housekeeper and cook. I was naturally very alarmed and could not accept his assurance that he was in no danger of contracting the condition, yet this was another occasion when I felt it wiser to say little, even though, having that knowledge would always be a source of worry to me. I did wonder though why he thought it necessary to tell me; he must have known it would make me anxious for him but, in the end, I decided that it was probably a pre-warning – just in case.

I saw Alex frequently during my visits to London during the next five years or so, at the flat, in the city centre during my frequent stays at Maureen and Ken's home in New Barnet. Maureen was the eldest of Alex's cousins and both she and her husband Ken and their two children made Alex very welcome. Considering Alex, in his troubled teenage years, had on several occasions been very rude and off hand towards them, this demonstrated the depth of their tolerance and understanding of my son's family situation and their acceptance of his homosexual nature. In fact, because Maureen was nearer Alex's age than me, I think she understood him better than I did, he certainly benefited from her advice to me, which caused me to change some of my outdated attitudes to parenthood.

There are two such occasions which I remember clearly. The first took place when Alex was eleven, in his first year at secondary school and still very small and slight in build. Clothing him was a problem. One day, I noticed Alex in very earnest conversation with his cousin after which she came to me and said "Alex wants you to stop making his trousers and to buy them from the shop like other boys' mothers; the other boy's are teasing him about his homemade clothes". So I bought his trousers, but spent almost as much time in altering them to fit, as I did making them from scratch, particularly when, on his instructions, I had to be extra careful, under his watchful eye, to preserve the designer labels intact and on show.

The second occasion was a family Christmas in New Barnet during Alex's turbulent seventeenth year. We were expecting extra family for Boxing Day and I sternly warned the truculent Alex to be on his best behaviour and not show me up. I must have overdone the admonitions because Maureen turned to me and said very sharply, "For goodness sake Doris, stop picking on Alex for small things that don't matter, he has enough big problems to contend with and you are making things worse for him". I was very taken aback and offended by this reprimand, but it made me stop and think hard. I took her advice and tried to be less critical, but it was hard work at times with Alex, who on occasions appeared to suffer from an intermittent deafness.

Alex often came home for breaks and occasionally brought friends with him. I always made them welcome, even though sometimes the apparel and manners of both Alex and friends caused me to raise my eyebrows in silent dismay. During his childhood, I grew used to his tendency to seek out and identify with 'lame ducks' that he brought home for my support. On these occasions I hid my disapproval but hoped that the neighbours would not notice these weird visitors, or if they did, would not identify me with them. I must say I was relieved when Alex tired of this extreme self-expression and reverted back to more conventional standards of dress and behaviour and, when outside, I could stop walking behind and pretending he wasn't with me.

For about six years, Alex seemed reasonably happy in choice of city life and partner although after several attempts at short term employment in menial jobs which adversely affected his asthma and eczema, he seemed to accept unemployment as a way life. It was a kind of apathy which I am told, often develops in the long term unemployed. This attitude to unemployment did not please me at all and I often reprimanded him for his lack of ambition, but as it did with his father, my criticism went over his head. My disapproval didn't prevent Alex from cheerfully visiting me for a spell of home comfort, but gradually at each visit I noticed Alex showing increasing signs of strain. His air of independence became more subdued than on his early visits, and I also began to detect the signs of deep distress. At first he avoided giving me an explanation for coming home so often except to insist he needed a change from city life. After a few days of rest and good food he would return to London and to Steve. It was very clear but distressing to me that the situation between Alex and Steve was deteriorating. I also suspected some violence was involved. When I tentatively attempted to sound Alex out on this point he angrily dismissed my suggestion. I hastily backed down, but was not convinced by his vehement denial.

Eventually, though, the strain of coping alone with the situation grew too much and he confessed he was having difficulties with Steve because of his increasingly erratic and uncontrolled behaviour, due Alex thought, to his serious illness and the effect of the prescribed and non-prescribed drugs he was taking. I tried to persuade Alex to leave Steve and find other lodgings, but he felt he owed him too much to desert him. Yet on at least two occasions this erratic behaviour led to Alex fleeing the flat and being housed in temporary, emergency accommodation to wait to be allocated permanent housing. On both occasions Steve persuaded Alex to return to him on the promise to improve. I had to accept that, like it or not, there was a deep attachment between them, that they needed each other. From my point of view it was a damaging relationship for Alex, but when I said this to him, he told me I should have more sympathy for Steve, who had been physiologically damaged by an abusive father in childhood and had been thrown out of his home at fifteen for trying to protect his mother. More than this he refused to say. Although I did feel more sympathy for Steve, I became very concerned about Alex's safety should Steve become more unstable.

Moreover, it was inevitable that having learned about Steve taking illegal drugs I began to wonder if Alex could also have adopted a similar habit. It was with great reluctance and dread that I asked him to be quite honest in answering the question 'Do you take drugs? His immediate reply was 'Yes'. He then went on to explain he used Ecstasy and then only occasionally as a mild recreational drug. He added 'I also use cannabis because it helps ease my breathing after a mild asthma attack'. I remember looking at him long and hard before deciding he was being honest, but I warned him to be very careful with drugs as I would never in any way supports an addiction to hard drugs. It is important to stress that he did not develop any serious drug problem, because, later, drugs were to become an important issue to police investigations into his death

**Part 2 – Alex rethinks his life**

During the early part of 1995, Alex and Steve appeared to have a more settled relationship. I could see that Alex was definitely happier, but more thoughtful than usual. We had a celebration meal in London for his 27th birthday and while we were discussing my imminent BA degree exams, he surprised me by saying it was time to reassess his future.

I like to think that this discussion with me, and an important event in my life, helped Alex into giving further and more positive considerations to what were to be changes to his life. In July 1995 he was present to see me receive a BA degree from De Montfort University in Leicester. He was quite impressed with the ceremony (although after I received my degree he did fall asleep during the rest of the presentations). He was however, most taken with second year students and spent most of the morning discussing university courses and student life with them. He said to me on the way home "I had the wrong idea about university life Mum. Did you know that people like me are more acceptable and that homosexuals have their own social group?" I did know of course, but I let him describe to me the life which those university students were experiencing, at the same time secretly hoping that this occasion would influence him into deciding on a full time university degree course. However, he made no further reference to the matter before returning to London in quite a contented mood.

Some weeks later it was a very upset Alex who rang me and told me that he needed to come home for a while, but hadn't any money for the fare. I arranged for him to collect tickets from King Cross station and within a few hours he was home pouring out, with tears, such a confused story of hurt and anxiety over a situation that had arisen between him and Steve. Alex was in effect homeless because of Steve's more bizarre behaviour after becoming involved with a bondage group. He had wanted Alex to become a practising member with him but when Alex adamantly refused, Steve became violent and Alex, for the first time, retaliated and hit back. He then quit the flat to let Steve cool down, and took refuge with Lisa and Mathew, a couple who actually were good friends of both men. After two days, or so Alex returned to the flat only to find he was locked out and that Steve had taken a new partner.

Alex, in describing these experiences was obviously quite shocked at his rejection but especially so, as it had resulted from Steve's fascination with bondage. He said to me, as he had apparently said to Steve, that under no circumstances would he ever subject himself to such revolting baseness and added bitterly to me "It is bad enough being homosexual."

This was the incident I believe which shocked him into amending his life and to say "I've got to change, Mum, I've done nothing with my life; it's not worth living like this, I have been too dependent on you and Steve. I want to take control of my own life". This time I did move into action quickly and, as diplomatically as possible, suggested he consider further education of some type. "Oh" he said "You mean University" and to my glee continued, "Well Mum, I think you could help me there". Obviously the discussions with students at my graduation had taken root and it hadn't been entirely my example which won him over to the advantages of studying for a Humanities BA degree, to the extent he already had ideas about which courses to take.

With my help he sorted out suitable colleges, but he insisted they must be in London. We sent off several applications. At the same time, as his only residence was in Lincolnshire, he applied to the County Council Grant Office and was given the full student grant. He was actually called for interviews with two London universities for which he had returned to London. He was accepted by both for the next academic year 1996-7, with the proviso that he took the preparation course designed to reintroduce mature students to higher study. Alex decided that he would do the course in London before he made his choice and, on his return, he lost no time in registering for the course at an East London Sixth Form College, to do revision in English, English literature and his preferred subject, History of Art, and probably others, which he continued until the Christmas vacation.

I am not sure just how relations with Steve were restored or if Alex ever stayed in his flat again, but Alex became Steve's close friend and paid carer as apposed to his partner, without any of the old animosity. I do know that Alex stayed with various friends, but in the main found a temporary home with those two very good friends Lisa and Mathew, who not only provided Alex with a bed when he was homeless, but were also instrumental in him gaining tenancy of a Housing Association flat. It was a very small but self contained flat near King Cross Station, not a very salubrious area, but it was Alex's own home and he relished being in charge of his life for the first time.

Alex received his tenancy just before Christmas. During the settling in process in early January, and following a short flare up of glandular fever, Alex suspended his studies. When I met him in London on 23$^{rd}$ March 1996 to celebrate his 28th birthday, he told me that he had recovered and was well settled in his new home. He intended to restart the preparation course after the May Bank Holiday, but was worried about the cost of retaining the flat as a full time student. I was so very pleased with this new and more self-confident Alex and promised to help him maintain his flat when he started University in the autumn. I had already set aside a sum of money for him, following the sale of my house and the purchase of a home in a retirement park, so retaining his flat for three years would not be a problem. I was aware though that it might be a difficult period of adjustment for Alex and he would probably need, and certainly have, my constant encouragement and support throughout the three year course.

My own future was already mapped out and I had started a two year post-graduate course in Modern History. Life at that time seemed so good for both of us.

# CHAPTER THREE

## Part 1 - The Last Meeting

Very often before fate is about to inflict a cruel blow on an unsuspecting individual, it creates an incident which at the time seems to be of little significance, but later will become a small, shining memory, to lessen the awful darkness of grief which can engulf a person who loses a loved one by a violent and unexpected death. I have such a memory in the last, unplanned meeting I had with my son ten days before his death.

For two years I had been one of many women taking part in an Ovarian Cancer study. I was asked to attend for an interview with a team member at the Royal Free Hospital in London on 26th April 1996. As I expected that the interview and the journey time would occupy most of the day, and as I was tied to a particular train departure time by the terms of my railway ticket, I had not arranged to see Alex. The ticket and a taxi fare cost me about fifty pounds and I was very indignant when the interview consisted of merely writing my signature which I considered could have been done by post and at the cost of a stamp. Without much hope of finding him at home, I rang Alex about midday and was delighted when he answered his phone. So you see it was a price well worth paying for one last meeting with my only child.

The memory of this last meeting is special because it was only ten days before he died, so every minute of that afternoon is locked into my memory. It began with a reversal of the normal roles in that it was I who got off the underground and walked into Kings Cross Station, where Alex was waiting for me. It was a wonderful moment when Alex, unusually demonstrative, strode towards me with arms outstretched and then gave me the biggest and closest hug I ever had from him.

Naturally the first thing we did was go for a meal. Alex chose a Greek restaurant but as I didn't like my cheesy choice, Alex had no difficulty in scoffing both meals. We then did quite a big shopping in a nearby Sainsbury's supermarket. After topping up his electricity payment card, he escorted me back to Caledonian Road and I paid my first visit to my son's very own home. It was a small compact flat but he revelled in the fact that it was his territory and he was no longer dependent on someone else's whim for shelter. We had a lovely afternoon with no one to disturb our warm mother and son discussion. It was a very private conversation which would comfort me during the very dark days which lay ahead. When it was time for me to catch my train, Alex walked me to the station where we said goodbye and he promised to ring me some time during the next week. As the train drew out of the station I waved until he was out of sight and on the journey home I contentedly mulled over the way things were shaping for Alex and felt optimistic about his future.

But I didn't know then that Alex's future was already fading and that I was never to see my son alive again.

**Part 2 - The end of a life which was far from gay**

The previous chapters dealt with events in Alex's life which I consider were significant episodes and encounters which shaped his character and his nature, but are based almost solely on my recollections.

The chapters which follow deal with Alex's death and its aftermath are based on the end result of my comparative analysis of the volume of substantiated evidence I acquired from various official and semi-official departments of the justice system.

Much of this evidence was not easily obtained, as little was issued willingly by the justice officials. More often than not it was released with unbelievable reluctance, and on occasions, I am sure, released quite unwittingly. It includes recorded interviews, telephone calls, forensic and medical evidence, witness statements and important legal documents.

I waited for Alex to ring me as he promised, but as days went by and there was no call, I began to ring him, first in the evenings then after a week, morning and evening. I felt disappointed and a bit niggled at his failure to call me, but how could I have known that death had intervened and that the ringing tone of his phone was echoing throughout a silent, empty flat and that Alex would never again pick up the receiver and say his warm,' Hello Mum.

.

There was no sense of alarm though, not until Maureen my niece called me on the afternoon of Sunday May 12th 1996 and said, "Doris I don't want to alarm you but Steve Jones has been in touch and wants to know is Alex with you?" I did feel a sense of fear as I replied 'NO!' She told me that Steve was very concerned because he had not heard from Alex for ten days and had contacted everyone he could think of, but no one had seen or heard from Alex during all that time.

I rang Steve at his home in Fulham, in south west London, and he explained why he was so worried over Alex's absence. Alex had spent the day with him in his Fulham flat then between 9 pm and 9.30 pm he left to travel by tube to visit the London Apprentice pub in East London intending to arrive before 11pm to avoid paying a £5 late entrance fee. Alex had asked Steve to go with him, but he was too tired and they said what proved to be a final goodbye as Alex went on his way. At first, when there was no call from Alex, like me, Steve was annoyed, but as the days passed and there was still no call, his annoyance changed to worry. By the tenth day he was growing quite frantic. It was then he rang Maureen, hoping that she would be able to assure him that Alex was O.K. and he was with me. He asked Maureen to contact me and explain his concern and for me to get in touch with him.

Steve and I discussed the various reasons which could explain Alex's long absence, carefully avoiding any reference to death, and settled on the most feasible explanation namely that Alex had met someone unexpectedly and gone off with him for a break. Although it was not unusual for Alex to go away without warning, he normally contacted Steve or me within a day or so. He had on one such occasion rung me from Czechoslovakia (he needed help with his fare home). So, just in case Alex was merely visiting friends, we agreed to wait until 6pm Monday, because if he did turn up, we knew he would be very annoyed with us for creating an unnecessary fuss. In the meantime I asked Steve, who had a set of keys to go to Alex's flat, to check for signs of packing. Steve did so, but reported back that were none that he could see and Alex's passport was still in the flat. However, we agreed to stay with the plan and wait until Monday evening.

At 6 pm on Monday 13th May, 1996, Steve who was at Alex's flat rang to say he had not returned. As previously arranged, he and several friends were leaving the flat to report him missing to the nearest police station, which was in Islington. I waited and waited for Steve to call me and repeatedly rang his and rang Alex's numbers without success until about 11 pm when Steven finally answered Alex's phone. I demanded to know what was wrong with Alex, but Steve's reaction was on of shock when he realised that I had not been contacted by the police. He thought by now the police would have contacted me to tell me that there was very little doubt that Alex was dead, because an 'unidentified male' listed on the police computer as a missing person and who died on May 4th, very closely fitted his description. The body was now at Poplar Mortuary and it was Limehouse police officers who were in charge. Steve had not rung me himself as he had been specifically instructed by the police not to pass any of this information on to me as Limehouse Police had told him that they intended to officially inform the next of kin themselves. They had been provided with my full details

Steve very considerately offered to identify Alex, but I told him it was important and necessary for me to actually see Alex's body and preferred to do it myself. I then rang Maureen to break the bad news to her and Ken that Alex was probably dead.

I waited for Limehouse Police to call me, but by 12.45 am, when no one from London police attempted to contact me, I could wait no longer and rang Gainsborough police who I had assumed would have been requested to take over the task of contacting me. I told the duty officer who I was and asked if they intended to get in touch with me. The duty officer, totally at a loss asked "No, why should we?" I replied that I was waiting for confirmation from them that my son was dead and explained the circumstances. I could hear from the background noises; the obviously disconcerted officer checking the log book, then asking colleagues if they had any information, before he reported to me that no police officer from either of the two London police stations had contacted Gainsborough police. I gave the duty officer all the information I had received together with Alex's London address. He promised to make immediate enquiries and to send an officer to my home to report back to me as soon as possible.

After another long agonising wait, at approximately 2.30 am on Tuesday 14th May, a full eight hours after Islington police had been told Alex was

41

missing, a police officer from Gainsborough called at my home to advise me that they believed the body was that of my son. The reason for the delay was because Gainsborough had been referred to the officer in charge of the case and they had had difficulty in contacting him. Eventually they received a photo-copy of a police computer entry with the following details, "A post-mortem examination, carried out the 4th May on the body of an 'unknown male', had established the cause of death to be irreversible heart failure following a very severe asthma attack". The description of the body and the given cause of death removed any doubt from my mind; Alex was dead. The police officer who came alone to give me the news expressed his concern that I was on my own and offered to find a neighbour to stay with me. However, as I was new to the retirement park I said I preferred to be on my own until members of my family arrived.

I rang my niece Maureen, who was waiting for news, and told her I was now certain that Alex was dead. She began to make arrangements to leave New Barnet with Ken and the children immediately, but I wouldn't allow this; the children were fast asleep and too young to be dragged out of bed at a late hour for such a sad reason. Instead, we arranged that Ken would contact Limehouse police early next morning and make arrangements for me to identify the body. She promised they would be with me as soon as they had made suitable arrangements for their two children, Rachel and Simon.

It was a long and weary, sleepless night, most of it spent walking in the park or on the canal banks. At about 6.30am a neighbour, Gaynor Cook, who I barely knew, while seeing her husband Bob off to work, saw me standing outside my house, and, as she told me later, something about my attitude made her aware that I needed her help and she came over to me. She kept me company until Maureen and Ken arrived, comforting and supporting me during some of the worst hours of my life. Gaynor was to continue that true friendship in supporting me through all the difficult years ahead, during which time I tried to obtain the truth for myself, and justice for my son. Strangely, it was Gaynor who almost intuitively first declared that Alex had been murdered.

It is to my great regret that Gaynor died two days after I had finished writing this book, and that she would never read how I recorded her friendly compassionate action. It is quite certain though, that I will always remember her with affectionate and gratitude.

## Part 3 – Meeting Limehouse Police - to whom my naivety was a gift.

It was however, a huge relief when Maureen and Ken arrived at about 10am, and so very comforting for me to be with closes family members in a time of grief. Both my brother and sister were unfortunately out of touch at the time. Ken told me that he had informed the police of my intention to identify the body but had agreed to their request that we visit Limehouse Police Station first. We drove non-stop to London and as Ken is a Londoner, he had no difficulty in locating Limehouse Police Station, arriving there about 2.30 pm.

When we walked through the entrance, we did not realise that not only were we entering a police station but I was also to be confronted with an establishment cover-up. I was walking into a situation where, through ignorance and naivety, I would allow the truth to be woven into a tangled web of official deceit, secrecy and collusion. It would take me thirteen years of tenacious effort of opposition to partially tear down the web of lies and deception and begin to expose the truth, that Alex's death was in fact a homicide.

On entering the station, we found three officers waiting to greet us, Detective Inspector (DI) Baff, Detective Sergeant (DS) Bathie and Detective Constable (DC) Hardy. They were in reality the team designated to investigate Alex's suspicious death but who, at the time, we understood to be just a formal welcoming group. Although DI Baff is featured prominently in subsequent events and in documentary evidence, our acquaintance was brief. He stayed only long enough to express his condolences and then made a rapid exit. Maureen, Ken and I did not remember seeing him again until the inquest as from then on, DS Bathie took over police contact and proceedings, both at Limehouse and at the mortuary.

We had expected to be taken straight to the mortuary, but instead we were shown in to an interview room where, and to our surprise, DS Bathie proceeded to conduct an official interview. When the necessity for this was questioned, I think, by Maureen, he told us it was nothing to worry about as it was a mere formality. (A phrase I was to hear many times in the future.) We accepted this without further questions but with some uncertainty as to the need for an interview at this time.

DS Bathie opened the interview, without any preamble, by asking if I knew Alex was homosexual. If he had expected this to unnerve me, he was disappointed I told him quite sharply that I had been aware of Alex's sexuality even before he told me but positively since 1990 when he admitted it to me, also that I had always known about his relationship with Steve Jones and was well informed on his lifestyle and accepted it totally.

DS Bathie went on to give me a version of how Alex had died. Without any sensitivity he told me Alex had been engaged in 'a form of homosexuality' and was quite naked when he developed a very severe asthma attack, which led to irreversible heart failure. He then described more kindly, but quite graphically, the actions of 'the man' who was with Alex, how he had quickly dialled 999 and under telephone instructions from the Ambulance Service had made 'heroic attempts' to keep his heart going until the paramedics arrived to take over. Unfortunately all attempts at resuscitation had proved unsuccessful, but, DS Bathie assured us **"Alex had died quietly and peacefully"**. It was a very moving account and I felt the deepest gratitude towards the man who had tried so hard to save my son. Unfortunately, as I learned at the inquest, it was all a pack of lies.

One thing had been puzzling me since we arrived at the station; there had been no mention of any measures taken by the police to identify Alex when he must surely have been well known at The London Apprentice when he was accompanied by Steve and when he was on his own. I asked DS Bathie why the police had not identified Alex and was told "There were no personal effects of any kind with the body". I found this hard to accept. I queried this statement with DS Bathie but he insisted **"There were absolutely none at all"**. He was unable to tell me what had happened to Alex's cigarettes, lighter or his inhaler and keys. Both of these latter items would unquestionably have been in his possession.

This 'no effects found' was repeated by the then acting DI Bathie, in January 1997, after the inquest. But at least three items with information

44

should have been with his clothing, 1. His Lloyds bank cash card, 2. A small notebook containing emergency telephone numbers, which he always carried and he most certainly would have had his keys, both my house key and especially his flat keys, otherwise how else would he have expected to get back into his flat? None of these items were listed by the hospital. They were not mentioned in police records, nor were Alex's clothing. In February 1997, when I asked that it be returned, DI Bathie to my astonishment told me that Alex's clothing had been destroyed **at my request**. I strongly refuted this and demanded that a search be made for the clothing, but no one could account for it going missing and it was never located. After this interview we were left on our own for a while but DC Hardy, who was a very considerate and polite young man, came into the room to say they weren't quite ready for us and apologised for the delay.

Eventually about 4.30pm. We were taken by car to Poplar Mortuary, shown into a waiting room where we had to wait for another half-hour, as they still weren't ready for us. Maureen commented it was odd that after twelve days they **still** weren't ready for us. DC Hardy returned and called Mr Amphlett out of the waiting room to tell him of his concern that I would be distressed because Alex's face was very blue. Mr Amphlett told him not to worry because as an experienced trained nurse I was used to the sight of death.

I had no hesitation in identifying my son in the presence of DS Bathie, DC Hardy and the Coroner's Officer, Mr Davies, but was upset at the poor standard of preparation of the body. Alex was covered up to his chin in a green operating sheet, only his face was visible, as his head was completely swathed in a green operating towel. It was distressing to see there was a trickle of apparently fresh, bright red blood from both his right nostril and right ear. None of this conformed to the usual standard of preparing a body for family viewing that I had expected. It gave the impression of an unexpected procedure carried out in some haste. I have my own views on this action, which I will explain later.

However, the peaceful expression of Alex's face and the pale, natural tint of his complexion were very consoling and seemed to uphold DS Bathie's statement that death had been quiet and peaceful. The blue discoloration mentioned by DC Hardy had disappeared, but at the time I gave it little attention; all my thoughts were concentrated on accepting the difficult

45

reality of my son being dead. I had deep desire to see and touch him. Viewing him through glass was unreal, so I asked the Coroner's officer, Mr Davies, to allow me to go into the viewing room. Mr Davies, with some hesitation, allowed me to see and touch my son and to embrace him as I said a final good bye. He was so cold.

Regardless of the revelations and the deception which followed, seemingly condoned by Mr Davies, I will always deeply appreciate and treasure the coroner's officer's act of kindness. Apparently it is not the usual practice in a suspicious death, still under investigation, to allow the body to be touched by the family.

On our return to Limehouse police station I was extensively interviewed by DS Bathie. He concentrated most particularly on Alex's medical history in relation to his chronic asthmatic condition. Because it was so important I gave him full details of all his medical conditions. In reply to the DS's question on asthma I told him that, as a trained nurse, I was fully aware that sudden death from heart failure was a complication which could arise from a severe asthma attack *(status asthmaticus)*, and that Alex had several severe  attacks in the past, two of them having brought him very near to death. Alex's homosexual life style was discussed and to my surprise I was questioned closely about Alex's body piercing. DC Bathie then left the room.

He returned shortly with a prepared, hand written statement, which he asked me to read over and sign each page. I only skim-read the document as it did not seem necessary to do more and I was beginning to feel I had as much as I could take for one day and was ready to leave. Therefore it was only when I managed to obtain a copy of my statement four years later that I realised all details of Alex's very important asthma history had been omitted, but a lengthy account of the body piercing, which had no relevance whatsoever to his death, was included.

To our surprise we were then taken to the office of the apparently sympathetic Superintendent who was in command of Limehouse police. He discussed in detail the circumstances of Alex's death as DS Bathie had described, referring at all times to it being due to an asthma attack and cardiac failure, confirmed by post-mortem. I had the impression he was questioning my understanding of the situation and assured him with my experience in nursing I had no difficulty in accepting the report that Alex had died from such known complications. Why shouldn't I, when in a period of less than a day, three police from different area stations, a Coroner's Officer and a Superintendent established that death was as above. The superintendent gave no indication of knowing that the cause of death was **not** from natural causes or that he was even aware of the fact that from the very first it was treated as 'a suspicious death' by his own police team led by DI Baff. Whether he had or had not been given the full facts at that time was a matter I had occasion to question much later.

We left the Superintendent's office and returned to the interview room, where DS Bathie advised us that an inquest was to be held on Thursday 16th May 1996. However he strongly advised us not to attend because, as he explained, the inquest would only be a formality as the police expected a verdict of 'natural death,' He then went on to tell us that an inquest, under any circumstances, is very unpleasant. He would strongly advise us to avoid this experience. He then added that we could expect to be able to arrange the funeral in about ten days. His inquest advice was accepted as being sound and considerate and it did not seem necessary to attend the inquest. Unfortunately for us, we did not realise until much later that his advice, which I was to bitterly regret taking, had been ploy to prevent us attending the inquest.

Before leaving Limehouse police station at about 6.15 pm, I requested the name and address of the person who had made those **'heroic attempts'** to revive Alex in order to write and express my deep gratitude for his efforts. This request obviously disconcerted DS Bathie. I was similarly disconcerted when he refused my request. He said it was not possible at that time, but if I were to send a letter via him (DS Bathie), he would personally see it was delivered; we then left for New Barnet. I didn't write that letter, I found that I couldn't express thanks to someone without knowing his name.

What a fool I would have felt later if I had written a letter of thanks to the man who I now believe is responsible for my son's death.

47

# CHAPTER FOUR

## Part 1 -The Importance of Forensic Science – Accuracy in assembling facts

I do not think that the average man and woman really understand the importance that forensic science has in the investigation into a sudden or unexpected death in determining whether or not a crime has been committed. In my opinion, a family faced with the sudden and unexplained death of a close relative should have some knowledge of the processes involved, so that they do not find themselves in the same deplorable state of affairs that I was unwittingly drawn in to by the highly irregular way the officials handled matters in my son's case.

For over thirteen years, since I first heard of my son's untimely death, right up to the present day, all because of my initial naivety and ignorance of the legal processes, I have had to struggle to free myself from a quagmire of misinformation and official irregularities in the mismanagement of my son's case. This morass was created to prevent my access to the High Court in order to overturn the inquest verdict of 'accidental death' given by the coroner who held the inquest on my son's death. This verdict was completely against the ample forensic and medical evidence presented to the Coroner's Court, which provided positive proof that my son's death **was** an unlawful killing; the verdict should have recorded that fact. The coroner's verdict was the last of the sequence of processes normally used to establish that a crime has been committed, but in Alex Barrack's case appeared to have been almost ignored.

Not I fear from ignorance of the rules but a deliberate policy of official secrecy to hide the facts, and ignoring the recognised practices of forensic science. Forensic science deals with both the gathering of evidence by Scenes-of-Crime-Officers (SOCOs) at the scene where a body has been found in suspicious circumstances, and the interpretation of the forensic medical evidence found on the body by the pathologist, who carries out the post-mortem examination. To my mind the clearest and by far the simplest definition of the forensic science, is that of the crime historian Brian Lane, in referring to a suspicious death:

'The basis on which the investigation of a crime stands is in the assembling of a sequence of facts, this will allow the judicial process to be carried through to a satisfactory conclusion. It should prove that a crime was committed and it should present evidence that a named person or persons were responsible for committing that crime'.

The sequence in a suspicious or unexpected death begins when a doctor is unable to certify the cause of death and informs the coroner that there is reason to believe that it has occurred in suspicious circumstances. The coroner, as in the case of my son, can then order a post-mortem to be carried out by a forensic pathologist in order to determine, as far as possible, the cause of death.

How the next stage of the investigations proceeds depends on the pathologist's professional judgement on the cause of death, and whether or not an inquest should be held on the victim.

It is very important in the cause of justice that any autopsy should be conducted along the guidelines laid down (and there is quite a long list), to ensure that a medico-legal autopsy uncovers **all the facts** relating to the cause of death, or at least as many as the condition of the body will allow. This will enable the pathologist, and others who may follow him in investigating the case, to arrive at the true cause of death. The pathologist's report must fully record his findings. This should be submitted to the coroner as soon as possible, probably by phone in the first place, but this should then be followed as soon as possible by his written report, preferably within days. If later, further information requires him to make changes to his original conclusions, then these changes must be recorded as such in his first report.

The police also have a most important role when a suspicious death is reported to them. Their investigations start even before the post-mortem is ordered by the coroner. Obviously, in a suspected homicide, securing the crime scene must be done as soon as possible by the Scenes-of-Crime Officers (SOCOs), as this is the most crucial stage in the investigation. It is at the crime scene where vital contact traces are to be found on the victim, on any suspects, on physical artefacts, at the scene and also to establish the circumstances in which the death took place. These items can assist the pathologist in his findings and the coroner in his decision on the necessity of holding an inquest. Especially as both the autopsy finding and the coroner's decision on the cause of death will determine whether or not the police should continue with their crime investigations.

Textbooks on crime forensics and forensic medicine stress the crucial importance of early examinations of the scene of crime to preserve any evidence from contamination and to ensure specimens are labelled correctly. What is also very important to remember is that if the specially trained SOCOs overlook any clues in the first examination, they are extremely unlikely to get a second chance. Also of vital importance is that all the above mentioned officials work together in a spirit of co-operation in a common aim, that of solving a crime.

Once the Police Investigation Team consider that they have enough evidence for a prosecution they will pass the case to the Crown Prosecution Service (CPS), who will decide if the case is strong enough to warrant prosecuting a suspect or suspects in court.

On receiving the pathologist's judgment on the cause of death the coroner will then decide whether or not to hold an inquest. In general, the coroner has no duty to hold an inquest when the death is from natural causes. When an autopsy confirms that death was due to natural causes, the coroner can issue a certificate to the family for cremation or burial without the need for further enquiry. However, the coroner cannot dispense with an inquest when there is reasonable cause to suspect the deceased has died a violent or unnatural death.

**Part 2 – The Inquest - The Role of the coroner in 1996/7**

A coroner' jurisdiction over inquests is governed by the statutory provisions of the Coroner's Act of 1988 and the Coroner's Rules of 1984. The Coroner's Act contains powers for **regulating** the rules and procedures at, or in connection with, inquests and post-mortem examinations, whereas the Coroner's Rules contains the power to **make** those rules regulating inquests and post-mortems. At the time of writing, no changes had been made to these rules.

When the coroner has opened an inquest into a suspicious death, it is usual for it to be adjourned 'pending further police enquiries'. The coroner during his examinations of the witnesses and the evidence can only establish certain facts at the conclusion of the inquest:

    *1.  The identity of the deceased*
    *2.  Where, when and how the deceased came to die.*

One important point to be made is that neither the coroner nor a jury can directly blame, or name any individual as being criminally responsible, for negligently causing the death. That is a matter for the criminal or civil courts alone to decide.

If the police arrest or charge a person with homicide and the CPS proceed with a court prosecution, then the inquest cannot be completed until there has been a trial in the criminal courts.

Once the inquest is resumed, with or without a jury, a verdict must be reached even if it is an 'open verdict' in circumstances where recommended procedures of evidence cannot produce a definite conclusion.[2]

In considering the theory in relation to Alex's case the simple question is: 'Did the police, the pathologist, the coroner and the CPS put into practice the above sequence?' The answer is also simple; it is an emphatic 'NO.'

My son Alex's case seemed at first to be so straightforward, when I was told and accepted that he had died of natural causes. However I will leave the readers to make their judgement as to whether or not I have proved there are sufficient grounds for my accusations that status, money, inadequate investigations and influence did pervert the course of justice and the coroner into giving an inappropriate verdict, which had the effect of prematurely discontinuing police enquiries into what was an obvious homicide.

---

Under the Coroner's Act **section 8 – (1)** whether or not a jury is called at an inquest is a matter for the coroner concerned and he has a wide discretion whether or not he calls a jury. However there are certain cases where it is mandatory for him to call a jury.

## Part 3 – Oh! What tangled web

On our return to New Barnet we tried to make some sense of the proceedings we had just gone through and we agreed that for a natural death, some of them were unexpected, but decided it was probably part of normal police routine. Maureen undertook the difficult task of informing friends and relations of Alex's death, but I rang Alex's greatly shaken father to tell him of the loss of our son. It was another very grim night for me, as I struggled to come to terms with the unfairness of my 28 year old son dying before me, his 70 year old mother.

The following day, Maureen, Ken and I discussed funeral arrangements and decided New Barnet would be the most central and convenient area for family and friends to congregate. We delayed deciding on the form of the ceremony because I thought, in fairness, Steve Jones should have some involvement, but we agreed to cremation which is what Alex wished. (Actually, he would have preferred a Viking's funeral)

Towards midday on Thursday 16th May, DS Bathie rang us and we were stunned to learn that although the coroner had opened the inquest at 10 am, he had almost immediately adjourned it. He then visited the mortuary and viewed the body himself. After this examination he had instructed the police to make further enquiries that would delay the inquest verdict, it would be about three weeks before the coroner could consider releasing the body for the funeral and the issue of a death certificate. He then asked if we had decided on burial or cremation. We received no explanation for the coroner's action and DS Bathie gave Ken no opportunity to ask questions.

We were left in a state of utter confusion and had no idea what to do next except wait. Had we not been so ignorant of the law and had not been misled into believing Alex's death was due to natural causes, we may have realised that we needed, and should have obtained, legal advice. This left me in quandary as to what I should do in the meantime but, after talking things over with Maureen we reached the decision to go ahead with the funeral arrangements and she made an appointment with a Barnet undertaker for the Saturday morning.

The next step was to inform Alex's Housing Association of his death, only to be told, incorrectly, by an official that we had to clear the flat within the week. I asked Steve Jones to help me with this very painful task. On the next day, Friday, he brought with him several friends and between us we cleared the flat of Alex's possessions, mainly by distributing them amongst his friends and bagging the rest to take to charitable organisations. This last job was undertaken by Steve later in the week. One thing which is very important to note is that there were no signs in the flat that any forensic investigations had been undertaken by the police between 13th and 17th May. His cash card and notebook were not in his flat and have still not been found.

Once these two tasks were completed, I decided there was no reason for me to stay in New Barnet for the three weeks wait, so I returned to my home in Torksey, Lincolnshire, where I could occupy myself in continuing my study for a Post-graduate degree. I was very grateful that Maureen and Ken had undertaken to liaise with DS Bathie on my behalf and to deal with any urgent matters should they arise.
.
As it happened, there was very little for them to see to. In fact, for the next eight weeks it seemed the police were woefully inactive. I know differently today because I have learned that the police scrupulously, (or perhaps I should say unscrupulously), concealed from us that investigations into Alex's murder were underway. Yet throughout all the frequent calls Ken or Maureen made to DS Bathie, he exasperatingly refused to divulge any information on either the coroner's actions or the nature of police investigations. The justification for the refusal was always the same "it would be prejudicial to police enquiries", and by the end of June we were becoming increasingly frustrated.

At the beginning of July we were losing patience, and acting on my behalf, Ken began to press the police for a fuller explanation for the coroner's refusal to release the body. DS Bathie gave the reason for the hold-up as 'due to the nature of the case', that is, death from natural causes. This gave it a low priority in the pathologist's heavy autopsy list; therefore, he had been unable to complete his report. He promised to apply more pressure to the pathologist and we would have news in a few days. I can say now that this was totally untrue, as in 2005, I learned the pathologist submitted his written report to the police and the coroner on June 16th 1996. Therefore when DS Bathie promised to apply pressure, he was already in possession of the pathologist's autopsy report. Obviously it was another delaying tactic

Nevertheless, we thought that for once DS Bathie was being as good as his word when on July 7th he rang Ken to inform him that the pathologist's report had been received. But he then went on to say that no date could be set for the resumed inquest, as in the coroner's opinion, **'the report indicated sufficient physical evidence to warrant a high level enquiry'** and also that **'someone was helping with police enquiries'**. These terms meant nothing to Ken, or to any of us. DS Bathie was asked to explain them more fully but again he refused because to do so would be **'prejudicial to police enquires'**. He was then asked if these official actions were because Alex had been subjected to a violent attack earlier on the evening of May 3rd which had later triggered the fatal asthma attack. DS Bathie refused to confirm or deny this repeating that any answer could prejudice police enquiries.

This evasive behaviour led us in our ignorance to the conclusion that violence had indeed been perpetrated on Alex and was the reason why someone 'was helping the police with their enquiries'. During the next three weeks several more, unproductive, phone calls were made to the police asking for information on the progress in the case. All requests were refused.

On July 25[th,] quite surprisingly, DS Bathie did have information for us, but it wasn't what we expected. We were told that police investigations were now completed and the 'Investigation Team' was preparing a case for the Crown Prosecution Service to consider a prosecution which would be ready in about three weeks. To say we were flummoxed is an understatement 'WHAT PROSECUTION AND WHY? DS Bathie, when urged by Ken to provide an explanation for the CPS involvement refused to say. He did state that **"no malice or drugs were involved"**, but would not clarify this statement either. We were more confused than ever as we were not aware that drug use had ever been considered. But at the same time it seemed to annihilate the family's theory of inflicted violence. We felt that we were once more in a vacuum of ignorance and betrayal. Furthermore, that statement 'no malice or drugs' proved to be another fabrication. Drugs were involved as was confirmed by the toxicology report read out during the inquest, and, the subjects of both malice and drugs, were recorded in the Murder Review Group (MRG) report issued ten years later. This Report was initiated by the then Police Commissioner Sir John Stevens in 2005, at my request.

Ken and Maureen had booked a family holiday in their time-share flat in Cornwell and I had arranged to visit another niece in Scotland, so the police were told we were taking a seven day break and would be back on 13th of August.

When I returned home, I found a message on the answering phone asking me to contact DS Bathie urgently. This I did, and the DS told me that the pathologist had requested to see Alex's medical records urgently but that his GP, Dr Mills, wanted my written permission before she would release them. This was ironic, really, as it was the first time I had been consulted on any decision concerning Alex's death. I was also warned that the police would obtain a court order if I refused. Permission was given to Dr Mills, first by faxing a letter and then by a letter of confirmation posted the following day. The practice manager rang me back to say that Dr Mills was very reluctant to comply with my request as she had great reservations about the propriety of releasing medical notes if a death was from natural causes. I asked that the notes be released as I did not want any further delay to having my son's body released, as the waiting was beginning to be intolerable.

I then rang DS Bathie to advise him that the notes were being released and also for him to explain to me why the request for the notes had been delayed for fourteen weeks after the post-mortem. Once more he failed to provide an explanation.

On August 27th or 28th DS Bathie contacted Mr Amphlett to report that the police case was now prepared and would be submitted to the CPS on Friday 30th August. The decision to prosecute or not would take about 2-3 weeks. Again he refused to give any further information on the subject matter or say why the case had developed the way it had. All he did was to repeat the deceptive explanation that the delay was due to the pathologist's failure to meet the police earlier requests to <u>complete</u> his report.

Unfortunately at that time our family situation was becoming more distressing as Maureen was undergoing prolonged treatment for recurring cancer and naturally Ken had to give priority to his wife and children, yet in spite of their own worries both managed to continue their support to me.

Anxiety over Maureen and grief over Alex was taking its toll on me. I consulted my most helpful and understanding GP who thought my best line of action should be to seek advice from the Citizens Advice Bureau. The counsellor who interviewed me decided my case warranted half an hour's free legal advice and arranged a consultation for me with a Lincoln solicitor, Mr Marshall.

Mr Marshal, after considering the meagre information I was able to give him, considered that it was essential for me to obtain a copy of the post-mortem report and he took my instruction to do this. Again, acting on his advice, which was not to read the report myself as it could be very upsetting, I agreed that the PM report when received should be sent to Ken who could then disclose the nature of its contents to me as he thought fit.

About a week later, Mr Marshall contacted me and asked me was I sure that Alex's body was at Poplar mortuary, because the Coroner's Officer claimed they did not have a body under the name of William Alexander Barrack in Poplar mortuary. He had given Mr Marshall the telephone numbers of several other mortuaries in nearby areas all of which he had contacted without success.

When I confirmed that it was at Poplar mortuary and that I had identified Alex's body, Mr Marshall rang Mr Davies and then told me that the Coroner's Officer's first attempt to locate the body had failed, because it was still labelled 'unknown male'. I was outraged; it was an insult to Alex's memory and affront to his dingy to neglect to give him his name after two post-mortems had been held, an inquest had been opened and the coroner had carried out his own examination of the body. It seemed to be unbelievable. Today of course I believe that that it was all a tactic to delay matters to enable the coroner's office to find a means to prevent me obtaining the post-mortem report.

Mr Marshal received the post-mortem report on September 24th. He immediately sent it to Ken as arranged, but the pathologist's conclusions on the cause of death, did not correspond to death being from cardiac arrest as described by DS Bathie. Maureen or Ken, I can't recall who, gave me this incomprehensible autopsy finding recorded by Dr Michael John Heath, A Home Office pathologist about whom I was to hear a great deal more later. They are as follows:

> **".....the changes (*noted on the body*) were the result of occlusion of the upper airway by pressure being applied to the neck and mouth.**
>
> **These changes could have been produced by the application of an apparatus and/or application of a balloon/bag...**" (Document 1 PM p7)

What came into my mind immediately was the distressing and overwhelming realisation that Alex need not have died. Unfortunately, none of us, including Alex's father, took on board the significance of that finding, only the fact that Alex had not died from a heart attack registered. Yet we wondered how a natural death could have resulted from 'an apparatus.'

Therefore we decided to ring DS Bathie and ask him just that. I do not know if at the time DS Bathie was told that we had obtained the post-mortem report, when he was requested to provide fuller details of the actual circumstances of Alex's death, which did not appear to us to have been from natural causes. He responded by stating he could make no comment on either the cause or the circumstances of death until the CPS made a decision on the police investigations. Once more he insisted that Alex's death 'had been quiet and peaceful'. He also advised us that as soon as the CPS made a decision, the coroner would release Alex's body.

The serious mistake I made was taking in the solicitor's advice not to read the full post-mortem report myself, when I could have understood its contents better than Ken and Maureen who had no medical background, and related only the eight report's conclusions to me. Although extremely disturbed at what the post-mortem conclusions revealed, and the reference to the balloon bag, Maureen, Ken and I naively decided to accept police advice to wait for the CPS decision and coroner's inquest which, we had been led to understand, would provide all the facts and give answers to our questions.

Around about this time Mr William Barrack, Alex's father, who lived near Leeds but had been in constant contact with Maureen, became very uneasy about police handling of the case and began to make his own separate enquiries. He hoped he could pressurise the police into being more informative. However, DS Bathie subjected him to the same infuriatingly evasive behaviour as we had experienced from the start.

Altogether we waited four weeks for the CPS to make their decision which, when given, was, 'that there was insufficient evidence to proceed with a prosecution'.  At that particular time I was overjoyed with the non-prosecution decision because, I thought it meant Alex had not been subject to any violence. We then expected the coroner to release the body almost immediately as had been promised by Mr Bathie.  However, when we were still kept waiting, we contacted him to ask for a release date to allow us to the make the final funeral arrangements. I was devastated to be told that the coroner had refused to accept the CPS decision and had requested that the CPS review the police evidence again. He would not therefore  release the body to the family. According to DS Bathie, if a prosecution was ordered a defence counsel may require a further post-mortem, even though two such examinations had already been carried out.  This was another puzzling situation for us.

Near the end of October, we had another call from DS Bathie, and this time we were sure we would be given a release date for Alex's body. We could not believe it when we told the CPS had again advised the coroner, they did not intend to proceed with a prosecution. Once more we expected an inquest date and the release of the body. It didn't happen, because,  DS Bathie rang to tell Ken that the coroner was still not satisfied with the CPS refusal, and was adamant that he would not release my son's body until he himself had made further enquiries, and then held an inquest. Therefore we should not expect the inquest to be resumed before early January 1997. As a result of this decision we were to endure another distressing bout of waiting and uncertainty.

DI Baff when asked why the coroner was holding on to the body of my son, when he could issue an interim death certificate, would only say that he believed the coroner was making his own enquiries. According to Mr Ensor of the York CPS in an interview he had with Mr Barrack and I in Jan 1999, there were no records of the coroner ever making any requests for further investigations.

Increasingly worried by these many unexplained developments, I contacted the Lincoln Coroner's Officer for advice. He gave his view that it appeared to be an extraordinary situation. In his opinion the conduct of the officials involved did not conform to the normal practice of most coroners and police forces, which is always to minimise any delay to holding the funeral, to treat the bereaved with compassion and understanding, and to keep them informed on every aspect of the case as fully as possible.

He also advised me to wait patiently for the inquest, as he expected that during the inquest, in accordance with the Coroners Act of 1984 and Coroner's Rules of 1988, the full facts would emerge, and could probably account for conduct of the officials involved. This I decided we would do.

Suddenly, without any explanation during the last week in November, we were told by DS Bathie that the coroner would release Alex's body to allow the family to make arrangements for the funeral and cremation, before the inquest which he would hold in January 1997.

The coroner issued a certificate of cremation on the 30th November and this was the first document, of any kind, to be received by me or issued officially, which confirmed Alex's death. This documentary authority, unaccountably withheld for seven months, at last allowed me to lay my son to rest. The funeral, a quiet family affair, was held on Friday, December 13th 1996. Alex's mother and father, stood side by side to say a final goodbye to our son.

Although the coroner had opened and adjourned the inquest on the death of Alex Barrack on May 16th 1996, he did not officially certify and record the fact until December 17th 1996, four days after the funeral, when a death certificate was issued. I did not receive my copy of this document until after the inquest and it was only then was I able to settle my son's affairs.

On January 7<sup>th</sup> 1997 Poplar coroner's officer informed us by telephone, not confirmed officially by letter as is the usual practice, that the inquest would be held at 11am January 9th 1997. Altogether we had waited eight months for the inquest to be resumed and during that period had learned very little of the true circumstances surrounding the death of William Alexander Barrack. We were not informed of a family's rights at inquest, including the right to have legal representation and to question and challenge witnesses. The only advice given by Mr Davies the coroner's officer was for us to wrap up well, as the central heating in the coroner's court had broken down.

Mr Bill Barrack (father), Mr and Mrs Amphlett and I with and two friends of Alex, attended the inquest, totally unprepared to hear the evidence to be presented during the inquest and totally ignorant of the dreadful truth, that the death of Alex Barrack was indeed a cruel and needless waste of his life, and should have been avoided.

# CHAPTER FIVE

**Part 1 - We arrive for the inquest– January 9$^{th}$ 1997 - the truth begins to emerge.**

Maureen, Ken and I left New Barnet for Poplar Coroner's Court to attend the inquest on a typical January winter's day. It was very cold, with a sharp wind driving rain and sleet into our faces as we walked the short distance to the Court room and we were then shown into a small waiting room where Alex's father was already waiting. It was almost as cold indoors as the outside temperature; Mr Davies had done right in advising us to wrap up warmly. Shortly afterwards, two friends of Alex arrived Matthew and a girl called Spike. A little later Mr Davies came into the room to inform us that the inquest, scheduled for 11am, would be delayed as the previous case was running late.

He was obviously much taken aback to see me there and said to me 'I wasn't expecting you to be here and I have arranged for Mr Amphlett to give evidence of the identity of Mr Barrack, I though you would be too upset. As far as I remember, I replied 'Why would you think that? I identified my son before and expected to do it again'. At the time, knowing very little about inquest procedures, it didn't seem to me to matter who carried out the identification, so I told Mr Davies to let the arrangement stand. (*In May when the inquest was opened Ken may have been improperly recorded as the person who officially identified Alex*).

Our little group were standing together and trying to make sense of the paltry information we had on inquest proceedings, wondering how we were expected to take part in the proceedings, hoping that someone would arrive and enlighten us before we were called into the court. Suddenly the door opened and a stranger was shown into the waiting room. He neither looked nor spoke to us but sat huddled in a corner on a chair. We all looked at him curiously, wondering who he was, and Maureen whispered to me 'Do you think he is the man who was with Alex? I replied 'I hope not', only because he wasn't at all the heroic figure I had imagined him to be. This man was older than Alex, shorter and I thought overweight, wearing a rather grubby ex-army officer's overcoat. He wasn't left with us long, because someone opened the door and beckoned him out, and the obviously relieved stranger jumped to his feet and speedily shot out of the room.

Not long after this, Mr Davies entered the room again, but it was only to hand out three documents. He left them with us but did not explain why we had received them. These documents were actually three police witness statements. One was that of Steve Jones, Alex's friend and ex-partner, the second that of a paramedic, Lee Butler and the third that of Dr Heyman, a Hospital Registrar. I received Steve Jones' statement, while Maureen and Bill Barrack were handed the other two. We barely had time to do more than skim read the contents of one document each before Mr Davies called us out. We followed him into the courtroom, each in state of shocked disbelief, at what we had read. This initial shock would be increasingly intensified as the inquest proceeded.

We walked into the coroner's court totally unaware that as 'interested persons' we had 'rights at an inquest',[3] and that because of the true nature of the case, we should have been advised to have a legal representative to exercise those rights on our behalf, and when necessary, question the witnesses or challenge the evidence. Unfortunately, we entered the court without legal assistance and completely unaware that we had the right to interrupt the proceedings. So we sat in silence during the entire inquisition, apart from one brief occasion, while the coroner conducted an inquest into the death of my son which, from start to finish, was a travesty of justice.

Looking back, I remember the court room as appearing large, grim and gloomy, more like Victorian chapel with its high ceiling, and the coroner's elevated podium rising above a vacant central area. At the two sides of the dais were two benches. Running parallel, but further back, were three or four tiered benches. In front of the well, and therefore, immediately under the coroner's eye, more benches stretched to the back of the courtroom.[4]

Mr Davies directed family and friends to the tiered benches on the far side of the court room and seated us at the right hand of the coroner where we were not only well back, but also out of his direct line of vision. I was indignant to find myself sitting next to an obviously very junior,

---

[3] Interested persons
[4] seating diagram

inquisitive newspaper reporter, an arrangement which I considered to be an insensitive gesture towards me and the family. Occupying the front bench in front of the podium were four persons, who, were in fact official witnesses. The recently promoted police officers DCI Baff and DI Bathie, the pathologist Dr Heath and, I think one other person, who took no part in the proceedings. We were not told who he was or why he had been called.

One other individual sat alone on a bench below the dais, and after we were all seated another man was shown to a seat, which we all noticed, was as far away from us as possible, and very close to the exit. This person was the stranger who we later learned was an important witness, who had been mistakenly left with us in the waiting room. As the inquest proceeded and we learned the nature of the stranger's involvement, it began to dawn on us that the separated seating arrangements had been a deliberate, strategic move to keep us apart and also to distance us from the coroner.

I now know that this seating arrangement was out of keeping with the normal practice which the coroner's officer, acting as clerk and usher, should have followed. When a family is legally represented, their advocates should sit in the front row and have easy access to their clients.[5] When the family are not represented, they should be seated in the front row as this allows them to easily engage the coroner's attention and he to engage theirs.[6] I believe that denying us this important contact was intentional. Also, it is not the practice at an inquest to give reporters such easy access to a family.[7]

In fact, we felt completely isolated from all the officials and the witness Simpson. The following sketch will make show just why we believe that it was the coroner's intention to distance us from the proceedings.

---

[5] legal access Levine
[6] Levine on Coroners Courts family no reps
[7] Diagram of Court Layout p31

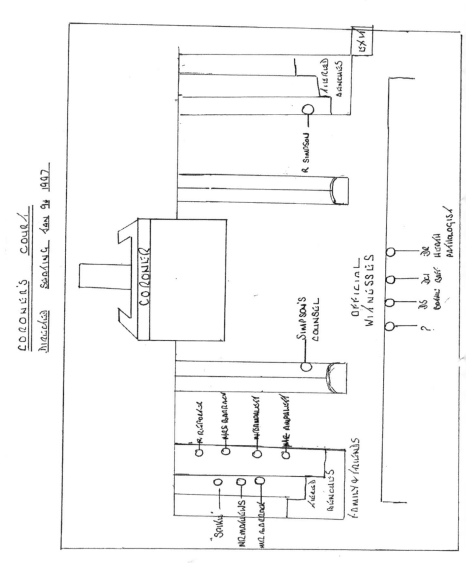

Diagram of the seating, which did not conform to the normal practice, because we should have been seated immediately in front of the coroner.

64

Unlike other judiciary officers, the coroner is not restricted by detailed rules of court procedure. Nevertheless, the proceedings are formal and should be conducted punctiliously along established lines. His duty is to "seek out the truth and record the facts concerning the death as the public interest requires" by obtaining reliable answers to four important factual questions[8] in order to ensure that "justice is not only done but also seen to be done":

1. The identity of the deceased
2. The place of his death
3. The time of death
4. How the decease came by his death

Unfortunately, as all too many families have discovered to their cost, coroners can interpret this duty in different ways. Factual questions don't always receive factual answers and justice is not done. In conducting Alex's inquest case, the coroner excelled himself in the "irregularity of his proceedings, in rejecting evidence and making insufficiency of inquiry."[9]

**Part 2 – The identification of the deceased**

Eventually, at about 11.30am, the coroner made his entrance into the court through a door at the back of the raised podium. We rose dutifully to our feet as requested until the coroner Dr Chan, had taken his seat. There was no jury present at this inquest, but according to Section **8.** – (1) (a) of The Coroner's Act 1988, there should have been, as there was reasonable cause to suspect that the deceased died a violent or unnatural death.[10] It would have been very instructive for the family because, had a jury been called, been sworn in and taken the oath, the coroner would have had a duty to fully explain to the jury the functions of the court and the purpose of an inquest.[11] Therefore, this explanation was denied us.

In fact, the number of people in the court was very small. There were three

---

[8]          "                    Factual truths
[9] Coroner's Act 13 –(1)  grounds to order to hold anew inquest
[10] Jury not called unnatural death act
[11] Explanation to jury

official witnesses who gave evidence and one other who did not, all of whom would be familiar with inquest procedure. In addition there were four members of the family, the two friends of Alex, all of us were totally ignorant of inquest procedure, and the miss-seated cub reporter. Another person present who was seated in the well of the court was a top barrister, a Queen's Counsel, and no doubt an expert on inquests. He was the legal representative for the last witness who was seated near the exit. No members of the public were present but whether this was a deliberate exclusion or one due to the inclement weather, I can't say. However I do have my suspicions.

The coroner's opening address was brief, in fact so brief, it didn't register with me, but, one thing I am certain of is that he purposely disregarded the family's presence except for one occasion when he had to call a family member as an identification witness. He most certainly did not offer any condolences on our loss, as is the custom.

Dr Chan made no reference to the fact that this was a resumed inquest which had been opened and adjourned on 16th May 1996. According to the Coroner's Act when an inquest is resumed without a jury, it carries on from where it left off. In that case, surely the coroner should have made a statement to that effect, but he did not. So anything that was discussed at the opening of the inquest was never disclosed, including the reason why it was adjourned. *(Later, when a copy of the opening record of the inquest was requested, the Inquest Unit was unable to trace the original.)*

Dr Chan then lost no time in calling the first witness to begin to fulfil his obligation to obtain reliable answers to the first factual question, 'the identity of the deceased.' This was the role, which, had procedure, been followed should been mine. Ken, having been selected by the coroner's officer was, called to the witness stand and sworn in.

The coroner began by asking if Ken was a friend of the deceased but Ken corrected this, stating his relationship was that of husband to a cousin of the deceased, and therefore a family member. The coroner's next mode of questioning was unexpected, he made several more statements and asked Ken to confirm them, two of which was disconcerting to his witness.

Dr Chan informed Ken that on the 16th of May 1996, (the only very

66

oblique reference made to the adjourned opening of the inquest) that Detective Chief Inspector Baff had confirmed to him that **he** had identified the body of the deceased to be William Alexander Barrack. This threw Ken off balance because he knew that the DCI (then DI) had not been present during **my** identification of Alex and therefore that statement was not strictly true. Then Dr Chan asked him for the purpose of the record to confirm that Alex was born on the 28<sup>th</sup> March 1968 in Lincolnshire. Once more Ken was at a loss. He knew neither were correct but couldn't recall the right details. So, I interrupted the questioning and gave the correct information.

I was quite taken aback and nonplussed when the coroner failed to ask me to identify myself and give my relationship to the deceased. I had expected him to query my right to challenge his statement. His only comments were brusque:

> "There is some doubt here......Born on the 23<sup>rd</sup> March 1968 in Birmingham.
> Thank you very much"

And that was it, I was just an interruption. The identification was over and Ken was dismissed.

One question on Alex's identification that has never been answered is why the post-mortem was carried out in such a rush and before any attempts had been made to identify him. Experts in forensic medicine hold that identification of the body is of foremost importance in the practice of forensic medicine and should normally take place before the autopsy is held. According to one of the foremost experts:

1. **The dead body must definitely be identified before the autopsy**
2. **A relative or a police officer must confirm the identity of the body before the autopsy begins.**[12]

When I queried this point with forensic expert Professor Bernard Knight

---

[12] Identification before autopsy

he said in a letter to me that there could be special circumstances which do require an urgent post-mortem. This confirms that there must have been special circumstances which justified such a hasty post-mortem on Alex's body, but these were withheld from me at the time. I did discover at the inquest, that the circumstances had lead to a suspect being questioned over a suspicious death and then released on bail.

**Part 3 – The absent witnesses - the importance of their written statements.**

The next witness called was Chief Inspector David Baff who was greeted warmly by the coroner before he was sworn in.

The coroner then told the court that he had received a medical report concerning the witness Steven William Jones from a psychiatrist requesting, that he be excused giving evidence. The coroner told the court he had agreed to this request. He then asked DCI Baff to read Mr Jones statement.

There were in actual fact three statements from absent witnesses and DCI Baff read all three aloud, one after the other to the court. We had received copies of these documents just before the inquest started:

1. Statement provided on 17$^{th}$ May 1996 by Steven Jones, age over 21 and unemployed. Read in full.

2. Statement provided 8$^{th}$ May 1996 by Lee Jane Butler a London Ambulance paramedic attending victim. Read out in full.

3. Statement provided on 15$^{h}$ May by Dr Timothy Heath, no other details provided.

After giving this evidence DCI Baff then temporarily vacated the witness stand.

Although the coroner has control of the witness list, he examined remarkably few, and I quote "In any event, the coroner must examine on oath concerning the death, **all** persons having knowledge of those facts whom he **considers** it expedient to examine"[13]. The coroner offered no explanation why he chose to use so few witnesses nor why he had excluded the two medical witnesses from giving evidence at an inquest on a death which, he knew perfectly well, had been investigated as an unlawful killing He simply stated that he would mark the three statements as Exhibits C1, C2 and C3., and informed the court he intended to use all three as documentary evidence to assist him in his inquiry. But apart from few very perfunctory references he did not. However, I know from a reliable and sympathetic source that there were at least eleven documents which she considered should have been introduced as evidence. She was of the opinion that their use could have ensured a different and more suitable verdict [14]

The two medical witnesses should have been called to give evidence in person to him, as they had given evidence to Dr Heyman and the police which was important in establishing the time, place and cause of death. Like many other families we found to our cost that the coroner's control over an inquest exceeds that of a judge in a High Court and it appears that Dr Chan's control over this inquest was excessive and, in my opinion, interfered with the course of justice. I won't quibble over his excusing Steven Jones, as I had reason to be very aware of his fragile state of mind, but the answers he gave to certain questions asked by the police could have been used more extensively to introduce other areas into police investigations and to provide more details important in establishing the true circumstances, including the cause and of time of death

Two paramedics from the London Ambulance Service, who received the call to the address given in a 999 call, had both attended Alex and attempted to resuscitate him. Due to the information received from the Emergency Call Centre, they separately looked for physical artefacts and other evidence possibly related to the patient's collapse. Even though the coroner admitted only one of their statements, I do know that both paramedics gave statements to the police. Both of them would have included information concerning vital information on the signs of death on the body and the circumstances in which it was found.

---

[13] Expedient to examine
[14] transcriber

In 1999, in an interview given to Mr Barrack and myself by Mr Absalom, the London Ambulance Service Senior Incident and Claims Assessor, he told us that he had been prepared to accompany the witnesses to the inquest as their legal adviser and that he was very surprised that they were not called. He considered it was most unusual for any coroner not to call the paramedics as witnesses to give evidence in court, especially when they are first on the scene of a sudden death and the circumstances appear suspicious. In his opinion, paramedics can be the most important witnesses at an inquest on a sudden or suspicious death. Mr Absalom very kindly gave us the opportunity to hear a tape recording of the full 999 conversation between a witness and the 'Call Taker' in the interval before the ambulance arrived and issued us with a transcribed copy.[15]

The omission from the list of the third witness, Dr Heyman, was even more incomprehensible, as he was the person responsible for reporting the death to the coroner, when Alex was taken by the Paramedics directly into his charge in the Accident and Emergency Department of the Royal London Hospital. After futilely attempting further resuscitation and upon making an assessment of the condition of the body, he decided that he could not reach a conclusion on the cause of death and asked for the matter to be reported to the coroner and the police.

All the above documents and events will be discussed more fully as I progress through the inquest details.

What was becoming clear to me after the reading of those three statements to the court was that the accounts given to me by the police of the events and circumstances of my son's death bore no relation to the facts whatsoever. It was in no way the simple uncomplicated case they had persistently encouraged me to accept. By the time the inquest reached its close, we were becoming convinced that the conducting of every area of official investigations and the conclusions they had reached, had been contrived to prevent us delving too far into police *modus operandi*[16] until the inquest verdict had been given. The conduct of the investigations and the way the inquest was run, allowed the police to close their investigations and it was too late for me to avoid the tangled web of deceit.

---

[15] 999call Police refused me a copy
[16] Method of operations

I will always deeply regret not taking further advice from Mr Marshall after receiving the post-mortem report. But then, it was not offered and unfortunately, I did accept the advice of the Lincoln Coroner's Officer to wait for the inquest.

# CHAPTER SIX

*"O that though thou should give dust a tongue*
*To cry to thee*
*And then not hear it crying*

## Introduction - – The Inquest continued

In the previous chapter I dealt with the fairly straightforward question of establishing the true facts of Alex's identity, which was the first of the four factual questions which is incumbent on any coroner to ask at an inquest held on a sudden or suspicious death.

It was a great deal more difficult to research true facts relating to the time, and how and where he died because it involved so many other people who had made decisions affecting the investigations into the death

Looking back, I am appalled at how little information I had when I first doggedly set out to refute the blatantly specious official versions of how, where, and at what time Alex had died. It has entailed a great deal of analysis over many years and cross referencing of police records, the inquest report, witness evidence and a variety of other types of evidence into which all three questions are interwoven. After thirteen years, I think I can now give what I firmly believe are true and accurate answers to those questions, which is more than the coroner did.

I cannot stress strongly enough that had the coroner called a jury, I would never have had to face such an uphill struggle. I truly believe that having a jury present would have changed the manner in which the inquest was conducted and that any verdict given would have had integrity.

Unfortunately, under The Coroner's Act **section 8 (1),** whether or not a jury is called at an inquest is a matter for the coroner concerned and he has a wide discretion whether or not he calls a jury. However, as I said earlier, there are certain cases where it is mandatory for him to call a jury.

I would argue that the particular circumstances in which Alex died are prejudicial to a section of the public. Both the High Court of Justice and the European Court have condemned these circumstances. I will say more about this later on.

Furthermore, a coroner, before the inquest, is in possession of all the evidence, and he may have already formed a bias towards a particular verdict which he must set aside, as during the course of his inquisitions of the witnesses, a different verdict may emerge. Where a jury is present, its verdict may well differ from the coroner's opinion. In my opinion, a more appropriate verdict would have been achieved had a jury been there as, quote;

*." The court is obliged to submit the case fairly but let the jury do the deciding".* [17]

The Coroner's Act **Section 8** is very often used unfairly at an inquest into a sudden or suspicious death by allowing the coroner to act alone. But a jury can, often and do, speak successfully in defence of the silent dead. So it doesn't take much commonsense to work out why a jury was not called in this case and why witness numbers were restricted. I believe Dr Chan did have a bias towards a particular verdict. This became obvious to us from the manner he adopted when questioning his witnesses. We, as a family, did detect that he was applying some pressure to obtain the answers he sought, particularly in setting the time of death to be much later than the factual evidence suggested.

The discussion in this chapter is mainly concerned with establishing the true time of death, and to do that I must go back to the 999 call to the Emergency Services, which is when agents of the Public Services first became involved. I will then discuss the flawed account of events given by the caller to the Ambulance Service operator, referred to in the transcript of the call as the 'Call Taker'. It is also the time when the web of secrecy surrounding my son's death began to be woven. At the very centre of the web is the man who had been with Alex when he died.

In this chapter I query the soundness of the answers given by Simpson to questions asked by the Call Taker. This conversation was recorded on tape

---

[17] Levine? Page.

and then transcribed by the Ambulance Service. I hold a copy of this transcription and it has been used in conjunction with witness statements to support my analysis of the time Alex actually died and why Dr Heath at the inquest, described the death as **'query suspicious'** from the outset.

We had already learned from the written evidence of the paramedic and the hospital doctor that the police account of the time and cause of death did not accord with the facts. After nine months waiting, we were faced with the distressing knowledge that Alex's death could not have been from natural causes, and there never was any 'heroic attempt' to keep him alive between the 999 call at 4.54 am. and the paramedics' arrival sixteen minutes later at 5.10am. Far from taking immediate action to save a life, I suggest the supposed hero had waited over two hours before calling for assistance for a man he knew to be already dead.

**Part 1 – The 999 call – The Ambulance Service transcript - the false witness**

The deception and I suppose the secrecy, surrounding Alex's death, started the moment the caller dialled 999. Unfortunately, I could not obtain a transcript of the actual call, but I was told by a manager that if the caller had indicated a possible overdose of heroin to the operator, then this information would be passed to the Ambulance Service as urgent. The tape transcript of the Ambulance response call identifies the caller as Robert Simpson, the owner of the flat in London E3 where Alex met his untimely death

I will show that although Robert Simpson knew that Alex was already dead, he attempted to deceive the Call Taker and the ambulance crew over the time of death.

Question – "Ambulance service, can I help?"

Reply – "I think someone has **just** died in my flat".

After giving details of the address, Simpson continued:

"...I mean... this chap, he is a friend of mine, and I think he'd

74

been taking drugs this evening and he came back this evening, and I think  he is dead".

The problem here for the Call Taker is that he would have realised that some minutes must have elapsed since the time of collapse given by Simpson and that the chance's of reviving the patient were extremely slim. But he was duty bound to ask Simpson to carry out the CPR[18]resuscitation technique until the ambulance arrived. When he asked if the patient was still breathing Simpson answered: "I don't think so….he's gone blue".

Throughout the remaining conversation with the Call Taker, Simpson attempted to give the impression that resuscitation was being carried out.

Simpson was asked if there anything in the patient's mouth, and, if so to take it out. At this point there was some problem with the phone, and the full answer was not recorded except that the patient had just 'gone limp'.

> Call Taker – "Is he flat on his back?"
> Simpson – "No, he's sitting up",

Simpson was instructed to lay him flat and the question on the mouth was repeated.

> Call Taker – "Anything in his mouth?"

> Simpson – "Nothing in his mouth".

From the background noises heard, it seemed that Simpson was apparently acting on his instructions because the transcript states that gurgling sounds were heard by the Call Taker and Simpson was instructed to tilt the head further back to stop it. (When I heard the gurgling sounds I recognised them as escaping gas formed after death, and forced out by pressure from a moving a body. A sound I became familiar with during the laying out of many bodies).

Simpson was then given the instructions for cardiac massage and induced

---

[18] Cardiac Pulmonary Resuscitation

breathing and during this Simpson exclaimed "He's gone an even stranger colour".

A little later:

Simpson – "There's vomit **now** coming out of his mouth".

Call Taker –"Right scoop it out, just using your two fingers scoop it all out for me".

Simpson – "I think there is blood amongst it".

Simpson was told to continue the compressions once the vomit was cleared, but Simpson reported there was no pulse. Then:

Simpson – He's bringing up more sick".

.The reason I have recorded the above with detail is because most of what Simpson told the Call Taker was untrue. This was only one of several versions that Simpson gave to officials.

The next question dealt with drugs:

Call Taker –"Is he an addict?"

Simpson – "Ah well he's someone who takes a bit of drugs but, em he's...not....he's just someone I know relatively casually and we were out at a club and I think he's taken something".

Notably, Simpson makes no mention of a heroin overdose to the Call Taker or to paramedics when the ambulance crew did arrive.

A little later, the Call Taker asked Simpson to open his front door and turn on all his lights to help the crew to locate the flat. In asking Simpson to leave the patient the Caller must have felt that the patient was probably beyond recovery.

On his return, the resuscitation was restarted until Simpson was informed that the ambulance was outside and was asked to show the crew where they needed to go. Discontinuing CPR again at this point confirms that Alex was already dead and it would be quite safe to leave him.

The significance of this transcript is that it clearly shows that life was extinct before the 999 call was made, and therefore the trained Call Taker, even in the absence of any response within six minutes of the so called collapse, carried out the resuscitation advice to Simpson, in the full knowledge that the chances of revival for Alex were virtually nil and would prove to be futile. The paramedics and the hospital team in their turn acted on Simpson's account and continued with the required procedure, although, fully aware they were dealing with a patient who was already showing signs of having been dead for considerable time.

Mr Absalom, the paramedic's manager told Alex's father and me that had this incident occurred today (in 1999); the crew would have had the authority to state that the patient was already dead without a doctor being present and discontinue treatment. In 1996 they had not yet been given that authority.

**Part 2 –The importance of the paramedic's statement - establishing the time of death**

Lee Jane Butler stated to the police that at 4.54 am on the 4th May 1996 that she and the ambulance driver Terry Walsh, responded to an emergency call at 14 Driftway, Grove Road, E3, but owing to inadequate directions took 16 minutes to locate the address and arrived at 5.10 am.

On arrival they were led by Simpson into the bathroom, where they found Alex naked and lying on his back, face upwards. Because the bathroom was small, the patient was dragged into the hallway by Mr Walsh, where there was more room to work. The first thing she attempted to do was to introduce an airway into the mouth but she found it difficult 'because the jaw was rigid'. She did however manage to force his mouth partially open, but found that the mouth contained a great deal of vomit.

Hoping to elicit more information about the patient, M/s Butler asked "Do you know this man". But Simpson said, "No, I met him earlier on the night

77

in a club, I know his name is Alex".

Because M/s Butler had responded to an expected overdose of Heroin she records in her statement the following question:

M/s Butler – "Has he taken any Drugs i.e. Heroin?"

Simpson – "No, he might have taken an 'E' (Ecstasy) earlier at the Club, but he has taken nothing here".

Simpson was asked what had happened (to cause Alex's collapse) and he replied that Alex had felt sick and wanted to have a bath, so he went into the bathroom with him and was there when he was being sick, went blue and stopped breathing. Simpson told her that, "I started mouth to mouth and called the ambulance", and then added "I couldn't do much because of the vomit" and **"It was my worst nightmare come true"**. He did not say at this time that Alex had actually been in the bath or that he had to drag Alex out of the bath because he was unconscious.

This does not correspond with the account he gave to the Call Taker which was, that vomiting commenced after starting CPR under instruction, and as I shall show later, he gave yet another very different account to the coroner. I suggest that none of these accounts was true.

During this conversation M/s Butler was working on the patient with Mr Walsh, carrying out CPR and applying a heart monitor. She noted there was a thin leather necklace around his neck and asked Simpson to cut it off. Intravenous drugs were applied via the arm. In her statement, she describes the changes she noted in the patient but these I will discuss later.

Certainly in her statement to the police there is no mention of Simpson saying Alex had been in the bath. She records only being told by Simpson, that he went to the bathroom with Alex and was with him as he was being sick, and stopped breathing.

Leaving Mr Walsh to continue the resuscitation M/s Butler went into the bathroom for the purpose of looking for drugs because as she said "On the initial call from Ambulance Control, we were told the male had taken Heroin".

This search apparently caused Simpson some concern and although M/s Butler did not find any drugs, she did find several objects in a large toilet bag and on the floor which she described as 'sex aids'.

After this search, the patient was moved to the ambulance and at the paramedics request Simpson accompanied them with Alex's clothing.

Further attempts were made to resuscitate Alex during the journey to the Accident and Emergency Department of the Royal London Hospital, but with no good result.

There were other important signs of changes in a body which are important in determining the time of death which were observed by M/s Lee Butler, and they are developed further By Dr Heyman following his discussion with the Ambulance crew.

Although Alex's asthma was to become an issue at the inquest, it is noteworthy that Simpson made no mention of Alex being an asthmatic to the Ambulance Crew or to any member of the Hospital Crash Team. Obviously he was not in possession of that information at the time.

After my interview with Mr Absalom, he sent me a letter in which M/s Butler confirmed the following:[19]

> "She did not believe that the man present would not have boarded the ambulance if they had not asked him".
> "He was asked to do so in order to provide further information to the police and hospital staff."

Later, Mr Absalom allowed me to speak to Lee on the phone. Although it was some time after the event, she had a fairly clear recollection of the unusual events at the flat. I put several questions to her:
> First Question – "How rigid was the Jaw?"

---

[19] Letter dated

Answer – "I couldn't carry out CPR fully as the stiffened jaw and throat prevented me inserting a suction tube correctly to clear the vomit, and I couldn't insert the introtracheal tube into the trachea."

Second Question – "Did you find a great deal of vomit on and around the patient?"

Answer – "Not that I recollect, only that the mouth was full of vomit but I am sure I would have remembered if there had been, it would have been an additional problem to deal with."

M/s Butler hesitated before e answering the next question

Third Question – "Was the patient wet and lying in water, indicating that he had been in the bath?"

Answer - "I don't recollect if there were any signs of a bath. Had there been - as during the initial call from Ambulance Control, we were told the male had taken Heroin, I think I would have checked for a drowning".

M/s Butler said that the reason she remembered this particular callout was because of the unusual circumstances and the difficulty in finding the address due to initial incomplete directions.

**Part 3 - The Hospital Crash Team's actions - relation to the time of death – death reported to the coroner.**

The ambulance arrived at the Royal London Hospital at 5.40 am., approximately thirty minutes after arriving at 14 Driftwood. The patient was taken immediately to the Accident & Emergency Department as an emergency 'crash' case.

Dr Heyman, the Medical Senior Registrar who was on call, took charge of the operations. In his statement to the police he reported that he found the patient 'suspended'. " That is to say, neither breathing spontaneously, nor

80

with any cardiac output." He asked for the CPR to be continued with artificial ventilation, cardiac massage, appropriate drugs and routine blood samples for blood gases.[20] Dr Heyman then did an assessment of the patient.

In 1999 I learned from a Royal London Hospital consultant, that the ambulance crew had given their assessment to Dr Heyman before and while he carried out an examination of the patient. They had considered him to be already dead when they arrived at the flat. They reported they had found the patient to be 'asystole' i.e. showing the classic signs of cardiac arrest, and commenced the appropriate treatment. M/s Butler had noted that the patient "Had no pulse and no breathing and his pupils were dilated. I saw that his face was very blue". (All these were signs that life was extinct). She had also reported to Dr Heyman the stiffness of the mouth and throat.

Dr Heyman in his assessment also recorded that the patient was cold and stiffer than might be expected from a patient whose heart had stopped only recently. He noted too that that the pupils of the eyes were fixed and dilated 'beyond that reasonable with drugs given during ambulance crew resuscitation'.

He also noted the blue discolouration of the patient's face and in addition the fact that there was a striking purple discolouration with a clearly defined line from the portal neck upwards. **"The patient had clearly been dead for a considerable time"**. Dr Heyman decided that further resuscitation was clearly futile and with the agreement of the other members of the crash team, discontinued all attempts to revive the patient.

**At 6am. Alex was declared to be dead and was then a victim.**

On further examination of the now officially dead body, Dr Heyman noted there was an abrasion over the back of the neck 'perhaps consistent with the rubbing of a necklace', but that no focal bruising was apparent. This bruising was to be further discussed at the inquest.

During the above CPR, the Medical Senior House Officer spoke to the

---

[20] Blood gases

ambulance crew who told him that Simpson had claimed the patient had felt cold, gone to the bathroom where he had vomited and then collapsed. So, within less than an hour Simpson had provided several different versions of the time and events.

The integrity of the accounts of the trained paramedic Lee Butler and the qualified Medical Registrar cannot be questioned; they are based on the forensic medical evidence present on the victim's body which confirmed a much earlier death. In contrast, Simpson gave two versions of the time Alex Barrack died to the ambulance and medical personnel.

> 1. To the Senior Medical House Officer – he had collapsed at 4.50 am., and died a little later.

> 2. To the Ambulance Control at 4.54 am. - I think he has just died

At the inquest he was to give a more elaborate account of the death of the victim including a third time of death.

> 3. In a scenario described to the coroner at the inquest – he died between the 999 call and the arrival of the ambulance.

Body temperature and stiffness *(Rigor Mortis)* are two of the four signs on a body that assist in estimating the time of death. Dr Heath was to provide detailed forensic medical evidence at the inquest on all four changes, which take place after death to a dead body. These will be discussed in the next chapter.

# CHAPTER SEVEN

*"It is a capital offence to theorize before you have all the evidence.
It biases the judgement."*(Sherlock Holmes)

**Introduction — When the victim died – The pathologist's and the coroner's views**

In 1997 I first started to compile my Comprehensive Analysis with, as I said, very little information to work on. However, as I went through the various processes and failures in trying to overturn Dr Chan's original verdict of 'accidental death'' I did extract bits and pieces of information from the reluctant authorities to add to and improve my analysis, but not enough to convince them that my case had merit.

That is until December 2004 when I sent a comprehensive and very strongly worded letter to Sir John Stevens, the then Metropolitan Police Commissioner, with a complaint against the way the police had handled the investigations into my son's death. Sir John did find merit in my arguments and through his good offices the case was referred to the Murder Review Group (MRG) who were ordered to re-examine the police investigations into the case.[21] This Review Report was completed in mid 2005. Even then I faced another obstacle when a copy of the Report was refused me. It was only by invoking the Freedom of Information Act and involving some delay that a redacted copy was issued to me.

This report though, did not meet my expectations as the case was not reopened. Nevertheless it did reveal a number of useful and enlightening details which had been withheld from me and the family during the original police investigation. These details, where appropriate, I will include in further chapters of this book to increase the strength of my claim that that there was interference in the course of justice by the authorities and that they harmed my son's right to have his case argued impartially in a court of law.

The MRG Review will be discussed in detail throughout the remaining

---

[21] Describe role of MRG

chapters, please note though, that my discussions on the various issues raised at the inquest are not necessarily in sequence, as this account of the events, is mainly structured on the changes to body in death, and relate to, when, how and where my son met his death, but all these subjects are of course interlinked.

**Part 1 -The Changes in death** - *The sole aim of a Pathologist at any post-mortem is truth or the nearest approach to the truth that is possible; he cannot be 100% certain[22].*

To arrive at the truth should be the aim of every branch of the justice system but it is a sad reflection on the integrity of many of its officers who handled Alex's case that their aim was, and is, deflected away from the truth by unworthy motives. This is certainly true in the coroner's inquisition of Dr Heath in which he did his best to deflect Dr Heath's evidence away from the truth of, when, how and where Alex met his death.

Dr Michael John Heath was examined under oath and the coroner identified him as being a Consultant Forensic Pathologist who had carried out a post-mortem on the 4th May 1996.which he (the coroner) said 'I understood was treated as 'query suspicious death' from the outset'.

The pathologist replied 'That is correct sir'.

But was that correct? For eight months the police maintained to the family that death was from natural causes, yet the coroner does not ask Dr Heath why the police on the 4th May were able to list this death on the 'Missing Person' File as being that of un unknown male and stated that, a post-mortem had confirmed that death was the result of a severe asthma attack and heart failure and certainly not one to be regarded as suspicious. However when Dr Heath eventually made his statement to the police on 26th June he did not say that the cause of death he gave differed from the original or why he had changed the cause from natural to unnatural.

I know that these officials, who led me such a dance, would love to be in a position to deny that such a cause of death was ever given to the family but

---

[22] Forensic Medicine

to their chagrin they cannot. I have documentary proof that we were so informed which was provided by the very helpful Lincolnshire Police HQ, It is a copy of a computer printout containing the Missing Person List entry, which Limehouse police sent to Gainsborough police[23] just hours before I identified Alex. In 2005, during an interview with Mr Ahern of the MRG, I raised this matter with him and asked that he trace the original PM report. In the MRG written report Mr Ahern stated that Dr Heath did carry out a PM on the 4th May, but, **"It is not clear from the papers available whether the Pathologist gave a cause of death at that time"**.[24] If Dr Heath didn't – then who did? Most certainly I have not managed to acquire a positive answer to that often repeated request from any official. Yet according to the later PM report Dr Heath did give the cause of death as by asphyxiation after the first autopsy.

One other thing that is not quite correct is that according to Dr Heath's PM Report he carried out a post-mortem examination on the body of a male identified as William Alexander Barrack, (previously Unknown Male). As this report was dated 26th. June, then this information is not based on fact because Alex' identity was not known on the 4th of May. Furthermore Dr Heath makes no mention of the original natural cause of death at the inquest and the coroner simply ignored it.

The inquest continued after Dr Heath confirmed for the benefit of the court, that Alex's death was suspicious, the coroner then asked him for an account of his PM findings.

Dr Heath in the first place stated the date of his autopsy examination and said that it was held in the presence of a number of senior CID Officers. He then asked if he could 'to assist the court', give his evidence in the form of conclusions 'as the findings are rather complicated....' and to this the coroner agreed.

It was at this point in the inquest that very important forensic evidence of changes in a body after death, crucial to estimating as closely as possible the actual time of death, was introduced into the proceedings. Not that the coroner spent much time on the time issue

---

[23] Computer data – Gainsborough Police
[24] MRG Report-2.19-p8

85

The pathologist had noted in his report that the deceased was a well nourished male with a tattoo and body piercing and in continuing his report on his forensic medical examination stated:

1.  There were marks of intensive hospital therapy. *(Previously described in Chapter six.)*

2.  More significantly – I found that there was hypostasis over the front and back of the body. Hypostasis over the back of the body is a normal finding at a PM, but over the front of the body indicates that the body after death had been lying on its **front** for a number of hours.

Dr Heath then moved on to the cause of death but I will leave that subject for the present and discuss the other two very important changes to the body after death.

Dr Chan in reference to the time of death questioned Dr Heath on the statement of Dr Heyman the A&E Registrar who had given as his opinion 'That death had occurred much earlier, because of the rigidity', *(rigor mortis)* that was noticed'.

The coroner then, quite obviously, set out to undermine the long-established medical criteria on the determining the time of death. In referring to the A/E Hospital Registrar's opinion that death had occurred much earlier, because of the rigidity of the body that was noted he implied that it could be unreliable:

> Really the dating of the time of death is indeed an extremely difficult process and it depends on many factors such as sexual activity which would throw a lot of leeway into estimating the temperature of the body.[25] (Both the Hospital Registrar and the Para-medic had commented on the unexpected coldness of the body).

---

[25] Inquest Report p5 Qs. 17

A short explanation of the terms used, as closely as possible, the time death occurred when it is considered suspicious. This is especially useful in breaking an alibi or proving perjury.

Generally death in most cases, whatever the cause, occurs after cardiac arrest and a whole spectrum of change begins when the heart stops, which soon becomes obvious to the naked eye and are important in determining how long since death occurred. [26]

1.Hypostasis - When circulation ceases plasma and blood cells seek the lowest level of the venous system and settle in the lowest areas of the of the body to form a pink or bluish zone of hypostasis. As most bodies are left in the supine position (face upwards) the hypostasis forms in the back, buttocks, thighs, calves and back of neck. However, those parts resting on a hard surface, usually the buttocks and shoulders will be blanched from the pressure. The time of onset is variable but is usually visible 2-3 hours after death.

Hypostasis on it own is most useful in indicating a body has been moved after death. If the pink to bluish zone is uppermost, then it must have been moved a few hours after death.

2. Rigor Mortis - Results from the physical and chemical changes in the dead body which react to form a gel which causes the muscles to stiffen. It is a complex variable process but as it is temperature dependent, it comes on more quickly if the body remains warm, and is delayed if cold in an average room temperature rigor may become apparent within 1-4 hours in the face and in the limbs in 4-6 hours. But in a hotter climate, could develop more quickly. Rigor also comes on more quickly in a person who dies during, or soon after exhaustion or exertion.

As a general guide, if a body is warm and flaccid – it has been dead less than 3 hours.[27]

---

[26] Simpson's Forensic Medicine pps. 20-21
[27] Simpson's Forensic Medicine

**3. Body cooling after death** - This is also a complex subject. But metabolic activity stops as the circulation ceases, and the mechanism for transferring internal heat to the skin also ceases. The body surface begins to cool immediately, but remains warm to the touch for some time. Even though there are many variables, together with the internal temperature, it is still considered the best means of estimating the time of death, and is used in estimates for important forensic purposes. For example in breaking suspect alibis in a suspected criminal death.

'When all three are considered together, then it is possible for the time of death to be to set within reasonable accepted limits'. *(Simpson' Forensic Medicine pp 20-25*

### Part 2 – The coroner & the pathologist differ on the time of death

The internal temperature of Alex's body was not taken at the hospital, as once the declaration of death was made it became a case for the coroner. The pathologist failed to record it at the autopsy, but the unexpected coldness of the body was recorded by both the paramedics and the Hospital Registrar. That degree of coldness together with the fairly advanced stiffness of the body, prove that death had taken place at least three hours before the arrival at the hospital.

Dr Heath did agree with the coroner when he insisted that factors would throw quite a lot of leeway into estimating the time of death. However Dr Heath made it quite clear that this did not apply to this death. He told the coroner that in this particular case he was relying on two post-death changes on the body:

'One is the presence of hypostasis over the front of the body.
'Two is the findings of the doctors regarding the stiffness'

He then continued,

88

'...hypostasis is not so dependent on other factors (*drugs alcohol, physical activity all discussed later*), and that hypostasis indicated that Alex had been left lying on his front for sometime after he was dead. That coupled with the findings of the hospital doctors on the stiffness, this suggested that the deceased was dead much longer than the time given to the ambulance people, 'which I understand was immediately prior to calling them, and these changes from hypostasis are inconsistent with that alone'.

Dr Heath in referring to the stiffness of the body being inconsistent with a later time of death was mindful of the fact that, even though rigor mortis can come within two hours - in early stages of death, that these findings on Alex's body are not consistent with sudden death and resuscitation immediately afterwards.

Additionally when Dr Heath began his autopsy on Alex's body at 2-30 pm on May 4th, it was then eight and a half hours after he was declared dead by Dr Heyman at the hospital at 6am. Dr Heath found that 'rigor mortis was complete and intense throughout all muscle group*s (a process which is generally complete within 12 hours)*. This indicates that life had been extinct for at the very least 12 hours i.e. is from 2.30 am at the latest. All this evidence proves that Alex died 2-3 hours later than the time claimed by the man sitting in isolation near the court exit, who was the last witness to be examined by the coroner.

All three changes after death cannot give the exact time of death, but can give the closest possible time, especially when, as in Alex's case, the changes were observed by reliable, qualified medical personnel very soon after his death. Dr Heath's estimation of the time was as close as it could be, but the coroner himself a qualified doctor[28] who would be well aware that total accuracy was impossible, asked

'...and you are not able to say exactly when.?'

Dr Heath very sharply told the coroner-

---

[28] Impressive list of qualifications listed in his affidavit to the high Court

89

'No I couldn't say that, but certainly I would put, sort of, a minimum of two hours, something of that order'.

The coroner – 'Prior to…?

Dr Heath – Prior to the events of the resuscitation process.

The coroner – By, for example, the Para-medics? *(Arrival time 5.10am)*

Dr Heath – That is correct.

The coroner – You were referring too, rather than the hospital?

Dr Heath – Well no. I'm really referring to the tape recorded interviews prior to that stage there. I don't know exactly when they were given. *(The 999 call was made at 4.54.am)*

The coroner – Right. Prior to the resuscitation efforts, you would leave it like that?

Dr Heath – That is correct yes.

Dr Heath' examination dealing with question of time of death actually ended his evidence and he was dismissed by the coroner.

However the how and when of the victim died were discussed at the start of Dr Heath's examination, but my intention in discussing the time factor first, was to demonstrate two things:

1. The importance of the time factor on the other two questions, how and where Alex died.

2. And how questions and answers at an inquest can be manipulated to fit a particular bias.

The bias in this case was an attempt fit the time factor into accounts of events yet to be discussed, by attempting to undermine Dr Heath's certainty over the time of death This was an attempt to reduce by about an

90

hour the time the period between the actual death, the three resuscitation times and the declaration of death at the hospital. This was a tactic to be used again by the coroner when he examined the main witness Robert Simpson.

However, Dr Heath very shrewdly would have none of it. In actual fact, to do so he would have had to have nullified the evidence of other qualified medical personnel involved, the paramedics, a whole crash team and the consultant in charge of the Accident and Emergency Department of the Royal London Hospital.

Realistically, had the coroner, in questioning the witness Robert Simpson, due to be examined next, conducted a more searching probe of his various statements, he could have established the time of Alex Barrack's death almost to the minute. However, for his own ends he chose not to do so.

# CHAPTER EIGHT

*Coroners and Doctors like other citizens must live and work according to a code of conduct established by society.*

## Introduction - How the deceased victim died

An inquest, as DI Bathie told the family, is an ordeal at any time, but as we listened to witnesses' evidence that an unlawful killing had robbed Alex of his life, it became not just an ordeal but a situation of confused horror. Had the code of conduct been fully observed by both the coroner Dr Chan and the pathologist Dr Heath, from the very first day Alex was found to be dead, as it should have been, we would have been spared such an ordeal.

What is so strange about the circumstances which followed the victim's death is that each doctor at first took a particular direction in their involvement in Alex's case, then without any explanation, each changed his course of action.

Dr Heath's change, of course, puzzles me most. On the face of it, he appears to have been responsible for halting police investigations within hours of the declaration of Alex's death on the 4th May 1996. The evidence first given to me suggested that he gave his autopsy finding as death from natural causes. Six weeks later, in a written statement to the police, he had changed this conclusion to 'death by asphyxiation', by the application of an obstructive head device to the deceased's head. I have tried many times, unsuccessfully, to obtain documentary evidence or oral confirmation that Dr Heath initially gave the cause of death as being from natural causes - and that this was the reason that police investigations were suspended. I believe this was also the reason for the coroner's delay in holding an inquest, until the 'unknown male' was identified as a member of a caring family. Had he remained unknown, I firmly believe the case would have been quietly shelved and forgotten.

There is no doubt that, at the inquest, the forensic medical evidence given by Dr Heath on the true cause of death is supported by other factual evidence. It is beyond doubt; my son's death was an unlawful killing. Dr Heath's opinion was that death was the result of the application of an

92

obstructive head device to the victim's head. Although the coroner attempted to undermine this conclusion, Dr Heath held to this opinion throughout the coroner's probing examination. In respect of this aspect of the case, I have to say that Dr Heath observed the code of honour.

However, I cannot say the same about Dr Chan. His behaviour is the more incomprehensible because, for eight months, he had determinately championed Alex's cause. It was he who twice instructed the police to institute enquiries at a high-level, and then he twice challenged the CPS on the decision **not** to proceed with the prosecution of a man, who had been arrested as a suspect in an unlawful killing. In withdrawing his championship, Dr Chan had a complete turn-about of attitude. Without any explanation, he released my son's body after refusing to do so for seven months and gave no explanation or an apology for the delay. Later, in conducting the inquest, this fickle coroner showed a distinct bias against the interests of the victim, whose right to justice he had once protected. In doing so, he failed to honour the code of conduct by which he was committed to uncover the truth.

**Part One – Dr Heath's cause of death**
*"We owe respect the living; to the dead we owe only truth"* (Voltaire*)*

Certainly, truth is the only thing that can give a victim of unlawful killing justice. I feel that should have been obtained without difficulty by the coroner on the basis of the positive forensic medical evidence given by Dr Heath and other witnesses to the Court. The pathologist was as certain as he could be in his opinion on the cause and manner of Alex's death, and quite clear in his explanations and in the judicious conclusions he drew from that evidence:

> Dr Heath: "Sir, as far as the cause of death is concerned, it was my opinion that death was due to - **Asphyxia due to – Upper Airway Obstruction."**[29]

The pathologist had arrived at his conclusion on the following forensic medical evidence:

---

[29] Inquest Report

93

1. Extensive congestion of the face, neck and upper part of the chest.
2. The presence of petechiae haemorrhages.
3. The presence of a linear bruise over the back of the left side of the neck.

The congestion was also referred to in his police statement by the Hospital Registrar Dr Heyman and that the paramedics made to him, when they expressed concern over the colour of the patient's face. The registrar described it as being purple and the paramedic as blue. This blueness was also mentioned by Robert Simpson to the Ambulance Call Taker, and later, by PC Hardy at the mortuary, before I identified Alex. It is a condition found in cases of asphyxiation by applied pressure to the neck and head. The congestion and petechiae haemorrhages, tiny haemorrhages into the skin, are caused by compression of the venous system.

Dr Heath had continued that it was apparent to him that there had been some obstructive apparatus applied to the upper part of the body, but at that point he told the coroner he would discuss that further when he talked about the exhibits he had examined. However I will discuss them together in this chapter.

These exhibits he had examined, he told the coroner, were Exhibit HH/36a, which the MRG report confirmed was the restrictive head apparatus referred to and several photographs recovered from the crime scene by the SOCO. According to the MRG Report, Dr Heath was shown these photographs just before he re-examined the body on May 15th, although he does not mention that date at the inquest. He said that they were photographs of the **body** of a man with such a device over his head, and then explained their significance:

> Dr Heath:
> "Sir, I was shown these photographs and in my opinion the apparatus that we see there, it could certainly have produced the changes I have described and his death."

The great significance of these photographs lies in three important factors. One is that they were taken at the flat where Alex died and two, they were taken on a Pentax camera owned by the witness Robert Simpson, and three, **were of the body of a man.** This matter was to become a very important issue after the publishing of the MRG Report ten years later.

Very surprisingly, the MRG report states that Dr Heath was not shown the balloon mask until the 9th August,[30] which is more than six weeks after the date given in his police witness statement. This late date was something else the pathologist failed to mention at the inquest.

The 'Balloon Mask' is the term used by Dr Heath when referring to the structure and purpose of the obstructive apparatus to the police. These were discussed in detail in the much later MRG Report, but not in the coroner's court. Therefore to have had to read the dreadful details on my own in 2006, so long after Alex's death, was a very, very painful experience. I should have been given these details in 1996, not 2006, and then I would have had time to come to terms with it all before the inquest. Although I am not at ease in doing so, I think it is important that I include the full MRG description, with additional details, in this book. This will reinforce my argument, and strong belief, that a chronic asthmatic like Alex would not have voluntarily worn such a lethal device.

It is described as a bag composed of two plastic membranes, with the outer bag having a bicycle type valve and an eighteen inch tube attached to the back. Through this tube, by use of a hand pump, air is forced between the two membranes to apply equal pressure around the head and neck, and simultaneously inflate the outer skin. The two skins are attached to a firm, close fitting and non-elastic, tough, rubber collar, which prevents further intake of air and therefore vital oxygen. This device needs at least two people to operate it, as a quick release valve is attached, which must be released by a second person.

The purpose of the bag is to heighten sexual pleasure by increased pressure or hypoxia, that is deficiency of oxygen to the brain causing fantasies, but once this is achieved, or if the wearer shows sign of distressed breathing,

---

[30] MRG Report

the valve must be released immediately by the non-wearer. Otherwise death from asphyxiation and cardiac arrest can speedily result. Dr Heath's emphatic, judicious conclusion was that its use caused the death of the victim.

It can be seen, from that description of the head device, that the wearing of it cannot be a simple 'spur of the moment' decision. It needs planning, and the agreement of at least two people, one who would wear it and one who would operate the pump and release valve. After all, it is a life-threatening device, and it is also a masochistic piece of apparatus where a wearer willingly risks his life by wearing it for his own sexual pleasure. It is also, as I have been informed, a device used by sadomasochists on victims who resist, to obtain pleasure from other peoples' pain and terror, even when there is a risk of death to wearers.

This then brings me to the question: did Alex voluntarily wear the obstructive apparatus, or was he compelled to wear it? This question should have been probed very deeply by the coroner, but he treated it very superficially. Dr Heath had been quite emphatic that Alex had worn such a device, and that it **had** caused his death, and therefore there is great significance in such a device being found at the scene. But earlier in his evidence he told the coroner that he had come to two negative conclusions:

1.  It did not appear that this gentleman had been struggling or fighting to remove any apparatus.

2.  He had noted that there were no restraint wounds - indicating that there was no one holding him down and forcefully applying any apparatus

These are amazing conclusions, because a few moments before, he had told the coroner:

> "Sir, I further found at examination that there was a cut to the outer aspect of the left ankle, (described in the PM report 'with clotted blood') this was consistent with having been caused by a sharp object and possibly indicates that some

object had been removed with a cutting instrument from the left ankle."[31] (There was such an object found at the scene)[32]

Furthermore in the PM report, he had given a list of six injuries, including the cut ankle, which he had carefully measured, two related to the superficial bruise/abrasion sited over the left and right side of the back of the neck, which he would later tell the coroner was made after death. Dr Heath did not stipulate whether the other three injuries were made before or after death. However, as he had described one of these abrasions as 'dried', it can be assumed that - as it had leaked fluid - it was made **before** death. I have prepared a chart of these injuries and it shows the abrasions are consistent with the body having been dragged on its left side. The abrasions therefore **must** have been made when he was dragged out of the bathroom by the paramedics, because Alex was dead and blood and serum could not have flowed.

It is an absolute certainty that Alex would never have willingly participated in sadomasochism, and Steve Jones vouched for that in his Police statement:

Steve.
"I have been asked about Alex's sexual preferences…His asthmatic condition prevented him from doing any sexual act which involved kinky games, where especially the air supply was restricted. To my knowledge he would not participate in any form of dangerous sadomasochistic activity, he was not into bondage."[33]

Steve Jones would know that better than anyone, certainly better than I. Yet, knowing Alex's asthmatic history so well, his lifelong fear of having his breathing restricted in any way, his mild claustrophobia and his low tolerance to pain, I am as certain as is possible to be that he was forced into wearing the mask against his will, that he **did** struggle and he **was** restrained, even though Dr Heath considered that he was not. In discussing the evidence of Robert Simpson, the last witness to be questioned by the by

---

[32] MRG Report p
[33] SJ police statement p2

97

the coroner, I will include the forensic evidence which contradicts Dr Heath's conclusion, and will also reveal the coroner's further bias which favoured the man who had been arrested on suspicion of unlawful killing of my son.

Very early in his evidence, Dr Heath stated that the cause of death was from asphyxiation by the application to the head and neck of a restrictive apparatus. He gave strong evidence to support that view. But the coroner seemed to be determined to find another more natural cause of death. He continued with what seemed to the family to be an unnecessarily long inquisition of Dr Heath to induce him into finding a different cause.

Dr Heath had, early in his evidence, provided Dr Chan with details of the microscopic examination of the lungs and the histological and toxicology reports which he had received from the Forensic Science Laboratory. The microscopic examination of the lungs at the laboratory confirmed his finding at the autopsy, that there was evidence of an asthmatic condition. Also he had been asked if it had contributed to the death. He stated to the coroner:

Dr Heath,

**"In my opinion the asthma was not the cause of death......as the changes I have described to the upper part of the body are not found with an asthma attack."**

Dr Heath had then moved on to discussing the toxicology report which showed that Alex had 79mgs of alcohol in his blood, and that Ecstasy at 1.1 micrograms per ml was also present. In both the toxicologist Dr Taylor's, and the pathologist's opinions, neither had caused nor contributed to death, and neither would they have produced the changes to the body that he had described.

The pathologist next discussed the histological report, which seems to have been concerned with the extensive fatty change to the condition to Alex's liver, which Dr Heath suggested, was due to his consuming large quantities of alcohol over a period of time. Obviously I am not in position to emphatically claim that this could not be the cause, but knowing Alex's limited financial means and the type of food he could afford for his normal diet, I think it extremely unlikely. He was born prematurely and was very deficient in fat cells. I was told by his consultant that he would always be a thin individual. More importantly I was warned by his consultant not to attempt to 'fatten him up' as it would only lead to excess fat being lain down in unwanted areas. One such area mentioned was the liver. Neither the coroner nor the pathologist chose to pursue this further. Of course it was irrelevant to Alex's death, but I hope it eliminates any assumption that Alex was a heavy drinker.

What was relevant to the discussion on the cause of death was that food was found in the air passages, and some had gone down well into the lung. Dr Heath twice referred to the singular, 'lung', **not the plural, 'lungs'**, but I don't know that this point was significant. He also said that food in the lung can cause asphyxial changes, but in his opinion they would not account for all the changes described in this case. But he then said that although he could not be definite, there were other reasons for the presence of food into the air passages:

> Dr Heath's reasons:
> 1. It may have been a terminal event, inhalation of food or aspiration[34]. (Up to 5% had been noticed in one case series.)[35]
> 2. It may have been driven deep into the air passages due to the extensive resuscitation which had taken place.

The forensic medical and witness evidence to follow will confirm that resuscitation and aspiration were the reasons for food being found in the lung.

> Dr Heath:
> "Finally, sir, as to the cause of death, I repeat that in my opinion it was due to:
> **1a: Asphyxia**
> **1b: Upper Air way obstruction**

---

[34] Inspiration by sucking or drawing in action by compression and decompression of the lungs during resuscitation

[35] Forensic Medicine p89

And those essentially were my findings".[36]
At this point the finality of Dr Heath's statement led the family into thinking the inquest[37] evidence was almost over. How mistaken we were. The coroner began a long examination of the asthma condition and the inhaled food evidence, and in doing this, he gave every indication, which, even to the least informed amongst us, showed that he was determined to have Dr Heath contradict himself, and to deny the evidence which the police considered was enough to prove and warrant a prosecution for an unlawful killing. He seemed intent on finding a natural cause of death, and to exonerate anyone from blame.

Dr Chan said that Dr Heath had already explained to him that there was fluid and food present in the bronchus and that he could not exclude that they were inhaled or aspirated (sucked in) into the lung. The coroner referred back to the bronchial asthma and noted that Dr Heath was quite emphatic that it had not caused the death. He was told that was correct.

That was not enough explanation for the coroner, because he persisted that the extent of the examination did not preclude[38] (I think he meant exclude here) an asthma attack at some time. He was given the answer that changes from an asthma attack do not include the ones he had described as due to asphyxia.

No joy for the coroner there, so he switched back to the head device and its collar-shaped attachment, and the mark on the back of the neck, even though Dr Heath had found it could definitely not have been caused by the apparatus collar. There is some ambiguity about what Dr Chan was trying to prove or disprove here, but from what followed, he appeared to be trying to eliminate the device as being the sole cause of death, and that the **belt** removed from Alex's neck at the flat could have increased the obstruction, as Simpson was holding onto the neck during the resuscitation.

The coroner's actual words were:
    :"Now if we have a scenario here, somebody frantically trying to resuscitate someone and there is an obstructive

---

[36]Inquest report Qs & As p?
[37]          ditto
[38] Preclude means prevent from happening

process going on and there is this **belt** with a collar round the neck which was still present, because bear mind that the **belt** was not actually cut until resuscitation measures were taken by the ambulance personnel with scissors..."

Then:
'Now in that scenario, then, would you say that it is quite possible that a frantic attempt at resuscitation effort, together with a restrictive collar, could produce further obstructive kind of findings?'[39]

Dr Heath must have found the coroner's reasoning quite bemusing. He had already stated that death had occurred at least three hours before the 999 call and before any resuscitation attempts were made. Also, that he had actually listened to a full recording of the resuscitation and therefore,

Dr Heath:
"That, the gentleman being dead - then the resuscitation - could not have exacerbated the asphyxial process. This was a bruise that was caused during life as an asphyxiation element, not as subsequent cause, and could not have caused the bruising, no matter how roughly he had been handled."[40]

I could not at the time understand Dr Chan's line of questioning. It was quite clear to me that any one of intelligence would not try to resuscitate an asphyxiating person, without first removing the thing obstructing the breathing. Also, the coroner was well aware that the mask was not on the victim during the resuscitation by Simpson. Also, Simpson had stated to the police that Alex **had never worn the mask**. Yet his question implied that the device was on Alex at the time Simpson supposedly tried to resuscitate him. Therefore this line of questioning appeared to be an attempt to lead those in court (the family) into misconstruing the facts. Or, perhaps the coroner confused himself. He certainly confused the family.

Lastly, although the coroner had stressed repeatedly that Alex wore a **belt** round his neck, probably to create the impression that it was it was thick

---

[39] Inquest Report p?
[40] Inquest Report p?

enough to cause, or increase the choking, it was actually a long, thin Doc Martins **bootlace** with a charm attached. Others had referred more correctly to a 'thong' or a 'necklace' and certainly it was too long to have caused any lethal effect without being twisted.

By then Dr Heath was growing increasingly testy and I think that at this point Dr Chan decided it was pointless to pursue a natural or accidental cause of death with the irate pathologist - and instead addressed the aspects of time of death, the hypostasis, the rigidity and the resuscitation which have already been well described.

The coroner then told Dr Heath that he had no more questions and he was dismissed from the witness stand.

## Part 2 – DCI Baff is recalled

*Manslaughter – 'An unlawful act must be such as all sober and reasonable people would inevitably recognise must subject the other person to some risk'*

Detective Chief Inspector David Baff was recalled to the witness stand and again questioned under oath.

The coroner began by asking DCI Baff to confirm that 'this death was investigated as a possibly suspicious death'. This was the very first specific confirmation that Alex's death had been considered suspicious from the beginning, and confirmed that we had been deliberately deceived over the circumstances of his death.

We also heard for the first time that the head device was only 'one of various types of paraphernalia' found at the scene, which the coroner queried as follows: '...but not actually scattered about the place...?'

> DCI Baff replied:
> "Indeed Sir, there were some devices within the bathroom area, both in a polythene bag, within the bath, and devices which had been suggested they had been used in the

bathroom area and indeed in the living room area of the flat itself."[41]

A year later, as I studied the Inquest Report for myself, it appeared to me that DCI Baff was describing what amounted to be a scene of group participation in sexual activities. This reinforced my growing suspicion, which now is a firm conviction that for Alex to have worn the mask, more than one person must have been present, and that it had been forced over his head against his will. The MRG Report later gave a more detailed list of forensic evidence found at the scene which further endorsed this view. I will leave that matter for the time being and go back to DCI Baff's answers to the coroner's questions. These dealt with the obstructive head device and the examination by the Forensic Science Laboratory.

The coroner asked DCI Baff if the use of the sexual aids, particularly the balloon, were used to increase sexual pressure and whether the balloon head device had been subjected to examination by the Forensic Science Laboratory. To these questions DCI Baff replied:

DCI Baff,
"Indeed yes, sir, it was subjected to detailed analysis by Mr Eames...His conclusions were that while the device had been used by a number of people and a number of Alex Barrack's DNA components were part of the DNA analysis in the bag at that time, others were not and it was inconclusive as to whether or not it had been used on him at that stage of the events. There was one small trace of blood within the back of the bag and that was proved not to be that of Alex Barrack."

The coroner remarked that the DNA conclusion was inconclusive and DCI Baff agreed.

The coroner then asked this strangely worded question:

'It didn't really suggest that the DNA material **isn't** from the deceased Mr Barrack at all?'

---

[41] Inquest Report p?

DCI Baff seemed to understand the question as he agreed it was correct, but I did not and am still not sure what he meant. Was he implying that it could not be taken for granted that the DNA **was Alex's** or that it **was not?**

That was the end of the coroner's question on the vitally important question of DNA analysis results. This in my opinion should more properly have been put to Mr Eames, who should have been called as an expert witness. Even Dr Heath, although not an expert on DNA analysis, could have given a more professional reply to the coroner's question on Alex's DNA analysis.

I am aware that in 1996 DNA sampling and analysis was limited to the techniques available at the time, yet even for the times, it still appeared to be a most inadequate answer. I noted that DCI Baff referred to DNA as only being **in** the bag as apposed to any **on the outside** of the bag. This was an issue I was to take up with the MRG in 2006 and again during 2008-2009 with the Metropolitan Police Specialist Crime Directorate when techniques for DNA analysis had greatly advanced.

Another matter which the coroner failed to include in his inquisition of DCI Baff was that of fingerprinting. That was another important issue which I raised with the MRG in 2006, and will talk about later on.

After his very short questioning on DNA, the coroner then returned to the police investigations on the device, in connection with the true role played by the witness Robert Simpson, during the events which lead to Alex's death, some of which have already been described

We learned that Mr Simpson had been extensively interviewed by the police, and had provided a very comprehensive statement in which he denied that any head device had been used, or indeed, that **any amyl nitrate** had been used by Alex Barrack that evening'. And, he was aware, because a **Ventolin inhaler** had been produced, that Mr Barrack was asthmatic, and that had been part of a conversation he had had earlier in the evening. Why he introduced these two items puzzled me, as neither the police nor the coroner had mentioned them during the inquest. This was retrospective evidence revealed by the police some time later, but not,

104

apparently, given to the coroner until after the identification process. These items were not included in the PM report or the pathologist's statement, which was not submitted to the police until 26<sup>th</sup> June. Yet these two items, especially the Ventolin, were to be taken up by the coroner when, after dismissing DCI Baff from the stand, he proceeded to question Robert Simpson.

In the final part of DCI Baff's evidence, he confirmed to Dr Chan that Simpson had been arrested on suspicion of having caused Alex's death. It was then that the family heard, for the first time, the reason why Alex's funeral had been so long delayed and why the CPS had become involved.

All this and Robert Simpson's evidence to the coroner will be discussed in the next chapter.

As a work of fantasy - Simpson's evidence deserves a chapter on its own.

# CHAPTER NINE

*Perjury, also known as foreswearing, is the wilful act of swearing a false oath or affirmation to tell the truth, whether spoken or in writing, concerning matters material to a judicial proceedings.*

**Part 1 Further details of when, how, where- the deceased victim met his death. By Mr R Simpson - his arrest.**

Throughout the previous chapters I have referred repeatedly to the witness Robert Simpson and the liability he had in causing my son's death, and to the fact that until the inquest I had no idea that it had not been from natural causes. I had certainly been unaware that there was any criminal element in his death.

The inquest changed all that. The evidence of Dr Heath showed us not only how Alex had died, but also how long he had been dead, and this inquisition also revealed the person responsible for the death. The first two inquest sessions also began to uncover the reprehensible actions of officials, who were intent on keeping the true facts from the public. The inquest did not disclose why these officials acted as they did; those reasons would only be revealed and confirmed slowly but surely over a long period. However, the inquest opened our eyes to the beginning of the truth - and was to govern all my later actions.

The coroner, in opening the inquest, said that he had been assisted by the police investigations, during which Simpson had denied any device or restraining apparatus was used at the time when the deceased was there. He added **'but certainly not used by the deceased'**. I found this a very odd comment as it seemed to me to imply that others used these apparatuses at that time, but not by Alex.

DCI Baff agreed with the coroner that Simpson had denied the use of any apparatus, and then added that no amyl nitrate had been used by Alex. Simpson claimed he knew Alex was an asthmatic as he had used a Ventolin inhaler earlier that evening. Throughout the inquest I had not noticed that amyl nitrate was mentioned in several witness statements, but at no time did any witness give a reason for including it, nor did the coroner, Dr Chan, even though it is a prescription-only drug. I will include this drug and its side effects when I write about the significance that drugs had in this case.

Dr Chan continued:

> "Now I understand too that the police evidence was submitted to the Crown Prosecution Service for consideration for any criminal proceedings and I understand it was decided that there was insufficient evidence?"

DCI Baff, after he had agreed to the above, asked if he could read a letter dated 19th September 1996 written by Mr Graham Martin, who was acting on behalf of David Kyle, who was acting on behalf of the Chief Crown Prosecutor of the CPS:

> "Dear Mr Baff,
>
> **Re Robert Thomas Simpson**
>
> Further to our meeting on the 30th August 1996, all of the evidence in this case has been the subject of careful consideration.
>
> Whilst the evidence suggests that the initial account given by Mr Simpson is not correct there is no evidence of any specific act by Simpson which could be regarded as grossly negligent.
>
> Accordingly, it has been concluded that there is insufficient evidence to provide a realistic prospect for manslaughter **or any other offence arising from the death of Mr Barrack.**
>
> Yours sincerely
> Graham Martin

This must be the most understated reason ever offered for a non-prosecution of a case which had taken the police four months to prepare. It is ludicrous considering **what a wealth of forensic and medical evidence the CPS had to hand, which completely refuted Simpson's changes in the statements he made to various officials**, particularly those relating to the time and cause of death, and the circumstances leading to that death. However I will leave the CPS decision for the present and comment on it later.

The coroner thanked DCI Baff warmly and he then left the witness stand. Robert Thomas Simpson prepared to take his place, with his attentive counsel ready to deal with any challenges which may be made to his client's evidence.

**Part 2 – The truth, the whole truth - or - anything but the truth?**

Mr Simpson entered the witness stand and was sworn in. He showed no signs of nervousness or distress, yet the coroner began his examination by noticeably bending forward to address Simpson in very benevolent manner, as if the witness was distressed and vulnerable. This was in marked contrast to the icy indifference he had shown to the bereaved family. This indifference was especially pointed to the parents who had just heard, for the first time, that this witness, the supposed hero, had been arrested and charged on suspicion of causing the death of their son. Also, we had taken note that although the CPS had decided not to prosecute him, this man had not been declared innocent – the letter stated only that there was **insufficient evidence** to prosecute him for manslaughters, and, notably to us, **nor for any other crime;** more on this point later.

Before his examination of Robert Simpson, the coroner explained to Simpson that he would make very clear to him one particular legal aspect of inquests:

> Coroner:
> '...that an inquest is not a trial and it is not the purpose of a Coroner's Court to apportion blame or to point a finger at anybody, really just to seek the truth of what had happened in order to assist me to come to a conclusion into the matter of death'.

That statement is correct as far as the coroner explained it to Simpson, and of course, it was given for the benefit of the family. However, that brief comment did not touch on the whole purpose of the rule governing a coroner's duty, in that it was not intended to exonerate or deny any responsibility which may have been incurred.

To explain the law more fully, and as I understand it, a coroner's jurisdiction over inquests is governed by the statutory provisions of the Coroner's Act of 1988 and the Coroner's Rules of 1984. The Coroner's Act contains powers for regulating the rules and procedures at, or in connection with, inquests and post-mortem examinations. Whereas the Coroner's Rules contain the power to make or change those rules regulating inquests and post-mortems. At the time the inquest took place, no changes had been made.

One important point to be made under these Rules is that neither a coroner nor a jury can directly blame or name any individual as being criminally responsible for, or being negligent of, causing the death[42]. That is a matter for the criminal or civil courts to decide. Yet it should not be taken (as it appeared to me to do so at the time) that this rule[43] restricts the coroner from raising issues concerned with establishing the criminal nature of any evidence.

Although under the Coroners Act 1988,[44] the coroner must determine how the deceased came by his death, therefore, the prohibitition of establishing any criminal liability applies to the verdict **'and only to the verdict'**. Obviously to determine a cause of death in a case of a conflict of evidence, the coroner and the jury must be able to explore all facts, even if they reveal criminal activities or negligence leading to a death. This applies especially where the verdict may reflect the nature of any criminal liability, for example, 'unlawful killing. This term covers murder or manslaughter, but without naming any individual, even supposing the evidence points towards a particular person or persons.

---

[42] Coroners Rules (rule 42(a)
[43] Coroners Act 1988 11(5)(b)(ii) [43] Coroners Rules 1984 36(1)(b)
[44] Coroners Act 1988 11(5)(b)(ii) [44] Coroners Rules 1984 36(1)(b)

Although this sounds very impressive and limiting when it is quoted fully, it is really only concerned with the anonymity of any possible guilty party. The coroner, although he actually has a great deal of licence in how he conducts his inquests, must conform to certain precedents laid down.

After his explanation to Simpson, Dr Chan continued by stating that it was his understanding that Simpson was the person who was with the deceased when he died, and had actually spent some time with him, and that he had heard various statements on Simpson's involvement in the matter.

The coroner also said that he was also very conscious of the fact that Simpson had been extensively interviewed by the police, and that he himself had been assisted by his seven-page statement 'which I have found very helpful'. He then said to the witness:

> "It is not my intention to have the entire statement read out, merely just to ask you on several points which will assist me further based on this statement".

In my opinion, the coroner should have rephrased that to 'I will ask you questions on **several selected points** of this statement which will assist **you**', because that was the impression he gave the family.

As the inquest continued, the economy of his wording of the questions, and the limited number which were asked on the vital issue of the time of death, made it abundantly clear, to all members of the family present, that Dr Chan was indeed doing his best to assist his witness to avoid liability. In fact, there was to be nothing really positive to come out of his questioning Simpson.

The coroner then asked Simpson, very kindly, if he was willing to be questioned, and, as he agreed, the coroner continued by asking:

> 'Mr Simpson, just confirm to me that the night in question was the 3$^{rd}$ of May 1996 and you attended The London Apprentice Public House in Old Street and you arrived here in the early hours of May 4$^{th.}$

Simpson agreed that this was correct; actually it was not. Because Simpson was not present on May 3$^{rd}$, he did not appear on the scene until after midnight on the 4$^{th}$ May. (This was only one of many inaccuracies we were to hear that day.)

The coroner then asked Simpson if it was there (the club), that he had met the deceased Mr Barrack and Simpson replied, 'Yes'. He also agreed that they had not met before, and, at the end of the meeting, the two of them left together and went to Simpson's flat.

Yet, even though we were quite unaware, at that time, that we were listening to two highly qualified individuals, the family considered that the dialogue - on all of the vital questions asked of Simpson about Alex's death; - fell far below the professional standards we had expected. Mr Simpson, I discovered two weeks after the inquest, was a senior lawyer and, significantly at the time, was still serving as a Senior Crown Prosecutor for the CPS.

The next questions asked by the coroner related to the time that both men left The London Apprentice. These questions should have had great importance in identifying the actual time Alex met his death, but they did not. The family, particularly Mr Barrack and I, who both had considerable experience in the nursing profession, and moreover, in the handling and care of dead bodies, could scarcely believe what we were hearing.

We had just heard from the pathologist and other witnesses that Alex had been dead for 2-3 hours **before** the 999 call, and then we heard Dr Chan conducting a line of questioning with Simpson, which was supposed to establish as near as possible the actual time of death. This mode of questioning had more resemblance to a Dutch auction[45] than an inquest inquisition, when Dr Chan attempted to take Simpson further and further back in time, apparently intending to increase the time interval between the arrival at the flat and the emergency call.

Coroner:
"The time you left the pub was approximately 3. 45 am.?"

---

[45] Dutch auction – where the price bid goes down instead of up.

Simpson:
"That was my recollection of the time, yes."

Simpson's answer was simple and direct. It established not only the time they left the club, but also the period between 3.45am and his making the emergency call at 4.54am, i.e. a total of 1 hour and 9 minutes. However, the coroner was not satisfied with the time given:

Coroner:
"Do you have any advance on that?"

Simpson:
"It is one of those things one simply can't be sure about the time. I was of the opinion that it was about that time."

Coroner:
"It could be 3.30am or 3.15am?"
Simpson:
"Absolutely, I wasn't looking; when one's in any situation you form your own view of time."

Coroner:
"So it would be right to think that you arrived back at your flat at sometime in the early hours of the morning, possibly 3ish, is that reasonable?"

Simpson:
"Yes I couldn't disagree with that."

That was a very puzzling way of laying the grounds for establishing a time of death in a court. Three-ish could mean just before or just after 3am, very odd, especially when Simpson had already agreed with the coroner the more accurate time of leaving the club was 3.45am. In fact, that in this line of questioning, it appears to me that the coroner had attempted to gain about one hour's extra time for Simpson, in order to account for the twelve activities he was to describe to the Court. Simpson had, in fact, told the police that he did not meet Alex until 3am and that they left the club almost

112

immediately, to arrive at his flat between 3.45am and 4am.[46] However, I can give a more detailed and accurate account of the time factors from the same evidence source used by the coroner and contained in the police statements, than the totally misleading ones the coroner appeared to be trying to coax out of Simpson.

Steve Jones' witness statement records Alex's intention to visit The London Apprentice Gay Club in East London but the time of his arrival is not questioned. It can be accepted that Alex most probably travelled by underground from Fulham to Old Street, as a tube ticket was found among his effects. The travelling time between Fulham and Old Street stations, estimated by the tube authority, indicates Alex would arrive at The London Apprentice between 2230 and 2245 on the 3rd May 1996 and in time to gain free admission.

The MRG Review records Simpson told the police, that after an evening spent drinking with colleagues, he went home and then decided to go to the club. One can speculate on the reason for that. He stated he arrived alone at the club at 00.30am 4th May, and this is supported by the taxi driver who picked him up from home at 00.15 am and drove him to the club.[47]

What are not consistent with the known facts are the times Simpson claims he met Alex at the bar, and the time that they left together. Simpson claims this was between 3.45am and 4am. Although Simpson asserted they travelled by taxi back to his East London flat, the police could not trace any taxi driver to confirm either the journey or the time[48] The MRG Report made no mention of any police check with other taxi firms, as to a possible earlier pickup of Simpson and Alex, even though the pathologist's opinion was that Alex died very much earlier than suggested in Simpson's statements. Therefore, if the pathologist was right, the two of them must definitely have met as soon as Simpson arrived and left the club well before 3am. Simpson claims this was at around 3.45am that morning, but we can deduce that they met no later than around 1am. Furthermore, the police claim they could not trace any witnesses who saw them together. Oddly, considering the circumstances, the MRG review makes no reference to any

---

[46] Simpson's police statement MRG2005
[47] MRG Report p4
[48]      ditto

113

enquiries being made to trace any witnesses who actually saw Alex at The London Apprentice between 11pm on the 3rd May, and when he left early on the 4th May in Simpson's company.

There is absolutely no doubt, that practically every point of evidence given in statements by Simpson to the police and the coroner, during the period 4th May 1996 to 9th January 1997, is nullified by the forensic and forensic medical facts. This factor is strongly supported by Mr Ahern in the MRG Review[49].

What is also indisputable is that when Alex Barrack left The London Apprentice he was alive and in good health, but the bizarre sadomasochistic situation[50] into which he unwittingly walked, led to his unlawful death; there was ample evidence to prove that. Also that categorical forensic medical evidence proves that he died in Simpson's flat, **two to three hours before the 999 call** which was made at 4.54am.

As has already been said the coroner failed to call any of the independent witnesses who had made statements to the police to give evidence. One such witness was a neighbour who claimed to have heard Simpson holding a normal conversation with another person, who said, and she was sure, it was no later than 3.30am. To have been able to recognise Simpson's voice and describe the conversation as 'normal' she must have overheard some of the dialogue. If she is as sure of the time as she claims, that is before 3.30am when she arrived home after a night out, two things are absolutely certain. One, the other voice was not Alex's, he was already dead at that time, and two, Simpson lied about the time of their arrival at the flat.

Strangely, it is Simpson himself who gives strong reasons to doubt his veracity in virtually all the statements made, to both medical personnel and the police on the 4/5th May 1996, and to the coroner on 9th January 1997. He had claimed, to both the police and Dr Chan that he did not leave the club with Alex until 3.45am. But the evidence of the neighbour, who I assume would have no reason to lie to the police, places Simpson in the flat by 3.30am,

[49] MRG Report - 4.1 p18
[50] That Simpson was involved in sadomasochist activities is confirmed by the police. MRG Report p4

114

So it can be seen that she exposed Simpson's versions of events, as described above and given under oath, to be nothing less than perjury. It also upholds my conviction that Simpson did not act alone, throughout all the circumstances and the aftermath of Alex's untimely, needless death.

That death occurred much earlier than Simpson claims, has already been recorded in an earlier chapter, and was mainly based on changes in the body after death. All which established beyond doubt[51] that these changes were well advanced and could only have resulted from a death occurring at least 2-3 hrs before any resuscitation attempts. This then supports my contention, that several persons were involved because, as the body was showing advanced stiffening, Simpson could not have handled it on his own, certainly not in the way he described to both police and the coroner[52].

Significantly though, future developments would confirm my belief that Alex **was in actual fact unlawfully killed** and that some senior officials, in making the decision to conduct the case in secrecy and to avoid any prosecution, ignored a very basic forensic medical fact**, that although a dead body can't move and is silent, the evidence on the body can give it a voice.**

The coroner then questioned Simpson on the drinks consumed at the club and in the flat, and he was told, that although Alex was a little intoxicated, he was chattering but comprehensive and quite ambulant. Simpson told the police that although he himself had an amount to drink when out with colleagues earlier, he was not intoxicated and had only consumed two beers at the club. (There was no mention him being tested for alcohol levels).

After having ensured that those in court were made aware that Alex was not drunk, presumably to imply he was fully aware in control of his faculties and his circumstances, the coroner proceeded to very briefly discuss the sexual activities.

---

[51] See 'Changes in Death' document
[52] Post-mortem Report, Inquest Report, Witness Para-medic Lee Butler's statement

115

Coroner:

'In the course of the evening then there were some sexual activities taking place. I understand this excluded full sex and oral sex?'

Simpson:
'Yes, there was no oral sex or any intercourse'

Coroner:
'This was by means of using sex aids basically, yes?'

Simpson:
'Yes.'

These oddly worded questions and answers, resulted in giving the impression to those present that that sex in any form did **not** take place and **that it was not done by not using sex aids.** I am sure a jury would have wanted those imprecise questions and answers to be fully clarified.

The coroner then dealt with the shaving of Alex's pubic area, (this shaving has been confirmed) and the stinging which Simpson claimed made Alex ask if he could have a bath to ease the discomfort. Also, he said, it took 5-10 minutes for the bath to fill before Alex climbed into it, after asking Simpson to join him which he refused to do. He then left him alone in the bathroom.

This was the full extent of the coroner fulfilling his duty to establish the full factors of the activities leading to the death of the victim and his failing to probe Simpson's obviously false evidence over the bathing incident when the right questions would have openly exposed in court that this first part of Simpson's evidence was undoubtedly perjury.

The truth fared no better in the rest of Simpson's evidence to the coroner relating to the events in the bathroom and the involvement of the ambulance personnel

**Part 3– The time of death according to R Simpson**

*"It has often been said, that it is not death, but dying which is terrible"[53]*

After telling the coroner how he had left Alex in the bathroom, Simpson was asked a question of great importance by the coroner:
Coroner:
'What time would that approximately be now?'

I think that this question caught Simpson unawares, as he seemed not to expect it, but he did succeed in avoiding giving any specific time, or indeed any answer, by telling the coroner that it would be easier if he worked backwards. The coroner, with unbelievable dereliction of duty, let that crucial question go unanswered and, in my opinion, allowed this witness to take control of the situation, by enabling him to describe fabricated events without any challenge as to their veracity.

The substance of Simpson's made up events is as follows.

1. He was keeping out of the way in the kitchen or the bedroom.
2. It was not very long before he needed to call an ambulance
3. He heard an alarming croaking noise from Alex who was still in the bath and who looked ready to be sick.
4. He helped Alex out of the bath, after asking him not to be sick on the floor.
5. He took him to the toilet where Alex knelt on the floor with his head over the toilet basin.

Everyone present in the court had heard Dr Heath state several times that death had occurred at least two hours before the 999call was made and none of the family, least of all the parents, could believe our ears when we heard Dr Chan ask Simpson the following questions as if he accepted Simpson's account of a much later death as the truth:

---

[53] Henry Fielding –Amelia- (1751)

Coroner:
'Was he breathless?'
Simpson:
'He was making sounds........I mean he was making sort
of incoherent sounds, although I didn't really understand
anything he said.'

Coroner:
'So you obviously would have conversed with him, you
enquired about what was going on?'
Simpson:
'I was saying "What's the matter, what's the matter, do
you feel sick?'

Coroner:
'Did you get any response?'

Simpson's answer was that he couldn't get any reply that he could
understand. He then gave an account of how he had tried to help Alex to be
sick, and that he had also noticed Alex's shoulders were changing colour,
so thinking he was perhaps cold, had rubbed his back with a towel to warm
him, and slapped his face to try and get a response. To my mind, these
actions were more likely to have been an attempt to camouflage the
discolouration caused by the petechiae[54] on the face and hypostasis on the
back resulting from the much earlier asphyxiation. After this, he then
propped Alex up against the bath.

What he said next is of great importance because, as I will demonstrate
later, it eliminates any possibility that the asphyxiations had resulted from
vomit inhaled into the lungs while the victim was still alive, as the coroner
maintained.

Simpson:
"I though at that point, well I mean it must be the fact that he's
terribly sick and can't vomit and I actually forced my fingers
into his mouth and you know, pushed them back as far as I

---

[54] Petechial haemorrhages are caused by raised venial pressure during asphyxiation

118

could without hurting myself. I couldn't produce any result from that, and at that point, you know, realised something awful had happened."

At this stage the coroner quickly brushed the matter of the vomit to one side, as if it were of no consequence, and briefly reintroduced the belt - but this time he called it a leather collar. Yet, Simpson, as with Dr Heath, attached no significance, to what he more correctly referred to as a leather thong with a pendant. He said he had he had not noticed it because Alex had gone a purple colour with a white rim.

Dr Chan then asked Simpson if he had pulled on the thong while he was trying to revive Alex, but Simpson rather obtusely, replied to the effect that when he was reviving Alex he would not be conscious of anything like that.

The coroner gave up pursuing the matter of the thong having any input into the death, as Simpson obviously didn't give the right responses and continued by asking what happened after he had propped Alex up against the bath.

Simpson's reply contained further inaccuracies:

1.  He had gone into the sitting room to use the phone and the Ambulance Centre call taker had asked if the phone was on a lead and, as it was, asked him to manoeuvre it into the bathroom.

2.  When he returned to the bathroom the victim had fallen over.

3.  He told the coroner that he wasn't sure what position the victim was then lying in.

4.  He was told by the ambulance man to 'sit on my knees' to perform the resuscitation.

None of the above events are recorded in the transcript of the Emergency call which I hold and which Mr Absalom of Ambulance HQ assured me

119

was a complete copy of the recorded call and that the police held the original the tape.

The coroner then asked another inadequately framed question:

> Coroner:
> "So by the time that he had rested on the floor, was he resting on his back or on his front?"

Simpson said in answer to the coroner that he couldn't be sure about that but that he had got the patient into the position the Call Taker had instructed, lying on his back, face upwards, but he could not be sure what position Alex was in before. He agreed the Ambulance personnel would have found their patient lying on his back.

The family by then realised, but Simpson didn't appear to, that the coroner was trying to get Simpson to confirm the victim had been in a prone position to give the impression of frontal hypostasis occurring during the resuscitation attempt and not much earlier.

The coroner explained:

> "The point the pathologist was trying to explain to this Court was that because of the hypostasis..............It suggested that the deceased had been lying on his front for some time., time enough to have caused most of the other changes (after death) suggested he had been changed to lying on his back. You don't dispute that do you?"

> Simpson:
> "Well I don't have any recollection of Alex lying for a long period on his front, the whole thing happened so quickly, you know, he just seemed to die in front of my eyes, you know."

At this point the coroner decided to abandon that line of questioning, Simpson it appeared, was not getting the message. Once again Dr Chan failed to question him on the time interval between the arrival at the flat and the actual time when all the twelve events he claimed took place.[55] Most certainly he made no further attempt to achieve any factual time of death, or any other related time, from Simpson.

The coroner then asked a somewhat jumbled series of questions relating to the arrival of the ambulance, the cutting off of the **belt** and Simpson accompanying the patient to the hospital. He then returned to the pathologist's evidence on the mark at the back of the neck and its significance to the asphyxia. Dr Chan, contrary to Dr Heath's opinion which was that it had none, seemed determined to have the belt cited as a cause of the asphyxial process. Once again Simpson failed to grasp this escape point, so the coroner went back to the head device:

'Now you heard the pathologist's evidence in respect of the mark on the back of the neck and his cause of death given as asphyxia consequent to obstruction of the upper chest?'

Simpson:
"Yes."

Coroner:
"And he gave an opinion as to the possible cause of death and he said that the device found in your flat, the balloon head device apparatus could cause that mark?"

Simpson: '
"Yes."

Coroner;
"Now the Chief inspector in his evidence already stated that in your statement made to the police you had denied that any apparatus was experienced by the deceased?"[56]

Simpson:
"It wasn't, because I wouldn't have dreamed…..he told me he had asthma so therefore I wouldn't even have used the poppers in those

---

[56] MRG Report

121

circumstances. I mean he was smoking a lot. I noticed he did smoke quite a bit and he had to use the inhaler and you know I simply wouldn't have dreamt..... "

At this point the coroner interrupted Simpson:
"You saw him use an inhaler?"

Simpson:
'Yeah, I simply wouldn't have dreamt of doing anything of that kind with someone who had problems with breathing.'[57]

I think at this point Simpson had said more than the coroner wanted him to. Dr Chan had up to that point ignored the question of drug use and its side effects, and nothing had been said about an inhaler, but Simpson had, perhaps inadvertently, raised the subjects. The coroner most obviously and very quickly, brushed those important matters aside and returned to the bathroom scene and introduced Alex's breathing into the questions.

Coroner:
"When you first heard the croaking noise and you went to the bathroom, was he gasping for breath?"

Simpson:
"He was sort of rising out of the bath and the noise that he made I formed the initial opinion that he was about to be sick, **but the noise he made could have been subsistent with gasping for breath,** you know not being medically qualified I can't comment, but there was a noise which gave me the impression that he was being sick, but it could have been consistent with other things."

If the coroner was trying to throw Simpson a life line he did not appear to have grasped it, because he appeared to become confused. He had not at any other time referred to Alex having breathing problems, but had made quite an issue of a copious but fictitious, vomiting incident, which the coroner had chosen not to discuss. Simpson seemed very relieved when the

---

[57] Inquest report p

coroner dismissed him.

Coroner:
"Very well, thank you very much; I have no further questions".

This completed Dr Chan's questioning of the very few carefully selected witnesses and he then began his summary of the evidence which will be the subject of chapter ten.

Although the coroner had lightly dismissed the use of drugs and the supposed use of the inhaler, I believe they both have great significance in accounting for Alex's predicament, Simpson's behaviour and his responsibility for Alex's death. These will be examined more fully in the chapters concerned with the matters the coroner omitted from his inquisitions, but included in the MRG report on Simpson's arrest.

**Estimation of Time Factors in Fictitious events Described by Robert Simpson at The Inquest held January 9th 1997 into the Death of William Alexander Barrack .**

| Event | Approx Minutes required |
|---|---|
| Distance from The London Apprentice to 14 Driftway (by car) approximately 2 miles. | 5 - 10 |
| Preparing drinks - settling in -taking drinks | 5 -10 |
| Undressing - preparation for sex activities | 10 |
| Pubic area shaved activity (minimum time) | 15 |
| Sexual Activities | 15 |
| Complained of stinging - washed area in bathroom | 5 |
| Setting taps - running bath | 5 -10 |
| Bathing | 5 -10 |
| Croaking noise heard - victim helped out of bath to toilet | 2 |
| Towel obtained - rubbed shoulders - slumped over | 5 |
| Helped to wash basin - head held over | 2 |
| Moved and propped against bath if victim helpless | 1 – 2 |
| Forced fingers down throat - slapped face | 2 |
| Walked to sitting room - dialled 999 - gave details | 2 |

**Minimum time allowed for event – 64 mines.**

**Maximum time allowed for event - 85mins.**

**Average time for events        - 7.54 mines**

**This is a purely academic exercise further demonstrating the extent of Simpson's lies, as the medical evidence proved conclusively that Alex Barrack was already dead by 3 am. when Robert Simpson claimed they left the club and the events began.**

124

# CHAPTER TEN

*"There is only one thing here worth minding,*
*and that is to be true and just..."*

## Part 1 – The coroner's Summary of the Evidence - The first three questions

Throughout the coroner's examination, we had sat in the freezing cold of the court room, listening to a mixture of factual evidence and perjured statements. It would be hard to describe how we felt about the course the case had taken, except that they we were in a confused mixture of shocked anger and disbelief.

Our state of shock and anger was not at all appeased when unexpectedly early, Dr Chan, the coroner began his summing-up of the of the inquest evidence. In a rather grand manner he reminded those present that the inquest was a fact-finding inquiry, which he was conducting on behalf of our Sovereign Lady the Queen, and that it was his duty to establish reliable answers to four important, but limited, questions. He forgot to add that 'the coroner has to ensure that the relevant facts are fully, fairly and fearlessly investigated,' because he then proceeded to give his interpretation of the facts in such a way - which even to us, as inexperienced in court practice as we were, could see - as to remove any element of criminality from the case.

In our discussions immediately after the inquest, our conclusion was that not only did Dr Chan refrain from implicating any one individual in Alex's death, but that he had clearly performed a role which would have been more suitable for a counsel defending a suspect in a trial. This is how the coroner chose to present his summary; Dr Chan listed and discussed the four important questions as follows:

1. The identity of the deceased.
2. The place of death.
3. The approximate time of death
4. **How the deceased came by his death**

## The Identification of the Victim

On the first question, the identity of the deceased, the coroner said he was entirely satisfied that it was William Alexander Barrack, and sadly, so was I. However, before the identity was finalised, I did have to amend two careless mistakes, which the coroner had actually quoted from the official identification evidence; they were, the date of birth and the place of birth.

## The Place and Time of Death

Dr Chan then proceeded to link the answers to the second and third distinctly different questions together, in the briefest way possible, and I quote from the Inquest Report Summary:

> Second answer
> "I am also satisfied that the deceased was certified dead at the Royal London Hospital in Whitechapel on the 4th of May 1996".

> Third answer
> "And that it was approximately 6.00am when he was formally pronounced dead by the doctor there".

These were the extremely inadequate answers to two very important questions, which by no means could we accept, as legally establishing the facts. I do not think that they would have satisfied a jury, they certainly did not satisfy me. The coroner had not only neglected to give any rationale for being so satisfied with his inadequately explained conclusions on such vital questions, but had, and very conspicuously, ignored the crucial information given by witnesses on the questions of both the time and place of death. He could have, from this information, positively established not only the facts relating to the place and time of death, but also, that the evidence had revealed the death to be one of an unlawful killing.

Furthermore, although several obviously perjured statements had been made by Simpson, relating to the time and the place of death, the coroner had not made any attempt to be fair and impartial, by testing the these statements made under oath, against the facts. In fact, he not only ignored some inconsistencies, but discussed others as if they were a feasible account of the circumstances and events leading to Alex's death. This, I

126

believe, was in order to give credibility to the verdict he obviously intended to present to the court, at the end of his summing up.

Considering all the reliable evidence given by the other witnesses called to give evidence in person to the coroner, and the statements read out on behalf of absent witnesses, he should have drawn attention to the many discrepancies in Simpson's very shaky account. So it is not surprising that the family were stunned when the coroner disposed of all three crucial questions and answers, in about 150 words; and actually spent no longer than two minutes in doing so.

It was quite clear to us that in his summing-up he purposely omitted a considerable amount of sworn evidence, which, we thought, had established, beyond any reasonable doubt, that Alex had been dead for at least three hours, before he was admitted to the hospital. Of special importance are those observations made by Dr Heyman in his written statement to the police. He recorded that although the immediate cycle of resuscitation was carried out:

- "The patient was very cold, stiffer than might be expected for a patient whose heart had only recently stopped."

- "That the Ambulance Team had reported to him, they were surprised how stiff the patient's jaw was, presumably noted as they tried to intubate him."

- "They also reported at that at the time 'There was no was no cardiac output, or electrical activity. His eye pupils were fixed and dilated, **(beyond that reasonable with drugs given during resuscitation)**"

- "The patient had clearly been dead for a **considerable time.**"

After this assessment, further resuscitation was considered to be futile. Therefore, Dr Heyman, with the agreement of the full Team, took the decision to discontinue the resuscitation attempt. Some time later, I received additional information from Dr Heyman's hospital notes, to the effect that the Ambulance Crew had attempted resuscitation for 38 minutes, before transferring him to the A&E Department, continuing resuscitation during the 5-minute journey. So, altogether, resuscitation techniques were carried out for about 46 minutes.

I believe that the Paramedics and the Hospital Team tried to give Alex every chance possible. They could have succeeded in reviving him if even one of Simpson's accounts of earlier times of collapse had been true.

The Senior Consultant Mr A. W. Watson gave me additional information in a letter dated 29 January 1999. He informed me that although Dr Heyman had made the declaration of death at 6am, the Ambulance Crew believed that Alex had developed rigor mortis **before** they arrived. (at the flat.)

It is incomprehensible that the coroner failed to mention any of those details, although in normal practice he would have received copies of all the hospital records relating to the incident. He referred only to that part of the Hospital Registrar's statement which gave the time that the death was certified. Dr Chan completely omitted Dr Heath's post-mortem forensic medical evidence, which made it quite clear that the length of time that Alex had been dead was 2-3 hours **before** the 999 call. Therefore, the patient was long dead before Simpson or anyone else had attempted any resuscitation.[58]

Although Robert Simpson had given varying accounts of the night's events and times to the police and the medical professionals who became involved, there can be no disputing that the place where Alex Barrack died was Robert Simpson's flat, at 14, Driftway, 182B Grove Road, London E3. The actual place of death is very important to establishing that a crime had been committed and also to placing a suspect at the scene at the time the death took place.

All this positive evidence on the time and place of death was once more ignored by the coroner, when he officially registered the death at Tower

---

[58] Inquest report Qs & As 19-23 p6

Hamlets Registration District, as the law required him so to do[59]. As the entries form a legal document, which may be required for use in any future legal action, all details should have been meticulously and accurately recorded. Yet this legal obligation was ignored by Dr. Chan, when he - knowingly and misleadingly - recorded on this document that the deceased **had** died at 6am, and that the place of death **was the Royal London Hospital**.

Much later on, I was to uncover the reasons why such a volume of evidence had been omitted from the inquest and the reason why the police were instructed to conduct the case in such great secrecy. At the inquest, though, we were unaware of the bizarre nature of the circumstances which had led to Alex's asphyxiation. It wasn't until a few weeks after the inquest that I began to get an inkling of the truth. Unfortunately for the victim and the cause of justice, our ignorance allowed the coroner to dispose of these three essential questions with brief and inadequate answers, without any challenge from even one of us.

There was no challenge from the family, either, when Dr Chan dismissed Simpson from the witness box, and then, without any delay, moved on to deal with the last of his questions: how the deceased came by his death?

**How the deceased met his death – the coroner's verdict**
When summing up the evidence on the cause of Alex's death, Dr Chan should have considered the factual evidence given by reliable witnesses on this very important matter. Instead, the coroner attempted to manipulate the forensic medical evidence by concentrating on Simpson's **patently unreliable accounts** of how Alex died, when it was so obvious to everyone present that they were nothing more than a pack of lies. The family's conclusion was that the coroner did so in order to achieve a verdict favourable to the police case - and wilfully disregarded the interests of both Alex, the victim, and his family. We have always suspected that he did this under pressure or influence.

Whatever the coroner's reason, his actions were so unjust. It is the pathologist's role to establish, as accurately as he possible can, the cause of

---

[59] Copy of Registration Form - on file.

death; (and is accepted that he cannot be 100% sure[60]), whereas, the coroner's role is to examine the evidence provided by the pathologists, and other experts, in deciding on a verdict. It is most certainly not in a coroner's remit to substitute a cause of death which he prefers, in flat contradiction of the pathologist who had already dismissed the reason given by the coroner as not contributing to the actual death. Also, it is the **pathologist** who should determine the mechanism of that death, based on the forensic medical evidence and the opinions of experts in other forensic scientific areas. In the main, Dr Heath had, in both the post-mortem report and his oral evidence, together with the physical artefacts the police found at the SOC, outlined very clearly the cause and mechanism of my son's death.

**How the deceased actually died**
Dr Chan began his summing up of the factors relating to how the deceased met his death by saying that the question was partly answered by the pathologist post-mortem findings. Although the points of evidence which the pathologist raised should have been of great importance in proving an unlawful killing of the victim, they received only a brief mention, and were then set aside by him, as if of little consequence.

The points of evidence, to which I refer, are listed in the same order as the coroner introduced them in his summary, and they will then be followed by my more detailed analysis of the evidence in the next chapter.

1. Restraint and defence marks
2. Toxicology analysis
3. Natural deceases -Bronchial Asthma
4. Food and fluid present in the Bronchus

**Restraint/defence marks**
The coroner said there was said no evidence whatsoever that the deceased was subjected to any violence or any force.

---

[60] Simpson's Forensic Medicine p

130

**Toxicology analysis**
Although some drugs had been taken, including Ecstasy, the coroner agreed that none of the compounds found were considered to have contributed to the death
**Natural deceases – Bronchial Asthma**
Dr Heath told the coroner that although there was evidence of bronchial asthma, he had firmly refuted the coroner's implication that the condition had contributed to the death. The coroner now indicated that an asthma attack could have contributed to the cause of death.

**Food and fluid present in the Bronchus**
Dr Chan then introduced the evidence that was found on microscopic examination of the lung and said that Dr Heath could not exclude the fact that food and fluid were **inhaled** or **aspirated** into the lung, but the coroner disregarded the pathologist's view that it could have been the result of a post-death resuscitation. Once again the coroner reduced the importance of pre- and post-death evidence concerning the cause of death to a mere inconsequential sentence.

Alex's family and friends listened in silent but mounting dismay, seriously doubting the competency of this coroner, as he gave his interpretation of the 'factual evidence'. He did this in such a manner that he not only exonerated any one individual from blame, but he also failed to describe any cause, incident, or circumstances which justified his giving an inappropriate verdict of 'Accidental Death'.

As Dr Chan closed the inquest and rapidly quit the courtroom, it is no exaggeration to say that the family were literally seething with rage at what we saw as a blatant **misinterpretation** of the evidence. We all felt that a great injustice had been perpetrated on the obviously murdered Alex.

While we had listened to the coroner outlining his conclusions, I don't think that any member of the family realised the full significance of the coroner's disingenuous summary of evidence, until his inappropriate verdict closed the case. By then it was too late for our intervention. We certainly had no comprehension how these events would shape my future actions, nor of how many years it would take for me to uncover the facts which top officials had intentionally concealed. Yet even before we left the

131

court room, DI Bathie was to reveal to me an item of information which confirmed that there had been official interference in the case.

In the next chapter I will give my analysis of the items of evidence in possession of the coroner during the inquest. Some of it which would have had great significance in establishing the true facts relating to all the above questions, was omitted by Dr Chan. Additionally I will include other very enlightening information, withheld from the family, by the coroner and senior police and CPS officials.

Later in the book, I will show how I fought to gain justice for my son, by challenging the establishment, over a period of fourteen years, during which I slowly and painstakingly compiled a thorough analysis of a great many facts, until it was officially revealed that my son's death was a undoubtedly a concealed homicide.

# CHAPTER ELEVEN

*"The coroner has to ensure that the facts are fully, fairly and fearlessly investigated"*
*Jameson* case ([1995] 1Q.B 1)

## Introduction - The Coroner's Summary of the Evidence

Theoretically, 'It is the coroner's task to seek to establish a probable course of events and resolve any ambiguity in the evidence...his overriding duty being to enquire how the deceased met his death.'[61] That is the official line, and that is what I believed before the inquest. On the word of the Lincoln Coroner's Officer, I had expected a fair and impartial inquest, but I didn't get it. The bias against Alex, from Dr Chan, the police and the CPS, made sure of that. When the inquest was over and the injustice of their conduct really began to sink in, I set out to find out more about the individual roles of those officials who had, to my mind, perverted the course of justice. I did this by purchasing expensive textbooks written by prominent experts on the subject of Police procedures, Inquests and Forensic Medicine. Additional information came from many other reliable sources, including the Internet and justice system officials. All these sources combined to provide very convincing proof that Alex's death was an unlawful killing. A fact that eventually was confirmed in a letter sent to me twelve years later, by a Metropolitan Police official.[62]

From Sir Montague Levine's much respected work on Coroners Courts I was very surprised to learn that a coroner need not be a qualified doctor. Considering the number of inquests held on sudden and unexpected deaths, I had assumed, from the medical nature of most such deaths, that coroners would be doctors. However, under section 7 of the Courts and Legal Act 1990, a Coroner is required to have either a five year general qualification as a lawyer, or to be a medical practitioner with five years experience in the profession, although some coroners hold both qualifications. In fact though, in 1996, the vast majority of coroners were lawyers.

---

[61] Levine on Coroners Courts p55
[62] Freedom of information letter

I had taken it for granted that Dr Chan was a medical doctor, but in fact he really was more than that. In 1997, in his affidavit to the High Court against my appeal for a second inquest, he listed several professional qualifications.[63] He had qualified as a doctor, a lawyer, and, for a number of years, had practised as a Senior Forensic Examiner for the Metropolitan Police. He had also held deputy coroner posts before taking up his coroner's duties in 1995.

I would have thought all these qualifications and forensic experience would have made Dr Chan an exemplary coroner, and indeed, until November 1996, it seemed me that he carried out his duties meticulously, as expected. I have already mentioned that, from the second post-mortem on Alex on May 14th to the end of November 1996, I have been unable to establish how far Dr Chan was involved in the events that took place during the first 10 days, following Alex's suspicious death, or, even if he was the same coroner. I cannot even be sure that it was Dr Chan who ordered the second, rushed, post-mortem, just a few hours before my arrival on the scene. Nor could I discover why it suddenly became necessary to re-examine Alex's body. Nevertheless, from that time onward until the end of November, the coroner seemed to have taken overall control of the case, and carried out his procedures in accordance with the duties laid down for coroners, in Coroners' Statutes and Rules and established precedents.[64]

I had taken it for granted that it was Dr Chan who ordered an inquest to be opened on May 16th, after receiving Dr Heath's further report, (probably given orally on May 14th). In actual fact, I am only assuming that Dr Chan was in charge at that time because I was given a copy of a document signed by the Coroner's Officer, Mr Davis, certifying that an inquest on Alex Barrack was opened and adjourned by Dr Chan - but the actual date of the inquest was omitted. Lately, in view of the many inaccuracies I have noted in other official documents, I cannot now be really certain that Dr Chan was the coroner in question at all times.

This inquest document, which was not issued until December 17th 1996, four days after Alex's funeral, states clearly that the cause of death was: **1. - Asphyxia; 2a. - Upper airway obstruction.** Therefore all actions taken by

---

[63] Coroner's affidavit
[64] Check ECHR list

the forensically experienced Dr Chan indicate that if he did run procedures from day one, he considered this death to be a possible homicide and acted appropriately. He ordered the police to make 'enquiries at a very high level', but, unfortunately for me and the family, he failed to inform us of these developments.

From May until the end of November, the coroner had obviously applied pressure on the police to continue to make a full and fair investigation. When the CPS twice refused to prosecute a suspect charged with causing an unlawful killing, he resolutely applied pressure to the CPS officials concerned. Very unexpectedly, the coroner's pursuit of justice for Alex seemed to evaporate into thin air at the end of November, which is when he decided to release Alex's body. This change in attitude became patently obvious when the inquest was resumed in January 1997. Dr Chan, throughout the inquest, quite definitely demonstrated a change in attitude, showing instead a strong prejudice against the victim's interests, and favouring instead those of the ex-suspect.[65]

I consider that my views and observations on the change in the coroner's attitude are fair comment, as are those I make on his reprehensible conduct at the inquest. My comments most certainly were not and are not the tenuous or spurious claims of a distressed mother, as the coroner was to infer later.[66] My conclusions are based on comparing his differing standards of behaviour before and at the inquest, using the same documentation, statements and forensic medical evidence he used at the inquest and official material obtained later. That material included a list of significant physical artefacts found at the Scene of Crime, although very few of these were referred to by Dr Chan. In the course of his examination of the witnesses, any significance these artefacts had to the circumstances of death was overlooked.

Although my inquest conclusions differ greatly from the coroner's, they are based solely on the same information he received. A great deal of this evidence was not made available at the time of the inquest. Departmental officials continuously denied me much of this evidence, until by using the

---

[65] Inquest Report pp????
[66] Letter from Coroner's official

135

Freedom of Information Act 2000 (FOIA); I forced the Metropolitan Police Service (MPS) to disclose a significant amount.

Even without this evidence released under the FOIA, I had collected other authentic information from sympathetic other public bodies who were also involved in the aftermath of Alex's death. With this information I compiled a comprehensive analysis which exposed the many deficiencies and anomalies in Dr Chan's manner of conducting his unusually short inquest. Altogether the whole procedure fell well below the standards of justice required from a Coroner's Court. What showed up with startling clarity in the inquest summary transcript was the coroner's bias favouring personal and departmental interests. The victim became a nobody; he was simply, 'the deceased'.

**Part 1 – The coroner's list of four points  he mentioned and others he omitted.**

### Point one. - Restraint and defence marks.
Both the pathologist and the coroner in reply to the question 'How the victim died?' stated in effect that, "There was no evidence whatsoever that the deceased was subjected to any violence or any force". Their conclusions, in face of the available evidence, go almost beyond belief.

**The importance of the bruises, abrasions and marks found on the body**
(A Diagram of the bruises and abrasions will be found below.)

In stating that there were no defence or restraint marks on Alex's body, both pathologist and coroner had ignored the detailed list of injuries found on Alex's body (with the exception of the neck abrasions) noted by Dr Heath at the autopsy, and these he had carefully measured and listed in his post-mortem report.[67] Also ignored at the inquest was the other significant forensic evidence found on the body which the pathologist had included in his PM report.

It was surprising that neither of them saw any real significance in this type of evidence, as one of the foremost experts on forensic medical evidence,

---

[67] PM Report

Professor Bernard Knight considers that 'in a medical-legal autopsy, the external examination is often of greater forensic importance than the internal dissection.' In Professor Knight's opinion the surface appearance of wounds and other features may often be of more importance in constructing the circumstances of the death than the gross examination of the internal organs.[68]

Also carefully omitted from the evidence by the coroner was the list of physical artefacts which included restraining devices and a prescribed drug, found at scene of crime by the SOCO. The existence of these artefacts and the drug, which I am sure were used on Alex, would reduce his ability to struggle and dull his mental awareness. These items were not publicly disclosed until the 2005 MRG Review. I am sure that it is most unlikely that the coroner would not have this information to hand during the inquest.

Marks, together with bruises and abrasions found on a body, are signs of violence of some kind having been inflicted on a body, before or after death. They are considered to be vital forensic evidence, particularly in cases of suspected homicide. It follows, then, that those marks and injuries found on Alex's body warranted the close scrutiny recommended by Professor Knight. This good advice was ignored.

Dr Heath told the coroner:
> "'Sir, ...finally I've two negative conclusions...I've noted that there were no restraint wounds on this gentleman, indicating that there was no one holding him down and forcefully applying any apparatus.'"[69]

If Alex Barrack was nor restrained or held down, why then was Dr Heath, in his PM report, able to list **no fewer than six** injuries on the back of his neck and trunk, which he described as being 'bruising' or 'abrasions'? They positively showed that violence and restraint were imposed on an unwilling victim. The position and size of these injuries, carefully measured by Dr Heath himself, are on the diagram below and speak for themselves.

---

[68] Simpson's *Forensic Medicine (11th edition 1997* p17)
[69] Inquest Report p2 Q & A 3

# Diagrams – slightly smaller than scale

ہ۔

## Bruises/Abrasions
### Found at Post-mortem Examination on the body of
### William Alexander Barrack

| | | |
|---|---|---|
| Left side back of neck | | bruise/abrasion 6.5cm x 0.3cm |
| Back of neck right side | | bruise/abrasion 0.3cm x 0.2cm |
| Back of left side of pelvis | | bruise/abrasion 2cm x 3cm |
| Left side chest middle third | | Incomplete abrasion 12.5cm |
| Left lower flank of abdomen | | Dried abrasion 4.5cm x 5cm |
| Outer aspect left ankle | | Incised wound with clotted blood 1 - 2 cm |

These abrasions are drag marks, skin scrapes, and are mainly sited on the left side, more or less in a line. This would have occurred during restraint when, it seems, Alex was twisted sideways and dragged by the hands or feet over a rough surface for a short distance. These injuries did not result from the paramedics dragging the dead Alex out of the bathroom, since one of the largest is described as a 'dried abrasion', therefore, the wound had bled or oozed serum, which shows Alex was alive when he received this and the other injuries - long before the emergency call was made and any resuscitation was applied.

Dr Chan tried to persuade Dr Heath that the long abrasion on the left side of the neck and the much shorter one on the right could have been the result of a frantic attempt to remove the thong from the victim's neck. He questioned whether that action could produce further obstruction to the restrictive collar of the head device.

Dr Heath dealt very sharply with this outrageous suggestion. He told the coroner he had listened to the 999 call transcript and was aware of the description of events given by Simpson. He told the coroner that such resuscitation on a dead man would not aggravate the asphyxia process and would not have produced the bruise on the neck. In his written police statement, he had been more positive in his conclusion that 'a bruise/abrasion could have been produced by the application of restraining and/or application of the balloon/bag' he had been shown by the police.[70]

> Dr Heath:
> "This is a bruise that indicated that it was caused during life and during that asphyxial element, not as a subsequent cause".

This was also a reminder to the coroner that Dr Heath had already settled the fact that Alex had been dead 2-3 hours **before** the 999 call was made and **before** the removal of the thong.

The Hospital Registrar, Dr Heyman, who had great experience in many types of injuries, was more specific in his description of the neck injury. It was much more definite:

---

[70] MRG Report p9 (a)

Dr Heyman:"

On more detailed examination of the body I noted an abrasion over the back of the neck, perhaps consistent with the rubbing of a necklace..."

At that time, the thong, the bootlace necklace, which caused the abrasion, had been removed from the body when at the flat.

Other evidence of restraint was found on Alex's body, which together with the abrasions, should have been subjected to a close enquiry by the coroner. These were two small oblique wounds which in the PM report were described as being 'consistent with having been caused by a sharp instrument used to remove an object positioned around the right ankle'.[71] Clearly the 'object positioned around the right ankle' was a means of restraint - and such an item was found in the bathroom by Ms Butler, the paramedic. She described it as consisting of an 18 inch long string, with four snooker type balls attached. In 2005 during an MRG interview I asked if this object was a form of restraint, and was told 'it probably was.' Physically restraining an individual does not necessarily involve great violence and severe injuries, especially if he were partially immobilised by such a gadget. There were other types of physical restraint apparatus found in Simpson's flat, known to be associated with bondage and sadomasochism, which may have been used on Alex, but the information of them being found at the scene was carefully withheld at the inquest, and was not officially disclosed until the MRG Review nine years later.

In actual fact, the extent of physical restraint needed would depend on the degree of mental awareness and the limb co-ordination of the victim, especially if the victim (like Alex) was of light weight, and had been under the influence of a combination of drugs, alcohol and 'other substances.' I will return to the questions on drugs and sadomasochistic practices later.

**Point one cont'd – Other Marks on the body**

In the PM report, Dr Heath listed other forensic evidence he found on Alex's body, which although they did not appear to be related to violence

---

[71] Pm Report p7

or restraint, were important in that they disproved Simpson's account of Alex taking a bath, immediately before his sudden death. Simpson's account was in fact flagrant perjury. No bath was taken.

Dr Heath had recorded that Alex's pubic area had been shaved. Whether this was carried out with or without Alex's consent I cannot say, but I discovered some time later that it is a feature in the practice of simulated-paedophilia. However, Dr Heath did not give this as a reason for the blood which had trickled over the right buttock crease, the perineum[72] and the back of the scrotum. Clotted blood from the two incisions on the right ankle was still present at the PM. In addition there was a smear of brown material on the right upper calf. He gave no reasons for the presence of any of them. The coroner too made no reference to any of these points during his inquisitions of witnesses, choosing instead to completely disregard their significance.

Therefore he also ignored the obvious truth - a truth of which the police were in no doubt - that these marks and injuries, the shaving, the restraining items, together with the presence of a frequently used head device, were all associated with sadomasochistic practice. In arresting and charging Simpson with criminal responsibility for Alex's death, they most certainly considered that it had taken place in sadomasochistic circumstances. Although Mr Graham of the CPS stated in his letter to DCI Baff (read at the inquest) that there was insufficient evidence to charge Robert Simpson with 'manslaughter or any other offence', the police have repeatedly refused to disclose the actual offences listed in the arrest documents.

What I stress is that the real importance of all this forensic evidence still present on Alex's body at the time of the autopsy lies in the fact that it totally refutes the account of the events given to the coroner by Simpson, which he claimed took place in the bathroom immediately before Alex died. As I will show in the next chapter, this account was only one of a series of concocted narratives Simpson used to disguise the true circumstances and cause of his victim's death.

---

[72] The region between the anus and the urethral opening

## Point two – The toxicology analysis.

Dr Chan in his summary stated that none of the compounds found in the toxicology analysis were considered to have contributed to his death; I disagree. The term 'compound' is a significant reference to the mixture of alcohol and drugs taken by Alex that night. Although the mixture did not chemically or physically contribute to or cause Alex's death, the combination would have affected his perception of the dangerous circumstance he was in, until it was too late to withdraw.

When the individual effects of alcohol and drugs are considered, it can be seen that the combination, even at a fairly low level, can enhance the effect on the brain. Research has shown that mixing drugs can be seriously dangerous.

1. Alex's blood alcohol level was 79mgms per 100mls of blood, a level which would reduce inhibitions, induce talkativeness, laughter and slight sensory disturbance.[73]

2. The toxicology report on MDMA (Ecstasy) showed that Alex had previously taken the drug within 6 hours of his death and would probably be under its influence during the time the events leading to his death took place. Users can, within ten minutes, begin to feel alert and very much in touch with their surroundings, while emotions, colours and sound are heightened, and life has never felt so good. Coupled with all those is the feeling of warm geniality towards other people. And these effects can last several hours.

3. The National Research Instituted advised me in 1997 that a research project was under way into proving the enhanced danger to the central nervous system from consuming a combination of alcohol, ecstasy and salbutamol, which is the drug in the Ventolin inhaler used by Alex to combat his asthma attacks. However, salbutamol, which must have been present, was not a substance mentioned in the verbal toxicology analysis,

---

[73] Simpson's - Forensic Medicine; p178.

so far as I am aware. But then the actual toxicology report was not introduced and marked as evidence and I have been refused a copy.

4. Another drug, which was several times referred to in both the inquest report in 1996 and the 2005 MRG report, is amyl nitrite, known to users as 'poppers'. Users get a very brief burst of energy and a rushing sensation from increased heart rate and light headedness. This is often accompanied by a sense that that time has slowed down and of sexual inhibition. The effects last only a matter of minutes and traces disappear very quickly from the blood.

The first three drugs (alcohol, ecstasy and salbutamol) were definitely used by Alex, but the coroner and the pathologist incompetently failed to take into consideration the well known adverse effects that they would have had on Alex's central nervous system, his emotional state, and his co-ordination. They most surely inhibited his ability to comprehend his danger, much less being able to offer much resistance to the sadomasochistic situation he was in.

However, although the use of amyl nitrite on Alex was not confirmed, I have little doubt but that it was, otherwise why would Simpson have denied using it when he had not been asked about its use? This was really odd omission, considering Mr Simpson admitted to using it on others. Indeed the MPS have confirmed that he was in possession of three bottles. No explanation was offered for him having it in his possession, and it appeared that no action was taken against Mr Simpson for being in possession of a Class B drug, legally available on prescription only. In the MRG report, an entry excuses the failure to test Alex's blood for amyl nitrite on the grounds 'it evaporates so quickly'. Without an expert toxicologist testing the blood, how could the police (who are definitely not experts) be absolutely certain there was no trace of that drug in the victim? There seems to have been a lot of such guesswork in this case.

At the time, I could not understand why both these doctors had been so unprofessional in overlooking the unfavourable effects that this combination of drugs and alcohol must have had on Alex's mental comprehension and physical co-ordination. It was obvious to us, nursing and non-nursing members of the family alike, with our limited knowledge, that this drugs mixture must have reduced Alex's ability to appreciate the

143

hazardous situation he had unwittingly walked into, and delayed his reaction to his danger.

I cannot stress strongly enough, that I am absolutely convinced that Alex, as a chronic asthmatic and with his fear of confined spaces, would have not have allowed that device to be placed over his head, had he not been affected by the drugs and **restrained by others**. The marks and injuries on his body are strong positive evidence that, even with his senses dulled by alcohol and drugs, he did put up some resistance to prevent a sadomasochistic rite, a perversion which he abhorred, being imposed on him

I try not to picture Alex's agony when the head device was forced over his head (there is no doubt that it was forced), and he suddenly realised the dangerous situation he was in. It would then be too late for him to offer any further resistance other than by instinctively raising his hands in a futile attempt to prevent his head being enclosed. With the device over his face and his breathing severely restricted, then terror and claustrophobia would have replaced his first state of euphoria. I try hard to suppress the recurring image of my son's despair when the horrible realisation hit him - that he was dying and - no one was going help him.

**Points three & four - natural deceases – bronchial asthma
-     foreign substances in the lung.**

The odd thing about this transcription of the coroner's summary is that although it consists of approximately 900 words, its contents are contained in just two block paragraphs. This may appear to be very poor English to a scholar, but on the other hand, having already experienced some of the coroner's deviousness at the inquest, it seems to me have been intentional. In reading such a solid block of printing in a brief one-off scrutiny, a reader, especially one sympathetic to the coroner's position, as so many officials of the justice system were, could persuade himself into accepting that it was a true record, in particular the questions put to Dr Heath and the answers he gave.

The truth is that these extracts from witness statements have little or no credence, because they have been taken out of context. It is certain that

144

much important evidence, indicating that Alex's death was an unlawful killing, has been omitted entirely from the summary. I have no hesitation in saying that these omissions were intentional, allowing the coroner to conclude, on inadequate evidence, that death was due to an unspecified accident, following a consensual sex act, and so give justification to the unbefitting verdict which was to follow.

My claim that the coroner acted reprehensibly in the structure of his summary, and deciding his verdict, is supported by the documents I obtained much later during my research. It is quite clear that in most respects, the police acted in accordance with procedure, even though much of the investigation, and the suspect's arrest, were conducted in secrecy - and no details were released to the family or the press until the inquest. However, in restricting his examination of witnesses and their evidence to the minimum, he presented a very different interpretation of the facts. Through this misinterpretation, he exonerated any person involved in the circumstance surrounding Alex's death from any criminal responsibility; by failing to acknowledge that a crime had been committed, thereby breaching Rule 42 of the Coroners' Rules 1984.

At the inquest, Dr Heath had told the coroner that although there was evidence of bronchial asthma, he firmly refuted the coroner's implication that the condition had in any way contributed to the death. The coroner, in his summary, said that Dr Heath **had** indicated that an attack could have happened which would account for the fluid and food found in the lung. That was because, **he said**, Dr Heath "had been **very careful in stating that he could not exclude** the fact that a mild attack could have happened **and if indeed it did, asthma itself did not play a part in the cause of the deceased's death**". However, Dr Chan ignored that part of the sentence and, taking only the first part, coupled it with the toxicology reference to food and fluid found in the bronchus by microscopic examination. This misrepresentation of an important fact, gave the false impression that these foreign substances had been inhaled or aspirated into the lung as the result a mild asthma attack occurring before death.

This definitely is not so; at the inquest hearing and in his police statement, submitted in June 1996, Dr Heath said that it was **not possible** to ascertain if there was an asthma attack at the time of death and that, had there been, it

145

had no significant effect. This is supported by an entry in the MRG Review taken from the written report:

Dr Heath:

"Had such an attack been present, in my opinion, it must have been mild. The overwhelming appearances were that death was due to an asphyxial process caused by an upper airway obstruction (pressure on the neck and over the nose and mouth)"[74].

This is in reality is very informative statement. Dr Heath is stating categorically that, in his opinion, asthma was not a feature in Alex's death, and that the obstruction was not from any natural cause or internal obstructive event. The pressure to the neck, nose and mouth had to be applied externally. It could not have resulted from either aspiration or inhalation. In his statement to the police, Dr Heath twice stated that death **was** due to 'asphyxia and upper airway obstruction' and in his opinion was caused by the application of a restrictive apparatus.[75]

After we had listened in silent dismay to Dr Chan's manipulation of the facts relating to all four points, we were startled when Dr Chan concluded the first part of his summary in this manner:

Dr Chan:

"I am satisfied with this evidence, so I will formally certify that the cause of death was as given by the Pathologist as that of **1a: Asphyxia consequent of 1b: Upper Airway obstruction.**"

The family heard this conclusion with great relief. It seemed that, after all, the coroner had finally accepted that Alex's death was unlawful and was caused by the application of the head device. This relief was short-lived. Dr Chan continued with his totally biased summary. By giving the

---

[74] MRG Report p9

[75] MRG review p9

146

incredible verdict of 'accidental death', he not only dashed our hopes to have justice for Alex, but also destroyed a family's trust in the fairness and impartiality of English justice.

In the next chapter I will continue with the second half of the coroner's summary of the evidence. I will give the reasons why I believe the coroner's biased conduct of the inquest was not in keeping with the spirit of the law. I will, through a cross-analysis of the medical and forensic evidence in relation to Simpson's and other witness statements, disclose a very disturbing flaw in the justice system. I shall demonstrate how personal and departmental interests can be deliberately used to eclipse a victim's fundamental and absolute 'Right to Life'[76], and pervert the course justice.

---

[76] ECHR (2)

# CHAPTER TWELVE

*It is enough for good men to do nothing, for evil to triumph.*

**What the coroner said - and what the coroner left unsaid.**
The second paragraph of the coroner's summary, which I have divided into short sentences for intelligibility, was also his closing statement of the inquest. It began with the almost meaningless, and certainly the briefest, and most incomplete, statement he could possibly give of his examination of the evidence and the reasons for giving this particular verdict

Dr Chan:

"In consideration of all the evidence presented - in this Court today - I am mindful that only the deceased and Mr Simpson know the truth of what activities took place that fateful morning."

No one would ever dispute that, only a victim and his murderer/murderers know the truth of the activities that led to someone's death (unless of course there were also other eyewitnesses), but that does not mean that only the voices of those suspected of causing a death can speak for the victim. On the contrary, a dead person does have a voice of his own; he speaks through the forensic and forensic medical evidence found on and around the body, and the circumstances in which the death took place. In actual fact, the dead can only speak the truth, whereas perpetrators can and very often do give accounts by which they either attempt to mitigate their crime, or totally deny it altogether. They always hope that such misleading versions of what actually happened will be accepted, and will minimise or even avoid altogether the consequences of their actions.

Mr Simpson was in luck; he was in the hands of a coroner who was deaf to the voice of the dead, and who was apparently prepared to ignore the strong evidence of an unlawful killing. This evidence, gathered together by experts in various fields of forensic science, contradicted Simpson's unreliable and varied versions of the time, the place and exactly how the victim lost his life. Yet the coroner chose not to hear their expert evidence.

This is demonstrated in the coroner's next sentence:

Coroner:
"Now if Mr Simpson evidence is to be accepted he emphatically stated that no balloon device or any other restraining apparatus was experienced in his flat."

That was it; end of explanation. Are we to accept, then, that because Mr Simpson tells the coroner that there was no such activity, it must be the truth? As I have explained already, that cannot be correct. The pathologist has in his professional capacity confirmed more positively - and not once, but several times - that Alex, the deceased, had died from asphyxia from the application of an obstructive head device. Any statement made by a witness under oath which attempts to contradict this fact, must surely be disregarded as not being worthwhile evidence. It must be classed as perjury and treated as such. However, it was not regarded as such by this coroner.

In the next sentence, Dr Chan told us that Simpson was aware that Alex was an asthmatic who had used his inhaler the sitting room of Simpson's flat.

The truth is that Simpson did not see an inhaler, and was not aware that Alex was a chronic asthmatic, until after the post-mortem. He was after all a very experienced Senior Crown Prosecutor, who would have known the value of such information. Had he known of Alex's condition, he would surely have passed on the information as a credible explanation for Alex's collapse and sudden death to the Ambulance Service personnel? Also, if he knew that Alex was an asthmatic, and carried an inhaler, as he claimed later, then in his call to the 999 he would surely have mentioned this. Instead, Simpson gave the false impression that he was asking assistance for someone who had taken an overdose of heroin. He gave a different story to the Call Taker, who also thought he was dealing with a heroin overdose; but Simpson merely said to him 'I think someone just died in my flat', and made no mention of either an asthma attack or heroin overdose. Nor did he make any reference to Alex being an asthmatic to either the paramedics or to the Hospital Registrar. **Quite obviously, he did not know that he was.**

When the police interviewed me on the 14<sup>th</sup> May and I asked why Alex had not been identified earlier, I was told it was because, **'there were no effects on the body at all'**, and this was quite true as Alex was naked. So it seems to have been me who introduced the inhaler into the case, when I listed the inhaler among the effects that I expected Alex to have somewhere among his clothes.

Furthermore, the MRG Review adds weight to my claim that Simpson was unaware of Alex's asthma in providing me with information regarding Simpson's first interview with the police at Limehouse Police station, on the morning of the 4<sup>th</sup> May. That interview took place before the PM. Definitely; the MRG has no record of him having mentioned either the asthma or an inhaler at that interview. Whether or not Alex did have an inhaler on him that day cannot be verified, because the MRG Review was unable to establish **when** Alex's clothing actually came into police possession, and it was not actually examined until 16<sup>th</sup> May. At that time, it was still in the hospital bag, not in an official evidence bag, as routine procedures dictated. There is no record apparently of the clothing and effects being listed in the police property file, before they went missing. Although this claim of Simpson that he knew of Alex's asthma condition was patently untrue, the coroner was happy to use such false information in helping him to decide on his verdict.

Dr Chan's next point dealt with Steve Jones's statement that, 'to my knowledge, Alex would not participate in any dangerous, kinky sex games which restricted his breathing'. That is also true, but Steve is only referring to **voluntary** participation. There is strong evidence that Alex was compelled to take part in such activities that night and very much against his will. Therefore the coroner, in accepting Simpson's unfounded claim that no sadomasochistic activities took place that morning, is once again accepting Simpson's word, and basing his conclusions on an unsound witness's statements. He totally ignored the solid physical evidence, and the documentary confirmation contained in the statements which recorded, that Simpson's flat was a centre of frequent bondage and sadomasochistic practices.

Dr Chan then moved on to the pathologist's evidence on the balloon or restraining head device and makes a surprising point that there was:

Dr Chan:

"...a suggestion of a discrepancy in concluding, that the overwhelming appearances that death was sue to an asphyxial process, caused by upper airway obstruction which could have been produced by the application or by the balloon device found in Mr Simpson's flat".

He next moved on to the DNA report given to him by DI Baff:

Dr Chan:

"However I am also mindful that the DNA test of the balloon device failed to confirm whether or not DNA materials from the deceased were present. Furthermore, whether any restraining devices or restrictive devices were used".

There was no suggestion of a 'discrepancy' in that evidence on asphyxia; death was established as being the result of manual nose and mouth obstruction. Yet, in these two sentences, one of which dealt with incomplete and inadequate evidence on DNA profiling, the coroner dismissed out of hand any likelihood of the device being used on Alex. What he was actually told by DI Baff was that some components of Alex's DNA were part of the DNA analysis found in the bag, but were inconclusive as to whether it had been used on Alex **at that time**, Advanced DNA analysis techniques were to become a serious issue after the MRG report was issued in 2005. For the present, I will merely say that I know from the MRG Review that the DNA analysis, combined with finger and palm print testing, were shown to be seriously flawed investigations.[77] It is a singular fact that any evidence relating to fingerprinting was omitted by the coroner in his the inquest inquisition.

Dr Chan's next statement is an anomaly:

---

[77] Even though in 1996 - fingerprinting techniques less advanced - MRG Review reveals that testing of both in Balloon bag were flawed. MRG Report and MPS Correspondence.

:"There is no evidence whatsoever to suggest that what activities did or did not take place was anything other than between two consenting homosexual males".

That is confusing. The coroner's role is to establish the actual facts and draw a conclusion from those facts. Here I cannot see that he draws any clear conclusion. He doesn't seem to be sure of whether or not there was any real evidence of sexual activity. He appears to be ignoring the evidence of the sexual activity given to him by Simpson, and the use of several artefacts of a sexual nature found at the scene by the paramedics and the police.[78] He also appeared to be expressing his uncertainty of the events, when he stated that he believed there was 'no evidence' that such activities did or did not take place. This was a court of law, and I would have thought that he should have reached a definite conclusion, which would have established either that:

1. There was no evidence of any sexual activity (Therefore consent was not an issue), or

2. There was insufficient evidence to prove that any sexual activity, which took place, was anything other than consensual.

But Dr Chan didn't commit himself to either conclusion. And considering the strong attempts he made before the inquest to secure a prosecution from the CPS, Dr Chan showed an unusual reluctance to express an opinion on the criminality of the same factual evidence.

The next sentence deals in the briefest possible way with criminal negligence:

Dr Chan:
"There is no evidence in my view, of any specific act which could be regarded as grossly negligent in the criminal sense."

---

[78] MRG Report & Lee Butler's statement

152

That is a surprising statement from a coroner examining the factual evidence, which demonstrated beyond any doubt that Mr Simpson, a Senior Crown Prosecutor, not only neglected to carry out several legal obligations in relation to a collapse and sudden death which he witnessed, or caused, but also, that there is evidence of several other criminal offences which could carry a penalty. In layman's terms they are:

1. Failure to carry out a duty of care and to immediately call for emergency medical attendance until 2-3 hours after the victim's collapse.

2. Neglecting to notify the police immediately of a sudden death on his premises, the result of a dangerous act.[79]

3. Evidence of perjury in statements made under oath to the Police, the CPS and the coroner.[80]

4. Offences committed under the Offences against the Person Act

5. Gross Negligence - Carrying out an act with indifference to obvious risk to health.[81]

Dr Chan also ignored the fact that Simpson had been arrested on a charge of manslaughter. That would not have happened unless the police had strong evidence. That the CPS did not prosecute him was not because he had not committed any offence, but on the grounds that there was 'insufficient evidence' to proceed with a prosecution.

This brings me to the conclusion, if it can be called such, in which the coroner reintroduced the subject already firmly dismissed by Dr Heath:

> Dr Chan:
> "There are of course other possibilities and I believe not an unreasonable scenario, which is that of a mild asthma attack, during which food and fluid…were inhaled into the lungs…"

---

[79] Information from Shropshire Police
[80] See previous reference.
[81] Criminal Law

Having previously told the Court that Simpson was emphatic in stating that no balloon device was experienced in his flat, Dr Chan now told the Court that there was a discrepancy in concluding that death was due to the balloon. He continued:

Dr Chan:

"...causing or contributing to asphyxia, either exacerbating the asphyxial process initiated by any restraining device or apparatus if indeed they were used..."

He appears at this point to be accepting what he had previously attempted to negate, that a restrictive head device could have been used. He concludes this convoluted piece of reasoning by repeating what he said at the beginning of his summary:

Dr Chan continued:

"...and nobody knows the truth except Mr Simpson and the deceased, *(adding)* or even in my view independent of it."

The coroner throughout the inquest had carefully omitted any reference to Simpson's accounts of copious vomiting and blood, even when he himself during the inquest, had made quite an issue of the food and fluid being inhaled, or aspirated, into the lung during an asthma attack. By contrast, Dr Heath's opinion was that these substances had entered the **lung** through the resuscitation processes, an opinion supported by Simpson himself. In the statement he made to the Call Taker (This was recorded and transcribed); he provides positive evidence that the food and fluid were aspirated into the lungs, **after death,** by vigorous resuscitation, and not while Alex was still living.

There is no doubt that at the time the dialogue between the Call Taker and Simpson took place, there was no evidence of vomiting, and Simpson himself said so, but by the time the Ambulance Service personnel arrived there was.

At the beginning of the 999 call to the Ambulance Service, the Call Taker had been informed by Simpson, 'Someone has just died in my flat'; the

Call Taker confirms the address details with Simpson and also the patient's age.

The Call Taker (CT) asked Simpson (S) to check if there is any breathing and on being told 'I don't think he is...' offered to give advice on resuscitation and Simpson agreed to try.

Call Taker:
"Right what you need to do, is to check that there is nothing in his mouth, if there is anything in his mouth, then, I want you to take it out..."

Simpson:
"...Em, he's just gone limp."

The CT then gave instructions on checking for a pulse, but S reported there was none. He was then asked if he was lying flat, when he was told the patient was sitting up, he told S to 'lay him flat'.

The CT then asked S again '**Nothing in his mouth?**' He replied, '**Nothing in his mouth.**'

CPR instructions were then commenced and S was given instructions on mouth-to-mouth breathing. On the tape one can hear quite clearly deep breathing sounds, indicating that he is performing mouth-to-mouth resuscitation. He confirmed to the CT that he could see the chest go slightly up and down. There is also some background gurgling.

The CT then gave directions for cardiac massage and the correct position for the hands.

Call Taker:
"Put your hands one on top of the other and push firmly down only using the heel of the hands about one and a half to two inches. Count out loud as you do it"

Simpson:
"...Six, seven, eight, nine, ten, eleven, twelve, thirteen, fourteen, fifteen."

155

The CPR routine was carried out for some time - and throughout there were sounds of Simpson apparently doing mouth-to-mouth breathing and of compression on the chest. Then he suddenly exclaimed: "There's vomit coming out of his mouth." It was at **this point** that the vomit entered Alex's mouth which had been empty until then, and **not** before.

Simpson was then instructed to scoop the vomit out, because it is impossible to carry out mouth-to- mouth resuscitation if the airway is blocked. Although Simpson gave the impression that he continued breathing into the mouth, and to scoop out vomit when required, there is no way that he would have carried out the mouth to mouth technique in what had become a distasteful task. It did seem, however, that he continued the compression of the chest.

Therefore, although there is no doubt that S did carry out CPR and that vomit entered the mouth as was described in the first part of the transcript, it was impossible for him have proceeded in the way CT told him to. He most certainly would have not been able to insert his finger into Alex's mouth and scoop out the vomit.

The trained Paramedic, Lee Butler, who reported that she had attempted to insert an airway but found it difficult because the jaw was rigid due to the advanced stage of rigor mortis, confirmed this. She had managed to force the mouth partially open and found it contained a great deal of vomit. Ms Butler also reported that she was unable to clear the airway of any obstructing vomit as she could not insert a suction tube.[82] It appears the that the mouth, although rigid, may have been slightly open, but free from vomit, at the time Simpson applied CPR, which is why he was able to say that at first the mouth was empty and to see that vomit had later entered the mouth. Incidentally the Paramedic saw no sign of the abundant vomiting that he described to the CT.

It should be noted that Simpson was not an expert in CPR, and it is possible that he was compressing the chest too hard and too far down, and pressed on the stomach to expel gases upwards, forcing some of the

---

[82] Check source of that report

stomach contents to be aspirated into the lungs. The paramedic's resuscitation may have also helped.[83]

Whatever the cause for the food and fluid to be present in the lungs, **it was not present as the result of an asthma attack**, nor during his death throes. Dr Heath was correct in giving his opinion that they were there as a result of vigorous resuscitation.

Not that Dr Chan appeared to take notice of Dr Heath's conclusions and findings, nor of any of the factual evidence he was supposed to examine fairly and impartially, before he decided on a verdict. He drew the inquest to a close as follows:

Dr. Chan:

"Well I have given careful consideration to all the available evidence and will state that I am satisfied on the balance of probability that the deceased death was accidental".

"The standard of proof for me to record an accidental death was that on the balance of probability whether it was more likely than not."

"Here I am not dealing in this Court with scientific absolute or near absolute and based on the available evidence, I will state that I am satisfied on the balance of probability that what happened was nothing more than a tragic accident."

The family waited in silence for the coroner to give details of which particular event had caused the 'accidental death' and what degree of probability he had based his verdict, but none were forthcoming. Instead Dr Chan closed the inquest in the brief terms he had used throughout:

Dr Chan:

"Finally, let me thank all the witnesses who have assisted me in this inquiry and I will record a verdict of 'Accidental Death'."

---

[83] This is not uncommon it occurs in about 25% of deaths

Then he was gone. Even before we could obey the coroner's officer's instruction to stand, Dr Chan had disappeared through the door behind the dais, while Simpson just as speedily headed for the exit.

The coroner had not expressed any of the customary condolences to the family for our lost son, and Simpson had neither expressed nor showed any regret over the circumstances of Alex's death throughout his inquisition.

Justice had been perverted and the inquest inquisition was over, as far as both the coroner and Simpson were concerned. Not for me though.

My quest for justice was just about to begin.

# CHAPTER THIRTEEN

*To no man will we sell, or deny, or delay, right or justice.* - Magna Carta-
On the other hand
*In England, justice is open to all poor men – like the Ritz Hotel.* - Irish
Judge - 1901

**Part 1 – DI Bathie helps me to take the first step to remedy an injustice.**

The inquest verdict had been delivered, and as far as the authorities were concerned, the case was closed, but not however for me. Even though I was not yet aware of it, I was on the first step of a campaign in which I would hound the justice system for years to come, working tirelessly to try to obtain the truth for me and justice for my son.

When I saw Mr Simpson heading for the exit, I was actually taking the first step in my quest for justice. I was on my feet in an instant and heading down the aisle, fully intent on catching up with him and demanding to know why he had waited so long to call medical assistance for Alex. I did not make it to the door because DI Bathie stepped in front of me, blocking my path. Whether or not this was a deliberate move, I have never been sure, because he held my arm and said, "I am very sorry that things have turned out this way, because we thought the police had a good case for a prosecution." (Referring to himself and DCI Baff). This admission shocked me and I demanded to know why there had not been a prosecution. DI Bathie replied, '**Because the DPP ordered the CPS that there was not to be a prosecution**' He then added, "That verdict, of course, closes the case and the police will take no further action".

The only thing that registered with me at that moment was that he believed Simpson should have been prosecuted. I hadn't a clue what a DPP was, and knew very little about the role of the CPS, or realised that an inquest verdict could be so final. I shook my arm free and hurried to the exit but Simpson had vanished with his QC.

The Coroner's Officer Mr Davis was waiting for me with the intrusive cub reporter, who was ready with his notebook. I was told that the reporter wanted to speak to me, but that I could refuse. I can't remember exactly what I said to him, but it was very brief and more in confusion than in anger. I am certain, though, that I did not say all the fiery things published later in two newspapers. I do remember saying to the junior reporter that I wanted to know why my son had not had the medical attention sooner. After that Mr Davis cut the interview short.

The Coroner's Officer told me that the whole of the inquest had been tape-recorded and would be transcribed and that I was entitled to a have a copy. I would, however, be charged for it. He could not give me an estimate of the cost, as the charge was based on the number of words in the report. Mr Davis obviously went out of his way to be helpful, because when I told him that I did not intend to leave things there, he gave me some good advice. He told me that the best way forward would be to get hold of the Inquest Report as soon as possible, to personally contact the transcriber, and to explain my feelings and intention. He also said I should also stress that it was important that for me to have a copy as soon as possible. Mr Davis then provided me with the transcriber's name, address and telephone number. I thanked him and accepted, but really, I could not see why it was so important to hurry the report along.

It was only a matter of two weeks before I learned how essential it was for me to have that document, therefore I would like put on record that I believe Mr Davis, in displaying so much sympathetic assistance, was in a small way trying to make restitution for the collusion and injustice in which, I really do think, he had played an unwilling role. I thanked him and we then left the coroner's court after saying goodbye to Nathanial and Spike, but before we left I asked Nathanial, who worked in a law office, 'What do you think of what we heard at the inquest?' I was surprised when he answered, "It is what we didn't hear that concerns me." It was weeks later before I was to realise the significance of his answer.

The family left the Court very cold and hungry in atrocious weather, and walked a short distance to the nearest public house. In a matter of ten minutes, we were sitting thankfully in the warmth of the inn, had ordered drinks and food, and began discussing the inquest in terms not too complimentary to the coroner. It was then that one of us, probably the discerning Maureen, asked 'Do you realise that it was a very short inquest, it can't have lasted more than an hour at the most?' That was true, because the inquest start was delayed until 11.30am, and there we were at ten past one, sitting waiting for our meal.[84]

A Lincolnshire Coroner's Officer confirmed later that it was an unusually short period for an inquest into a suspicious death, which had been adjourned for several months for further police enquiries. He would have thought that when the inquest was resumed, it should have been held with a jury and many more witnesses should have been called

Our conversation during that meal centred on the shocking truth that we had heard for the first time that Alex had not died from natural causes, but had been asphyxiated, and that Robert Simpson was not the hero we had been led to believe, but had actually been arrested for causing Alex's death. When I told them DI Bathie had stated that the DPP had interfered in the case to prevent a prosecution, and also of Nathanial's concerns, there was increased indignation at the irregular conduct of the judicial authorities. As we talked together, we began to realise how seriously detrimental the verdict of 'accidental death' was to Alex's case, in that it allowed the police to close the case and apparently block any future investigation.

Shortly after this, Alex's father took his leave and set off for Leeds, while Maureen, Ken and I returned to New Barnet. I think all three of us found it hard to grasp that Alex had been killed in such a manner. What was hardest to understand, when it was so obvious to us, was this: the witness Robert Simpson had been responsible for Alex's death. So why, then, had the CPS allowed him to walk free? There was further anger in our understanding that the coroner's verdict closed police enquiries and therefore he would stay free and unpunished.

Once back at New Barnet, the three of us discussed for hours all that the inquest had revealed and the many questions the whole procedure had raised for us. Probably the prevailing feeling was one of helpless finality, now that we knew the police would close the case. We could not see then, how we could remedy the situation, but I had it my mind that I would find a way.

---

[84] The total words of the transcript of the Inquest were 6387– estimated at 15ps x 30 words per line  of which 781 words comprised the summary.

161

I left the next day, Saturday, as Maureen was due to start another course of very unpleasant chemotherapy on Monday. Quite naturally, she and Ken needed time on their own to readjust to the routine they had established over the long period of Maureen's illness and treatment. And so saying goodbye to these very helpful relatives was difficult. It would have been different if the coroner's verdict had been favourable and less final, but I as I drove away it was with a deep sense of having failed Alex, and all because of my ignorance and naivety, I had let justice slip away. During the two hours journey home I went step by step through the details of Alex's case, and by the time I reached home, I had decided that I definitely was not going to passively accept that inappropriate verdict, and, come what may, I would take action.

**Part 2 – Waiting for the Inquest Report – Mr Hepburn of the Sun – his revelations on Simpson and the CPS**

The problem was, as for so many families who had found themselves in a similar situation, I hadn't much of a clue how to set about remedying such an injustice, but Mr Davis had recommended one line of action, so I took it. Within two hours of arriving home, I had written a letter to the PW Transcriber Services, in the manner which Mr Davis had suggested, and it was in the post that same night, Saturday 10th April 1997. That was my first step on to the rocky road to truth and justice. I followed the letter up with a telephone call on the Monday and spoke to the lady who was to handle my request, Mrs Woodward. She proved to be unexpectedly helpful and understanding when I explained I needed the transcript as soon as possible. I was quite relieved that she did not ask 'What is the nature of the urgency?', because at that time, I didn't know myself. Although later, on reflection, I considered that, as an experienced transcriber, she would already know the reason.

Mrs Woodward explained that she could do nothing until the coroner sent her the inquest tape, but she would try to hurry things along. Her system worked this way. Once the tape was received, transcribed and properly documented, then it would go back the coroner for his approval and signature. When the signed report was back in her hands, she would work out the charges and then advise me of the total cost. This charge I would have to pay by cheque, before I could have the report. Then she asked if I

162

wanted the documents sent directly to me, or to my solicitor. That question jolted me into the realisation that I was once again heading into a legal situation without legal advice. I asked for the report to be sent to me. I had it in mind that I would contact Mr Marshall, the solicitor who had helped me over the PM report, when I actually received the inquest report.

Before that happened, on 22nd January about 8pm, I had an unexpected telephone call from an investigative journalist, who asked if he could visit me at my home to discuss irregularities in the inquest on Alex, which a 'concerned, reliable' correspondent, had brought to his attention. This investigative journalist was Ian Hepburn of the *Sun* newspaper, who told me he was carrying out a special investigation into the CPS, which he would explain to me. I agreed to see him next morning, but told him that I had reservations about giving him a publishable interview.

Mr Hepburn, with a photographer, arrived very early and Mr Hepburn lost no time in telling me that he was conducting an investigation into Alex's inquest, because of what he described as 'his concern for justice'. The gist of the interview was as follows. His unnamed informant had read an account of the inquest in an Islington newspaper, and had become concerned, because members of the public had apparently been excluded from what appeared to be an inquest into a suspicious death, and found it significant that details of Robert Simpson's employment and place of work had not been revealed. This indicated to him that there was a 'cover-up', because he understood that Robert Simpson was a senior practising lawyer working for the CPS.

Mr Hepburn then stated:

> "My interest in the inquest stems from my concern for justice because, if Robert Simpson is who we think he is, then there is a possibility that his connection with the CPS has been used to pervert the course of justice."

Mr Hepburn then asked if I would be willing to be interviewed for an article on Alex's inquest revealing those suspicions. I hesitated over making a decision, even though if was true, and there had been a cover-up, it could explain the odd behaviour of the police, the CPS and the coroner.

After giving it some thought, I still hesitated, as I was not sure about his motives; frankly, I had a jaundiced view of newspaper reporting. I did not know if I could trust this investigative journalist, and it was, after all, a very sensitive matter to put before the public, and I said so. Mr Hepburn assured me that it would be tactfully handled without homophobic undertones.

The photographer asked if he could copy a studio photo of Alex, and I agreed, on condition that it would not be used unless I was sure that Simpson was a member of the CPS. Mr Hepburn wrote and signed a short note agreeing to this condition. He then left promising to contact me again when he had definite proof.

Everything to do with the case was now more confused and uncertain, except for one thing, and that was, if Hepburn was telling the truth, then the coroner had purposely failed to challenge Simpson's glaringly obvious perjury and I would certainly have to take some action. Nevertheless, I had to be sure, and so I contacted the only person I thought could help, and that was DI Bathie. He had said to me at our inquest encounter, "If there is anything I can do to help you, don't hesitate to get in touch."

Within an hour of the journalist leaving, I was on the 'phone speaking to the Mr Bathie. I asked him without any preamble:

"Is Mr Simpson a Senior Prosecutor with the CPS?"

There was a pause then he asked:

"Where did you get that from?"

I guessed then, that my question had thrown him off balance, and I said to him:

"He is isn't he? I can tell you where he works, at the Tower Hamlets CPS Office". *(Which was how Mr Hepburn described his position?)*

164

I knew from the tone of his reply, that bit of information had startled him and my question wasn't just guesswork, because he then demanded in an authoritive tone:

"Who told you that?"

His manner changed when I told him that the information had come from the *Sun*'s investigative journalist, Ian Hepburn, and he then said that he really couldn't answer that query. I told him that the family were already very dissatisfied with the coroner's verdict, and with the possibility that Robert Simpson was a member of the CPS; we now questioned the CPS decision not to prosecute a colleague. Therefore if Mr Hepburn confirmed Mr Simpson was connected to the CPS, I would agree to an interview. Later, I intended to take legal advice.

At that time I could not tell DI Bathie what action I would take, but he was very quick to defend the police position. He assured me that the police had thoroughly investigated Alex's death in accordance with the coroner's instruction. He repeated what he had told me after the inquest, that when the case went to the CPS, he and DCI Baff thought their results strong enough to warrant a prosecution. However the case had gone to the highest authority, The Director of Public Prosecutions, and this time he named her as Dame Barbara Mills, and that it was her personal instruction to the CPS prosecutors who were considering the case, they were **not to prosecute**. It was obvious to me that DI Bathie, in avoiding answering my question about Robert Simpson's occupation, was tacitly admitting that he was a CPS lawyer. I told him that if the *Sun* confirmed that he was a CPS member, then I would agree to an interview with Mr Hepburn. That was another unintentional error on my part, as I was soon to find out.

On the Saturday of the same week, Mr Hepburn rang and asked me if I had contacted the police. I told him I had, and that it was because I wanted confirmation of the *Sun*'s claim of CPS involvement. I was dismayed when he told me I had made a bad mistake, because the police had alerted the CPS, and that the CPS press officer had asked the *Sun* editor if he intended to keep Simpson under observation. He then told me that he had obtained the original shorthand transcript of the inquest (presumably the intrusive reporter's) and gave me a brief, but favourable, outline of the article he

165

intended to publish. I agreed he could go ahead and also use Alex's photograph. He gave me the day and the date, Tuesday 26th January, on which the article would be published nationwide.

Tuesday came, and I was out early to buy a copy of the *Sun*, but there was nothing in it about Alex and Simpson. I contacted several friends and family in various parts of the country, but they reported nothing had been published about the inquest in their areas. There was an article published in a London district paper, and although I never knew which one, a copy was sent to me later, headed 'Exclusive by Ian Hepburn', dated 26th January. I was incensed by its theme and contents. It was almost word for word from the earlier local London article Mr Hepburn had shown me, but with additional material researched by the journalist, which I had not and could not have known, until I read his article. However, what made me so angry was that this article was strongly homophobic, and couched in such a way which, although the views were Ian Hepburn's, he misled the reader into thinking that I had made these comments and accusations[85]. Certainly he had made his point about injustice, but at my expense.

When I managed to contact him, he admitted that it wasn't the article he had submitted to his editor, **who had flatly refused to allow the original to be published.** When I asked if the editor had been warned off as a result of my contacting the police, his comment was, 'Probably'[86] That was the last time I spoke to Mr Hepburn. Two or three years later I received information, from an independent journalist, to the effect that Ian Hepburn had for some time been conducting his own investigation into irregular activities of certain members of the CPS.

Before any legal action could even be started, I knew that it was necessary to have legal advice from a solicitor. There was however, an outstanding matter needing to be cleared before I approached a solicitor, which was what had happened to Alex's effects and his clothing? – which I knew should all have been returned to me. I contacted Limehouse Police, and as DI Bathie was not available, I spoke to Police Sergeant Martin, who promised to make enquires for me about the clothing and effects. He then

---

[85] The article was headed, 'TOP LAWYER LET OFF OVER KINKY DEATH OF GAY PAL'
' Mum blasts cover-up'

.

166

asked how I was coping with the situation. When I told him I was very unhappy about the inquest and the verdict and intended to take legal action, he told me that he would do the same if he was in my situation. I thought it significant that a uniformed police officer, who was not involved in the case, should repeat DI Bathie's comment that all Limehouse police were very disappointed at the way things had turned out.

A few days afterwards, Sgt Martin called to tell me he had been unable to trace either Alex's clothing or his effects. He apologised for the failure and offered to do anything he could to help, even if it was just to chat. He added 'I will make sure that DI Bathie rings you'.

I was out when DI Bathie 'phoned me, but called him as soon I heard his message. I just about hit the roof when he told me that Alex's clothing had been destroyed, 'on your instructions', when I went to the police station to identify Alex. It was a blatant lie, as I told him. While I was at the station, the question of his clothing had not arisen. Only the things that should have been in his pockets were discussed, and, even as early as that, they were missing. He made matters worse when he said that I must have given permission on my second visit. I sharply reminded him that I had only made one visit. He then said it must have been Mr Amphlett who had given permission. My reply was that excuse was absolute nonsense and I wanted the clothing and effects traced.

A short time later DI Bathie rang me to say that apparently Alex's clothing had been sent to the laboratory for examination and, as they would have been damaged as a result of the testing, then they had probably been destroyed by a member of the lab staff. I then asked, 'What was the reason for such an examination when Alex was not wearing them when he died?' DI Bathie couldn't answer that, because, apparently, **that report was also missing.** In actual fact, none of the effects were ever found, not even by the MRG during their search for missing items in 2005.

Furthermore, DI Bathie made no comment when I queried why I had been so misled over the cause of Alex's death, nor to my complaint that at no time had anyone given satisfactory answers to any of my questions. I told him that in view of the recent disclosures over Robert Simpson, I was consulting a solicitor over the CPS decision and the coroner's inquest.

167

DI Bathie warned me that it would be very difficult to overturn either the CPS or the coroner's decisions. I told him I was aware of that, but I would definitely take action and would go as far as possible to get the truth and justice. When I made that statement, I had no idea just how far I would have to go, or how long it would take me to achieve my limited success.

That was the last time I was ever able to contact DI Bathie or any other member of the investigation team. In less than a year, they too went missing from the scene, for one reason or another.

# CHAPTER FOURTEEN

*The Government's overall objective...is to see that the public has the*
*best possible access to legal services and that those services are of the*
*right quality for the particular needs of the client'...*
**The Courts and Legal Services Act 1990**

**Part 1 - The inquest Report is received -following Government guide lines - an appeal to the High Court is prepared.**

I must confess that I cannot remember the exact date I first contacted the solicitor Mr Marshal, but it was within days of my last conversation with DI Bathie. It was decided at that meeting, that until I received the inquest report little could done, but he had in mind an appeal for a Judicial Review. In the first week of February I again phoned Mrs Woodward, at Mr Marshal's suggestion, to ask for a progress report, but she had not received the tape from the coroner, but she assured me that she would give it priority when it was in her hands.

Mrs Woodward received the tape on about the 8th February and I spoke to her on the 16th of February when she told me that she had finished the transcription, and it was ready for the coroner's signature. She told me that she would write me a formal letter advising me of the completion of report, and the total cost to me. We talked a little about Alex's death and the inquest verdict, then she said, "Mrs Barrack, the coroner had instructed me to allow you only the three statements you had at the inquest, and to withhold six other statements, but really you should have them. I wish I could send them to you, but it is more than my job is worth.' I told her I understood, but then asked if the documents would help me? Mrs Woodward replied that they could be very helpful. The letter arrived on the 18th February and I sent the cheque for £87.47p, the next morning as we had arranged, so that when the signed report was received, she could send it to me without further delay.

On the 26th of February I was very surprised to receive a phone call from Nathanial Mathews, who, as I have mentioned was a friend of both Alex and Steven Jones. Indeed it was Nathanial and his partner Lisa who had given Alex house room when Steven had himself severed the relationship with Alex and made him homeless. It was Lisa who was mainly

169

instrumental in Alex being allocated a flat. I was shocked to learn that Steven was planning to take legal action, on the grounds that he was Alex's partner. He had contacted Mathew, who was employed in a paralegal capacity at Hackney Law Centre, and requested him to act for him in his proposed legal action, probably one which would challenge the coroner's verdict.

I told Nathanial in no uncertain terms, that I would not agree to Steven taking any independent legal action. As Alex's next of kin it was my right to act on Alex's behalf, and that under the distressing circumstances in which Steven had broken the relationship, and considering they had lived apart for almost a year, I did not consider Steven had moral grounds to act for Alex. I said that I had already engaged a solicitor who was preparing appropriate legal action and who was to engage counsel for me, once the inquest report had been received; I made it quite clear that I strongly objected to Steven attempting to take any action which duplicated, and therefore could interfere, with my own case. However, knowing that Alex and Steven had resumed a friend based relationship, and for Alex's sake, I was prepared to keep Steven fully informed of any developments in my intended action.

Nathanial also told me that although he was willing to advise Steven, for personal reasons he could not represent him. He had written to the CPS on Steven's behalf, to ask them to confirm the Sun Newspaper report that Robert Simpson was a Senior Lawyer with the CPS. On the 5th of March, Nathanial sent me a copy of the reply from the CPS, confirming that Robert Simpson was a CPS Senior Lawyer. Nathanial had also written to the coroner asking for copies of the additional statements he had used during the inquest, including that of Robert Simpson. I have no doubt that the request was eventually turned down, on the grounds that Steven was not an interested person as defined under Coroners Rule: 20.

The inquest report also arrived on 5th March and was handed over to Mr Marshal together with the correspondence from Nathanial Mathews. Mr Marshal informed me next day that he had written to Mr Jones asking what steps he was taking if any? My solicitor then asked if I wished him to go ahead with putting together my case for counsel without further delay, as he was very concerned about the time scale of three months for a

170

Judicial Review. I instructed him to go ahead and not to wait for a reply from Steve. I was quite sure that without Nathanial's support, Steve would not go ahead with any legal action. Apparently I was right, as I heard nothing more on any of the proposed actions, from either Nathanial or Steven.

In the meantime, my legal action was progressing quickly, with Mr Marshal carrying out many and varied legal procedures. I intend though, only to recount in detail the important ones, in which decisions were made and received, and those which required my consent or signature. Mr Marshal engaged Mr Timothy Spencer a London Barrister to act for me and to take the necessary legal steps to push my case forward. Mr Spencer agreed to accept a brief to challenge an inquest verdict recording an accidental death on Alex, when it had originally been investigated as a suspicious death.

Mr Marshal informed me on March 12th that he had sent all my papers to Mr Spencer, who had requested a short conference with us both on 21st of March in Lincoln, to discuss my case as fully as my evidence allowed. At this meeting I agreed to meet the estimated costs of my employing a solicitor and counsel to handle my case, and then we then discussed the process involved in applying to the High Court for a judicial review.[87] Mr Spencer's instructions to Mr Marshal were for him to apply, for leave to appeal for a Judicial Review of the inquest, by using the two avenues allowed:[88]

---

[87] Although I am not by any means an expert, my understanding is that a judicial review allows people considered to have 'sufficient interest' to ask a judge to review, in my case an action taken by a coroner. A person with sufficient interest is one who is affected by a decision and has sufficient substance (evidence) to make the challenge.

[88] Applying for Leave to Appeal is not at all easy as the applicant (or legal representative) must follow the official guide lines laid down in order to obtain that leave from the High Court. To ensure that trivial or misguided applications can be weeded out, the applicant has to lodge with the Crown Office, a completed official application form, an affidavit verifying the facts relied on, and copies of the affidavit.

1. An application to appeal to the High Court for a judicial review.

2. A memorial (application) to the Attorney General under Section 13 of the Coroners Act 1988.

In effect, both applications are alternate ways of seeking an order for a new inquest. But in the event of the Attorney General refusing to grant his fiat, then the judicial review application would become directly relevant.

Included in the 'bundle of documents' submitted to the Crown Office, was the **Notice of Application**, dated 1$^{st}$ April 1997, and on this form Mr Marshal stated that I was appealing against the verdict of the coroner in respect of Alex's inquest. On the application I was cited as the 'Applicant' and Dr Chan as the Respondent'. And in support of my case against the inquest verdict, Mr Marshal listed the following grounds for making the appeal.

- Failure to notify the Applicant of her right to ask questions of the witnesses at the said inquest.

- Failure to invite the Applicant to ask questions of the witnesses at the inquest.

- Failure to ascertain or disclose the occupation of a material witness at the inquest.

- The verdict of accidental death.

Mr Marshal stated that **the relief** sought (an order from a court granting a particular remedy) was as follows:

- An **order of certiorari** (<u>an order by a higher court</u>) to remove the appeal to a higher court (The Queen's Bench Division)[89] and to quash the inquest
- An **order of mandamus** (<u>a judicial remedy</u>) to the Respondent to require him to hold a fresh inquest before his Deputy or Assistant Deputy Coroner'

In addition Mr Marshal submitted his own affidavit made on oath and considering the restrictions placed on the material and the facts disclosed to me, made what I considered at the time was a full and comprehensive argument for me to be granted leave to appeal. Once the 'bundle of documents'[90] was delivered to the Crown Office, it was then a matter of waiting for decisions from the Attorney General, and the High Court, probably for several months, and for us to continue with any other appropriate action.

At our interview Mr Spencer had recommended that Mr Marshal contact DCI Baff at Limehouse police station and request an interview about Alex's case. This request had been made by telephone on March 27th and DCI Baff agreed to an interview at a future date, but advised that there would be a fee of £45.00. This interview would also entail Mr Marshal's travelling costs, and the total cost was estimated at about £200.00. I agreed to both action and cost. So far things had gone quite well. I had a further interview with Mr Spencer in Stamford and from our discussion, it seemed that both Mr Marshal and Mr Spencer appeared to have confidence in the merits of my case and I was happy to be guided by them.

In early April the Crown Office informed Mr Marshal that it would not be appropriate to list the application for a judicial review, until the outcome of the application for the Attorney General's fiat was known. :

While waiting for developments I occupied myself with my graduate course work, and preparations for a suitable memorial, which would help

---

[90] The bundle also contained the Inquest Report, PM report Mr Marshal's supporting affidavit and the only three witnesses statements allowed me by the coroner.

to preserve Alex's memory, and help to wipe away the horror of his death. This is something I will describe at the end of this book.

The meeting that Mr Marshal had arranged with DCI Baff never took place, because six weeks later I learned that on the 4th May 1997 the police officer had died by his own hand. This date was also the first anniversary of Alex's death but I did not, for even a moment, consider that remorse over his conduct in Alex case had anything to do with DCI Baff's suicide. A few days later, I received two newspaper cuttings which stated that Mr Baff had been a fast track graduate, due to be promoted to Superintendent in June, and recognised as being the MPS's highest ranked practising homosexual. One cutting implied that the suicide was over a row with his partner,[91] but another more explicitly implied, that he had associations with a convicted Scout Master paedophile, who was waiting to be sentenced.[92] This information at the time had no effect on the barrister's management of my case, which was not concerned with the police *modus operandi,* only with the inquest. I was to question the integrity of this information on DCI Baff, much later on in my campaign for justice.

Following the death of DCI Baff there was little we had to do in the matter of the court applications. Mr Marshal regularly kept me up to date on the accumulationing costs. This allowed me time to make arrangements with my bank to transfer the money I had saved for Alex's intended degree course, from a fixed term savings account, to a current account. The bank manager with kind understanding of my position allowed the transfer and waived the normal penalty charge, for an early withdrawal. This gesture was very much appreciated.

**Part 2 – The date for the High Court hearing is received.**

On the 9th of July 1997, Mr Marshal informed me that, unexpectedly, he had word from the Listing Clerk at the Crown Office, that the hearing for leave to apply for a judicial review was scheduled for 23rd of October. This was in advance of the outcome of the Attorney General's decision. On the 22nd of July, Mr Marshal was advised by letter, that the Attorney General, having studied my application, in conjunction with the coroner's

---

[91] Newspaper report
[92]     ditto

comments and Counsel's advice, did not think it appropriate for him to grant fiat. This decision was very disappointing because, had it been fiat granted, it would have strengthened my case considerably. Nevertheless, my application for a judicial review had been listed, and therefore, my hopes for a successful outcome were high, heightened by the confidence both Mr Marshal and Mr Spencer had expressed in the strength of my case. I wondered if the Listing Clerk had known in advance of the notification that the fiat had been refused.

Mr Marshal told me a few days later, that his senior partner, who was the Lincoln Coroner, had received a copy of a directive circulated to all coroners. I was not shown the actual document, but the gist of it was that coroners should carefully observe the process of my application for the review of an inquest and the grounds on which the application was made. Mr Marshal found this directive was very significant.

I had little communication with Mr Marshal or Mr Spencer during the three months before the hearing at the High Court. Looking back it seems that other than answering questions or signing papers, I had very little to do with the preparation of the appeal at all. Every thing else was in the hands of the legal experts and I just followed their instructions. To occupy my time and thoughts, while time dragged by during that long interval, I devoted even more time to the preparatory work for the MA degree.

It was a relief when the morning of the 23rd of October eventually dawned. Through family circumstances I travelled alone to the High Court and arrived much too early to meet Mr Marshal and Mr Spencer. It was an awesome experience standing alone and isolated in the hall of the High Court, while Counsels and their clients stood in groups in earnest discussion and countless others bustled to and fro as they went about their business. I panicked a little when I failed to spot my legal two representatives for some time, and it was such a relief when Mr Marshal located me, followed by Mr Spencer, clad in his gown and wig. I was most impressed.

Our case was due to be heard at 10.30, and we were called into Court on time. Within a minute Mr Spencer was requested to present his argument to the Honourable Mr Justice Potts, on my behalf, for leave to appeal to

175

the High Court for a new inquest. The language of the legal argument was difficult for me to follow and I was even more confused when after only ten minutes the judge withdrew and Mr Spencer left the Court room, while Mr Marshal ushered me out to join him. I thought the coroner's inquest had been short, but this hearing seemed ridiculously brief, especially when I seemed to have missed the judge's decision.

It was such a relief when Mr Spencer explained that we had only left the Court room temporally. Lord Justice Potts, following the usual practice, had left the Court room in order to consider Mr Spencer's argument. We would be called back into Court when Mr Justice Potts was ready, for further consideration of my grounds to appeal and to give his decision.

Although it seemed that we waited ages we were actually back in court at 1155am[93]. For the next twenty five minutes, Mr Marshal and I listened to a very politely conducted session of question and answers, Mr Justice Potts asking the questions and Mr Spencer replying with constant reference to his brief portfolio. After twenty five minutes, the Lord Justice announced his decision. I thought I heard him say 'Leave granted', but was uncertain because as he was leaving the bench, he said to Mr Spencer, 'You would do well to strengthen your argument in some areas'. As the Court arose I looked doubtfully at Mr Marshal, and he realising that I was unsure about the outcome said, 'It's alright Mrs Barrack you have your leave to appeal.

We three left the Court Room in high spirits and after a short spell of mutual congratulations; we prepared to leave the High Court. Mr Marshal said he would contact me in a few days to advise me on the next stage, and then we went our separate ways. It was then just after midday and the whole court procedure, excluding the interval, had lasted only 55 minutes I stood outside for the Court a few minutes feeling very alone, suddenly saddened at the thought that all this had happened because Alex, in death, had been denied justice. Such thoughts were soon dismissed because, in going through this appeal, I was attempting to remedy the injustice

---

[93] The official form of notification gives quite specific times "(time of the court:10.31 to 10.40 and 11.55 to 12.20)" 55 minutes, while the inquest had lasted only a brief 60 minutes maximum

176

imposed on him by a flawed inquest. So, more cheerfully, I went off to inform my family and friends of the successful hearing. It was only a small step forward on my road to justice, but just for once things were going well for me.

# CHAPTER FIFTEEN

*I find that the needs of a client must fit within restrictive Government guidelines, and that the interpretations of those guidelines by lawyers and coroners do not always go well with a client's rights.*

## Part 1 – Written confirmation of right to appeal – and doubts begin to surface

Within a few days, Mr Marshal sent me written confirmation that on the 23$^{rd}$ October, Mr Justice Potts had granted me leave to appeal for a Judicial Review of the earlier inquest verdict. I felt I was really making progress towards getting a new inquest, because Mr Spencer said he was very pleased with the outcome of the hearing. Even though it was only a test case at this stage, both he and Mr Spencer felt that they had clearly demonstrated there was an arguable case to put before the High Court. The following sentence, though, raised a slight feeling of unease. Mr Marshal wrote, 'The next stage **(assuming we proceed)**, is to ask for a full Judicial Review,' which needs to be requested within fourteen days. This surprised me, as I not ever considered that we would not proceed; a full Judicial Review was the sole purpose of my legal action.

My unease was increased even more, when he referred to: 'My slight concern is the question of costs, which Mr Spencer and I discussed with you briefly'. And he gave me details, which up to now had not been seriously discussed at all:

1. It is almost certain that the coroner would be represented at a full hearing.

2. Should I lose the case, I would almost certainly be ordered to pay the coroner's costs.

3. The amount of costs would depend on the amount of preparation time, which barrister was instructed, and how long the case lasted.

4. The costs could run into £2.000 or more.

178

That amount, compared with present day costs, may seem insignificant, but it was a very large sum to me in 1997. I had already advanced £500 to Mr Marshal to retain my barrister.

Although, up until then, the question of applying for Legal Aid had not been raised, he next advised me:

'Although Legal Aid is in theory available for Judicial Review, it is not available for matters involving inquests, and for this reason I do not think it would be granted to a case such as this'

Three days later, determined to go on, and suppressing any unease, I instructed Mr Spencer that the case should go forward. Mr Marshal then asked me to pay a further £1,500. Although the combined costs of my barrister and potential coroner's costs would consume the £5,000 that I had set aside for Alex, and leave me only a small balance in my savings, I considered the risk was well worth taking.

What I did not know at that time, was that when, on the 29th October, Mr Marshal received the official notification that Leave to Appeal for a new inquest had been granted, he also received another, related letter, the **Notice of Motion for Judicial Review** (Order 53 rule 5)" which stated:

'Take notice, that pursuant to the leave of a Divisional Court of the Queen's Bench Division, (or Mr Justice Potts) given on the 23rd October 1997, the Court will be moved, as soon as Counsel can be heard on the Applicant's behalf, for an order of relief in the terms and grounds, set out in Form 86a, herewith.

And the costs of and occasioned by this motion be paid by the Respondent to the Applicant, such costs to be taxed if not agreed.'

The letter also stated that the Notice had to be filed with the Crown Office within in 14 days of being granted Leave to Appeal. My interpretation of the terminology used on this form was that it did not mean that I would *definitely* receive such relief, but only that the case would not proceed until my counsel had made a formal application, on my behalf, and the Crown

Office had decided whether or not I could be granted these costs. I understood that if no application for relief was made, then after fourteen days the case could move forward.

What I find so very disturbing about this Form 86A is that, until 2003, I was not aware that it had been received, and that such an application for relief was open to me. Neither Mr Marshal, nor Mr Spencer, had even mentioned their receiving this directive from the Crown Court. It seems that they had either assumed, without checking, that filling in this form was not applicable in my case, or that they had pre-empted the Crown Offices refusal and had not applied on my behalf for this relief, and without the courtesy of allowing me to make that decision. I can tell you now that, had I been consulted, I would not have hesitated to direct Mr Spencer to make that application for relief, whether or not he thought it futile. I would have had nothing to lose, and could have gained so very much, had relief been granted.

Perhaps this was all due to his not having sufficient knowledge of the funding policy of the Crown Office Commission in relation to High Court hearings. The reason I say this was because at my first interview with Mr Spencer, he told me that he was keen to take on the brief as he had not had a previous case like mine - and welcomed the opportunity to act for me. Apparently it is, or was, a policy to issue Form 86A to all applicants requesting Leave to Appeal, but that granting relief for inquests rested on the decisions made by the Crown Office Commission. I learnt that all applications for inquest relief were considered on the merits of each individual case.

Why Mr Marshal had not encouraged me to apply for Legal Aid in the first place, and why he had this change of mind, was never explained. He had determined originally that Legal Aid was not available for a High Court review of inquest verdicts. Now he had apparently reconsidered that decision. Perhaps he had learned that it could be worth my applying on the grounds that the funding would be granted on different grounds, in that it would be for legal representation at the High Court hearing, and not for representation at an inquest. It all seemed a bit nebulous to me, but I complied with his advice, and in early November 1997 applied to the Legal Aid Board for funding.

There were no further developments in the case that I know of, until the 18ᵗʰ December, when I received a copy of Mr Marshal's affidavit to the High Court. It was a duplication of the statements originally made to the Crown Office. In this affidavit he affirmed his identity and confirmed that I had instructed him to act for me, and listed grounds for the appeal which are outlined in previous chapters. It was a very short affidavit, consisting of only two full pages, but the case seemed to be well covered in the full memorial[94] he resubmitted to the Crown Office.

This was in marked contrast to the coroner's affidavit to the High Court, actually signed on the same day as mine, and not, as I remember, received by Mr Marshal until well after the Christmas holiday. It covered fifteen pages, the same number of pages as the inquest report, and it covered practically every aspect of the inquest proceedings. The affidavit makes interesting reading because of the unusual number of mistakes and errors of interpretation which I consider distorted the truth.

I was surprised to see that the coroner repeated the mistake over Alex's date of birth. A small point perhaps, but as the date had been corrected in the inquest report, it was somewhat distressing to me that my intervention and amendment of the date at the inquest had not been registered by the coroner. Was it carelessness on his part? or was it an indication of his disinterest?

I was quite annoyed by the coroner's insistence that Steve Jones was Alex's full partner at the time of his death. Steve was, in fact, by his own actions and choice, an *ex*-partner. Alex, at the time of his death, was his friend and carer. It seems that referring to Steve as Alex's partner gives undue weight to certain details in Steve's statement, mentioned later in the affidavit, which I now discuss, in the order given by the coroner.

**Part 2 – The coroner's affidavit – the principle issues of the death**

In dealing with these issues in his affidavit, the coroner first stated that this was a resumed inquest, but gave no reason for postponing it in the first place. He then moved on to *the time of death*, and, in glib terms, but fairly

---

[94] A statement of facts as the basis for a petition (Application to a Court)

accurately, described the paramedic's and the Hospital Registrar's account of the patient's condition, ending his account with the pathologist's conclusion on the time of death. Dr Chan also very belatedly conceded that Alex had died at least two hours before resuscitation was commenced. He then added a very brief comment:

> "Mr Simpson, conversely, indicated that the deceased had been alive very shortly before he telephoned for an ambulance"[95]

That was all Dr Chan had to say on the matter, and, as he had at the inquest, he deliberately avoided testing the veracity of Simpson's version.

The next issue, *the cause of death*, was also as brief. Dr Chan stated that he did not doubt that death resulted from asphyxia, which was the result of upper airway obstruction, but added that there was some uncertainty over the precise sequence of events leading to the death. He totally failed, however, to explain this uncertainty.

He continued his affidavit by apparently re-wording Dr Heath's conclusions on the cause of death, stating, 'Dr Heath *thought* that "an obstructive device" [was] applied to the upper part of the body.' On the contrary, Dr Heath did not just *think* that such an appliance had been used, he was more positive than that. He stated several times that, in his opinion, the application of an obstructive head device to the victim's head was the cause of Alex's death.

Dr Chan gave more details of the 'sort of device' found in the flat and also that it had been forensically examined for Alex's DNA. Although, he stated, the tests proved that that it had been worn by several people, nothing conclusive about Alex's DNA had been found. He did not mention that four possible elements of Alex's DNA were present in the bag, but said that further tests were required for a more decisive outcome. However, Dr Chan, it seems, could not see that in this DNA testing, there was any evidence linking Alex to the device. By contrast, the police, in ordering the tests, had very clearly considered the possibility that there was a link.

.

---

[95] Coroner's affidavit p4

What Dr Chan did, in order to strengthen his view that Alex had not worn the mask, was to use Steve Jones' statement to the police, stressing that because of Alex's asthmatic condition, he would not indulge in any practices which restricted his breathing. Dr Chan appears to turn this statement round, trying to prove that, because of Steve Jones' opinion; under no circumstances would Alex have worn such a device. This, of course, was to ignore, as he did at the inquest, that there was a very strong case for it having been *forced* over the victim's head.

Another possibility, also ignored, was that any drugs given to him that night had weakened Alex's resistance to the device being placed over his head. Additionally, as he had at the inquest, Dr Chan entirely failed to mention the subject of sadomasochism. This was despite the subject having been raised with Steve Jones by the police and referred to in court, when Mr Jones' statement was read by out by DCI Baff. Nor did Dr Chan mention that the type of head device found at the scene had been frequently used in earlier sadomasochistic practices, presumably in the same premises.[96] The presence of several types of DNA in the device had been confirmed by forensic testing.

The coroner then gave, in his affidavit, his version of the vomiting episode. This, according to him, was that, "The deceased had vomit in his mouth and lungs at the time of death". That statement, he must have known, was incorrect and totally misleading. The vomit appeared in the mouth *after* death, not *before,* and *not at the time*. That was confirmed in the first place by Simpson's reply to the Ambulance Service Call Taker, when, at the start of the call, he was asked twice, "Is there anything in the mouth?" and Simpson replied, "Nothing in the mouth". That fact was endorsed by Dr Heath at the inquest, when he expressed his opinion that the vomit had entered the mouth through the resuscitation process *after death*, not while the patient was still alive, and therefore the vomit *did not* contribute to the death.

Dr Chan also referred to the very small bruises on the back of the neck and claimed that the thong, which Alex was wearing (not belt as he had

---

[96] The MRG Report 2005, recoded Simpson's interest in sadomasochism and that several other related items were
found in the flat

183

repeatedly stressed during the inquest), may have been tightened and could have caused these short and longer horizontal bruises and helped the asphyxiation process. That is nonsense, because the larger bruise (which was over the hard structures of the neck) was much too small and superficial to have been the result of any choking pressure applied by the thong. He also, without giving a plausible medical reason, linked the vomiting with a mild asthma attack, saying that both could have played a part in the death. Dr Heath had said, during the inquest, that he could not exclude a mild asthma attack, but he then, with some asperity, rejected the coroner's attempt to link both together. He was emphatic that neither the thong nor an asthma attack had contributed to the victim's death.

In the last paragraph of this part of his affidavit, the coroner very briefly summarised the cause of death saying: "...in the round, Dr Heath's *preferred version of events* was that the deceased died as a result of wearing the sexual aid...' This was the first recognition by the coroner of Dr Heath's evidence that Alex had died through wearing the device. However the term 'preferred version of events' is the coroner's phrase. Dr Heath had in fact given, as his *firm conclusion,* that the asphyxiation was the result of the application to the head of a lethal, obstructive device. Contrary to the coroner's affidavit statement, the pathologist had resisted all suggestions by the coroner for him to consider other possible causes. There was a one small but significant concession on the part of Dr Chan, when, for the first time, he agreed that the deceased "had been dead for a significant period of time, before the call was made for the ambulance by Mr Simpson". [97]

In the next paragraph, the coroner gave his abbreviated version of police investigations into the death, and acknowledged that it was investigated as a suspicious death, *from the very beginning*. He also conceded that the account given by Mr Simpson to the ambulance crew was not consistent with that given later by him to the police. He carefully omitted any reference to the other conflicting accounts given to other medical officers and the account recorded in the 999 transcript. Therefore Dr Chan, even in his inquest summary, carefully avoided establishing the circumstances leading to Alex's death. Simpson must have been very grateful to him.

---

[97] Inquest Report Question and answers

184

Dr Chan concluded his biased account of the police investigation by saying that the police found *no evidence* for the CPS to support a prosecution for murder, manslaughter or gross negligence. That statement is most certainly not true. The CPS decision not to prosecute, as Graham Martin stated in his letter to DCI Baff, was not that there was no evidence, but that the CPS considered that there was *insufficient evidence* to warrant bringing charges against Simpson for manslaughter or for any other offence.

The only reason Dr Chan gave in his inquest summary for the failure to prosecute was that the bruises and marks on the body were not consistent with defence or restraint wounds. I hardly think that such inadequate medical forensics would constitute a case of sufficient, strong, definitive evidence to warrant the personal intervention of the Director of Public Prosecutions, and other senior CPS officials. As he had during the inquest inquisitions, Dr Chan wilfully disregarded the abundance of other medical evidence found on the body, and apparently concluded that this evidence, and the other forensic evidence found at the scene, were of no importance to the police investigations.[98] He was to continue this negation of the evidence in the rest of his affidavit, which is to be discussed in the next chapter.

---

[98] Listed later in the MRG 2005 report.

# CHAPTER SIXTEEN

*The coroner's task is to seek to establish a probable course of events and resolve any ambiguity in the evidence by investigation at the inquest.*

## Introduction – Criticism of the coroner's affidavit

If the coroner had faithfully performed that task during the inquest on my son, he would have recognised the family's rights at an inquest and fully explored the evidence he had at hand. Then I would not now be censuring his affidavit for the purpose of my book. Nor would I have had to spend fourteen years of my retirement in trying to set right all the official injustices perpetrated on my son, arising from this coroner's mismanagement of the flawed inquest and his unsound conclusions. The affidavit that Dr Chan presented to the High Court gave a different interpretation of the inquest findings contained in the official transcript, and in this version the coroner appeared to attempt to convince the Court that he had carried out his duties in accordance with the rules laid down for inquests, and, that he had no case to answer. In my opinion it was a complete whitewash and I confidently expected that my legal team would be able to demolish Dr Chan's misleading account when the hearing took place.

## Part 1. The coroner's new version of events - he attempts to turn around his previous conclusions.

### Oral evidence

The coroner began this version of the inquest by stating that four witnesses had given oral evidence on the circumstances of the events, (presumably referring to the events leading to the Alex's death). One of the four is named as Kenneth Amphlett, a family member, but this is incorrect. Ken was not in a position to give any evidence whatsoever about the circumstances, he wasn't there. The only evidence he contributed was to confirm Alex's identity, on my behalf.

**Written statements**

The coroner then said incorrectly that the inquest had considered three written statements from the paramedic, the Hospital Registrar and Steve Jones. This implies that these statements were fully discussed by the inquest and also, that there were persons present other than the official witnesses, and who were in a position to discuss and question the evidence. These statements, apart from one item from Steve Jones's, were only read and not discussed. I have no doubt the coroner would not have skipped discussing and questioning fully these statements, **if,** a jury had been called, or if we had a legal representative. The official witnesses gave evidence relating to their own expertise, but otherwise, did not discuss or question with any relevance, the evidence of other witnesses.

Here the coroner jumped to the end of the inquest and gave his reason for selecting an 'accidental death' verdict.

- He accepted Dr Heath's opinion that the cause of death was consequent upon upper airway obstruction.

I agree with him there, because all the forensic and medical evidence supports that view, but I cannot accept that the verdict of accidental death in any way fits the facts, based on his reasoning.

- He recorded a verdict of 'accidental death' because he was satisfied on the balance of probabilities, that, **which ever version was in fact the correct one**, the deceased's death had indeed been accidental.

He does not indicate how many versions he did consider and whose they were, before reaching his verdict, or how he reached his conclusions. Nor does he give any the details of each version or accurately describe how they might have contributed to the death of Alex Barrack. In reality, only Simpson was questioned on his version on the actual circumstances and the obvious cause of Alex's death, But, instead of questioning the veracity of Simpson's very dubious evidence, the coroner merely stated

'Only Mr Simpson's evidence went directly to the circumstance which led to the death... There were inconsistencies in his

187

evidence as compared with his first account given to the ambulance crew.'

The coroner failed to give a comparative account of these obvious inconsistencies in Simpson's various accounts, which I have shown were completely at odds with both the medical and forensic evidence. These inconsistencies were many and varied and far from going directly to the circumstances, Robert Simpson sent all the medical personnel and the coroner on a tortuous route, to take them as far from the truth as possible. However, in spite of Simpson's interference with the evidence and the course of justice, the police had uncovered enough forensic and medical evidence to arrest and charge Robert Simpson with manslaughter.

Although, for six months the coroner had pressed for high level investigations and a prosecution, before the inquest, in his affidavit, he continued to demonstrate his bias which against the victim by favouring the CPS prejudiced decision that 'there was no evidence to support a charge founded on gross negligence manslaughter, and, nor were 'the ingredients for a verdict of neglect present'. This made it quite clear to my family and me that the verdict could have been a pre-judgment inquest decision.

**Part 2 - The inquest verdict.**

Although, Dr Chan introduced his verdict of accidental death very early into his affidavit, yet, as he had done at the inquest, he failed to provide any specific details of the actual sequence of cause and effect which any accident must have before a decision can be conclusive. He loosely misinterpreted the factual evidence of Dr Heath by linking together several suggestions that he had put to Dr Heath. He ignored the fact that that the pathologist had summarily rejected these suggestions, "as not in any way contributing to victim's death", and to emphasise, that in his expert opinion, death had resulted from the manual application of the obstructive device to the victim's head.

Why Dr Chan was so resolute in establishing death was anything but an accident, when the very strange circumstances surrounding Alex's death which, together with the very odd behaviour of officials, in the aftermath of his death, establishes that it was anything but accidental. This type of

188

conduct can only encourage speculation on there being a very sordid reason behind it all.

In the summary of his account of the inquest findings, Dr Chan stated that in his view death was a combination of three events, two of which were discounted by Dr Heath. They were the deceased asthmatic condition and the inhalation of food and liquid. The coroner's third reason was only partially correct, when he gave it as being "...the restrictive affect of some device i.e. either the balloon head or the leather thong".

I positively agree with the restrictive effect of the head bag being the cause of death, but the leather thong played no part in the asphyxiation. Dr Heath had told the coroner quite emphatically that it played no part in causing Alex's death.

According to Dr Chan all the above causes were identified by **both** doctors as possible causes of death. This was a very odd mistake to make when it is on record that the only other doctor, who attended to Alex and to actually examine his body, was the Hospital Registrar, but his was only a medical external study, not carried out for forensic purposes. The coroner seems to have completely overlooked the fact that the reason that the case was referred to him in the first place, was because this same doctor, Dr Heyman, was **unable** to determine the cause of death.[99]

The coroner concluded this section of his affidavit by reaffirming that there was no evidence that could be found indicating that violence had contributed to the death but, that the other factors clearly pointed to a verdict of accidental death because, 'I had no occasion to consider the last resort of an open verdict'. I totally disagree with him, there was ample evidence against his giving that verdict; an open verdict was more fitting when Dr Chan could not record with any accuracy, any circumstances by which he could clearly described the nature of the accident. An open verdict would at least have had the merit of keeping the case open, and allowing the police to continue their investigations. In 2009, under the Freedom of Information Act, I obtained confirmation of my earlier suspicion, that my son's death

---

[99] Dr Heyman's statement to the police.

was a homicide, and the true facts were deliberately concealed from the family and the public.

## Part 3 – The coroner – attempts to undermine my four grounds for complaint

The next part of Dr Chan's affidavit deal with the grounds that I put forward in my application for a judicial review.

Dr Chan was correct in stating that I listed three complaints and criticised his conclusion in my affidavit:

### CLAIM 1 -The right to examine witnesses.

On the matter that the coroner failed to notify me at the beginning of the inquest, of my right to examine witnesses and challenge the evidence under Rule 20 of the Coroner's Rules 1984, and during the inquest failed to invite me to do so, he had this to say.

1.  The coroner accepted that as an 'interested person' I had that right to question the witnesses but claimed that I was informed by the coroner's officer of that right before the inquest and also stated that Bill Barrack, Alex's father, had been in contact earlier and was aware of that right.

2.  Mr Davies had formed the impression that I was too upset by the inquest process and disinclined to take an active part. For that reason Mr Davies (or the coroner) decided that even though I was listed as a witness to formally identify Alex, my place would be taken by Mr Amphlett.

3.  The coroner also claimed that before the inquest started Mr Davies followed his usual practice and showed us a list of the witnesses he intended to call, the order in which they would be called and explained the nature of the evidence that each would give.

4. Then Dr Chan added that Mr Davies had believed that I was very distressed and as I said 'Let's get it over with' so therefore he may not have informed me of my rights.

5. The coroner continued by saying that he was aware of my distress and therefore he did not address the family members on the subject of the right to ask questions. But **he did pause after each of his examinations and looked pointedly at all interested parties, expecting anyone who wished to ask questions to do so.**

All the above is an incredibly fictitious figment of someone's imagination. Not one of those events ever took place, nor was I even listed as a witness. Kenneth Amphlett was always the intended witness, not me, as Mr Davies made quite clear, when he expressed surprise at my being at the inquest.[100] At that particular time there were witnesses available who could support me in this issue, but I do have today, three signed statements from three of those with me at the, including from one Maureen , who is unfortunately deceased. It was ludicrous to say that I was exhibiting signs of great distress, on the contrary. I was then, and still am a very composed individual. Indeed, I had had months to accept that Alex's death was from natural causes and had come to terms with the unfortunate circumstances of his asthmatic death. I was at the inquest, expecting to have all the anomalies, that had taken place before Alex's funeral, explained away, and to have the closure which any bereaved family needs to bring them peace of mind and to full acceptance of the loss of a family member, I was most certainly expecting only a verdict of natural causes, as DI Bathie had promised.

I definitely was not expecting the coroner's cold indifference to our party throughout the inquest, or for him to later untruthfully claim in his affidavit, that after his examination of each witness he looked pointedly in our direction expecting us to ask questions; that is an outrageous suggestion. The fact is that we were seated well away from him, on a tiered bench, and to his right, not directly in the centre front where we should have been, and

---

[100] I was later informed by the Lincolnshire Coroner's officer that it is the usual practice for coroner's officers to inform relatives of their rights and usually to provide an explanation booklet. It was inconceivable to him that relatives could be shown so little consideration.

191

therefore were not in a position see him face to face. The only time this coroner noticeably turned his head in our direction, was when I corrected the identity mistakes, and that was his only recognition of my presence. In all seriousness, how could we be expected to interpret a look as an invitation to ask questions on such a grave matter, especially as we had not been told we could do so?

After Dr Chan, having done his best in his affidavit, but deceitfully, to establish that he had conformed fully to the requirements of Rule 20 and that my accusations had no foundation in fact, he proceeded to say that it really did not matter whether I was right or wrong, as he was not really required to tell relatives about their right to question witnesses:

> " I am advised that Rule 20 of the Coroner's Rules does not impose any duty on a coroner to advise or notify a person who is entitled to ask questions, of their right to examine a witnesses or their right to be represented for that purpose".[101]

If a coroner can arbitrarily ignore a rule which was made in the interests of justice, how then can relatives obtain enough information to protect a deceased's right to justice? What then, was the point of making such a rule? Rule 20, misused in this way, becomes a meaningless sentence, a travesty of justice. Would he have adopted the same indifferent attitude in the presence of a jury or if we had been legally represented

It is my judgment, that this coroner had really gone overboard in his attempts to deny he did anything wrong, and it seems to me, that is very much a case of, *"The gentleman doth protest too much, methinks."*[102]

**CLAIM 2 - Failure to ascertain or disclose Mr Simpson's occupation.**
Initially, Dr Chan began by saying that he was fully aware of Mr Simpson's occupation in the Crown Prosecution service. He then continued:

> 'It is my belief that the applicant was also aware of Mr Simpson's occupation before the inquest started, because DCI

---

[101] Case quoted by coroner -
[102] Shakespeare – Hamlet -paraphrased

Baff had informed her in connection with the police investigation into the death of her son.'

This is also completely untrue. I have no doubt that it was a concocted story to excuse the coroner's failure to reveal much factual evidence which could have altered the whole tenor of the inquest. I hold to the belief that of Simpson's occupation, together with his perverted off duty practices, did influence the police, the coroner and the CPS into making decisions to protect the reputation of certain high profile professionals, and also departmental interests, from the adverse consequences of having the facts made public. This certainty arises from a letter from an MPS official in which he describes Alex's death as **"a murder such as this is required to be conducted in strict secrecy"**[103] That official statement implies very strongly, that that the reason why a jury was not called, was that in ignoring the demands of justice, which required the balancing impartial and balanced verdict of a jury, the authorities were able to set a side any rights the deceased Alex had under common law and the European Court of Human Rights.[104]

I found the coroner to have acted offensively in alleging that DCI Baff told me of Simpson's occupation before the inquest started; and is therefore clearly claiming that I lied. The only persons lying are the coroner or Mr Davis, or both. The truth is that I only ever met Mr Baff once, at Limehouse police station, and in the presence of Maureen and Ken Amphlett, when his conversation was limited to him expressing brief condolences. None of us had any further communication with him; we spoke only with DI Bathie on the telephone, never with DCI Baff. The only other time we saw the two police officers again, was on the day of the inquest when we entered the Coroner's Court and found them already seated in front of the coroner. At the time I identified Alex, I had accepted the police explanation that he had died of natural causes, and no one, as far as I knew, had acted criminally, therefore, there would be no reason for me to enquire about the occupation of the man who 'tried heroically' to save Alex. His job or his status was at that time, of no interest, only his (supposedly) heroic action concerned me. There is little doubt, that as DI Bathie had refused to give me this 'hero's'

---

[103] Letter from MPS Access Office
[104] ECHR Rule 2.

name or address, even if I had asked for Simpson's occupation, my request would most certainly have been refused.

There is only one period when such a conversation would have taken place, and that was the six week period between March 1997 and Early May 1997, after the coroner had been informed that I was taking legal action, when the coroner apparently found it necessary in his own interests, to establish that such a conversation had taken place. However by thee 4th May 1997, DCI Baff was dead, purportedly by his own hand. After that day it seems convenient that there was no one to support or deny the coroner's statement. Whereas I do have witnesses and statements to confirm the truth, **that DCI Baff and I did not have such a conversation.**

Dr Chan concluded his short explanation by repeating that he considered Simpson's occupation had no bearing on the circumstance surrounding the death, whereas his sexual preferences were material to the inquiry. This last of course is true, but the combination of Simpson's occupation and his sexual practices, do point towards the main reason why police investigations were conducted with such secrecy, and most likely is the reason why the coroner followed the police, direction and continued the secrecy at the inquest.

**CLAIM 3 – Alleged - inconsistencies in Mr Simpson's statements.**
The coroner stated that my objection to an 'accidental death' verdict was based on four stark contrasts between Simpson's accounts and the medical evidence and his failure to appreciate the differences.

The first inconsistency was the incident of Alex walking into the bathroom because he felt sick or because of the stinging and the coroner considering it was not his function to cross examine his witness on that point. Of course it was his function; it **was** his duty to have asked Simpson to explain, just exactly just how Alex had managed to walk unaided into the bathroom, at the time the pathologist had firmly established that my son had been dead for two hours.

The second consistency is a bit of a jumble. Even so, it appears that the medically qualified Dr Chan did not see any stark contrast in Simpson claiming that he was in the bathroom during the time he claimed Alex was having a bath and feeling sick, when Alex was already dead and actually in

194

the advanced stages of the changes that take place after death. As at the inquest, Dr Chan again ignored the fact that forensic evidence found on the body at autopsy, several areas of congealed blood and the presence of 'brown stuff' proved that no bath could have been taken by the victim; otherwise they would have been washed away.

Alex getting out of the bath and trying to be sick is also fiction, as is the account of the vomiting episode given to the Call Taker. The stark contrast rests in the fact that victim was not alive at the time when Simpson claimed the incidents took place and the coroner failed to question Simpson's veracity.

According to the coroner the fourth inconsistency I refer to is not an apparent fair reading of whether or not Mr Simpson did try to revive the victim by giving him resuscitation and that Dr Heath referred to this in his evidence. I found this statement somewhat vague, but take it Dr Chan is claiming that I do not accept Simpson's version and that there was actually no attempt to resuscitate Alex. On the contrary, my reasoning is fair, the coroner's is not. The 999 call merely records the **sounds** of an attempt to resuscitate being made. Having actually heard that tape recording I know it is not proof that he actually did so, and according to Simpson, he acted alone throughout, so there were no witnesses to support his claim or even the coroner's. So in fact, the coroner cannot positively claim, based on the 999 call transcript, that this was factual evidence that Alex was alive at the time, although beyond recovery. Certainly not, when positive forensic medical evidence proved that he had died sometime before, and Dr Heath, in referring to the 999 call at the inquest, actually established that as a fact. What the coroner should have done was to ask Simpson why he waited more than two hours to call for assistance after Alex's death, and why, knowing that he was already dead, he did not inform the police that a dead man was lying in his flat, when as a lawyer, he knew perfectly well that the law dictated he should have done so.

In concluding that section on drugs, Dr Chan implied that I had expected him to pursue the fact that heroin was referred to as a cause of death, which he had considered was not relevant to his inquiry. On the contrary I was not expecting any such action. I did not then consider before the inquest that the heroin and the other drugs had actually contributed to Alex's actual death.

However, as a result of the inquest evidence, I did conclude that that the drugs he had taken, would have had a serious detrimental affect on his comprehension of his dangerous situation he was in, and only then and in that context, did I consider the subject should have been discussed.

The coroner disputed the grounds on which I based my application to the Attorney General for a fiat for a judicial review, which was that deficiencies in his inquiry led to an inappropriate verdict. Dr Chan claimed that there was not enough evidence to warrant my claim that a verdict of unlawful killing was more suited to the facts. Such a verdict he stated required a criminal standard of proof that the death of the deceased was the result of murder or manslaughter or manslaughter by gross negligence. Well, I consider he had that evidence in his hands throughout the inquest

He did not agree that he should have cross-examined Mr Simpson on the inconsistencies between his accounts and the medical evidence. Surely that was Dr Chan's duty, to 'resolve any ambiguity in the evidence' by testing the factual evidence against the reliability of witnesses accounts. Apparently, Dr Chan did not think it was necessary, on the grounds that as the police had extensively questioned Simpson, without him providing evidence of unlawful killing, and also, that he would have been able to avoid answering any incriminating questions. This claim was very surprising. I had not realised that it was the suspect's verbal evidence alone, which decided on whether a case was one of unlawful killing or not, or that it was not necessary for the police to challenge a suspects accounts. I thought establishing that a case was criminal **was** an issue for the police to decide, based on the circumstances and the forensic and medical evidence found on the body, and at the scene. Apparently the coroner assumed Simpson told only the truth and that was good enough for him. The coroner omitted two other serious issues, and they were in fact, two very important issues, which even my counsel failed to record on my application to the Court. One was Simpson's negligence in not dialling 999 as soon as Alex died, which was at least two hours before the 999 call? And two - What was he doing during the period that Alex lay dead in his flat?

The coroner concluded by saying, 'I believe it was fanciful to suggest that an unlawful killing verdict could be more appropriate in this case'. Well, I think

196

the coroner's version and his verdict were as far fetched as Simpson's unlikely saga. Both are totally unbelievable in the face of all the evidence.

The last two explanations given by the coroner dealt with two possible versions of Alex's death. The first involves the use of the balloon bag and a sexual adventure going horribly wrong. That is all Dr Chan said on that. He once more evaded giving any reasons how or why Alex, a chronic, claustrophobic asthmatic came to be wearing such a restrictive head device, and, very significantly, omitted entirely Simpson's interest in such sadomasochistic practices. The alternate version given was that Alex was choked by a combination of, asthma, vomiting and constriction of his neck by a thong. Once again Dr Chan ignores the factual evidence of the pathologists, who in giving his expert evidence dismissed all three as not having contributed anything to the death.

Dr Chan rounded off his affidavit by saying:

"I believe that I conducted the inquest in accordance with the law and that my conclusions were founded upon a rational appraisal of the evidence before me."

I certainly don't believe that he did, I think that the term an 'irrational approach' would have best fitted his conducting of the inquest, and, yet, these are the grounds he put to the High Court to have my application for a judicial review refused. However, as shocking and as unacceptable as I believed the coroner's defensive affidavit to the High Court to be, the advice I received from my counsel , Mr Spencer QC, after he had considered the coroner's affidavit, was in its reasoning to be even more of a shock.

**Part 4 -The QC's change of direction – I exit the Appeal Court**

*It has been said that it is of fundamental importance that justice should not only be done, but undoubtedly be seen to be done.*
*But if a case is not allowed to reach court, how can justice be done or seen?[105]*

---

[105] Quotation

Up until the beginning of January 1998 every thing seemed to be proceeding satisfactorily. The coroner's affidavit had been examined; my response affidavit had been forwarded the Crown Office together with all necessary documents and, as far as I knew, we were ready to go ahead as soon as the date for the hearing was received. When I had a meeting with Mr Marshal on the second Wednesday of January, we discussed the progress we had made with the case, and he gave the impression that even though we had quite a tough task ahead, both he and Mr Spencer were reasonably confident of success. It was my impression that the coroner's affidavit had been scrutinised, his comments had been noted and an adequate response had been prepared, and that now, it was just a question of waiting. I left the office feeling well satisfied knowing that Alex's case was in good hands.

That feeling of satisfaction did not last long. On the 16th January, I received a letter from Mr Marshal, which I thought started well enough:

'I thought I would bring you up to date with events.

I have been notified that your case is likely to be on the list for a hearing before too long. I have not been given a date'.

That really lifted my spirits; at last things were moving quickly. Mr Marshall carried on by telling me that he had sent the papers back to Mr Spencer for his further advice, but he had already spoken to him on the telephone. As I read on, the disquiet I had felt but dismissed at an earlier meeting, surfaced in my mind again. The letter continued:

'Although I do not want to anticipate his advice, I think his initials reaction was that we were facing an uphill struggle. Obviously I will let you know as soon as his advice is to hand.'

I was confused at the sudden change in attitude, but I could not see that anything about my case had changed; yet I was obviously being warned to expect bad news. Mr Spencer had never said it would be easy, and I knew that Mr Justice Potts had advised Mr Spencer to strengthen my case, and he had promised to do so. Therefore, at that stage, I thought all that had been attended to and that my case had been strengthened enough to undermine the coroner's spurious affidavit version of the inquest, and that Mr Spencer would have located other inquest cases, which upheld Rule 20 of the

Coroner' Act against the coroner's claim that he was not compelled to apply that rule. Up until then, nothing had been said to indicate that the coroner's affidavit had caused any concern for either Mr Marshal or Mr Spencer. I was under the impression that my response affidavit had not been completed until Mr Spencer had studied the coroner's defence. Until I received that letter, I was confident that both solicitor and counsel would also have compiled a much stronger argument to combat the coroner's robust but inaccurate account of the inquest. During one of our earlier meetings Mr Marshal had suggested to me that we had a 60% chance of success and that had sounded pretty good to me.

Although I had not read the coroner's affidavit in depth or studied the implications as fully as I did much later, and reach firmer conclusions, which I have already summed up in part one of this chapter, I had recognised that the coroner's strategy was intended to discredit my claims against his prejudiced conduct of the inquest, but even so, the affidavit had not caused me any real worry; I had great trust in Mr Spencer's expertise. I was after all paying quite a lot of money for his top legal advice, and expected he would present a convincing argument to the High Court.

After receiving that discouraging letter, in a worried state of mind I contacted Mr Marshal by telephone to ask for a fuller explanation, He merely reiterated that he could not anticipate Mr Spencer's advice, and he would be in touch as soon as it was to hand. Ten days later that advice was received and it did nothing to alleviate the deepening feeling of apprehension that everything was going wrong.

Although I have thought long and hard on the matter, I cannot recall whether or not I had any further communication with Mr Marshal before receiving a letter on 28th January which conveyed the worse possible advice. That was a communication I will never forget, it consisted of a covering letter from Mr Marshal and a copy of Mr. Spencer's further advice on my application for a judicial review.

Of course I read Mr Marshal's letter first in which he said he would not repeat Mr Spencer's advice in full, he then continued in a manner which I now consider was meant to placate me against what was to come, but instead filled me with dismay:

'He does I think feel that we have achieved something in obtaining a concession from the coroner in clear terms, that there was significant inconsistency between Mr Simpson's evidence and the medical evidence'.

I had a sickening sensation that I was about to receive a heavy blow, because, he continued by saying that Mr Spencer's view was that at the end of the day the prospects of success at a full hearing were limited. To endorse the rightfulness of Mr Spencer's new view, he informed me, that in a case where the Attorney General had actually granted leave, the High Court had refused a new inquest. I did not see this as a rightfully upholding the counsel's view, I saw it as an excuse for him not to proceed, especially when I read the next sentence, which I quote in full:

'Although Mr Spencer feels that we have a case that could be argued, his judgement is that the prospects of success are significantly less that 50/50. Knowing Mr Spencer as I do, I am sure that he would be more than happy to argue the case for you. Both he and I are, however, very concerned at the likely outcome in terms of costs. If we were to proceed to a full hearing and lose, then the costs would be significant and could eliminate all your limited savings. I suppose, in the worst possible scenario, they might even be more than that'.

'If it was withdrawn at the present stage, it is likely we are going to have to pay the coroner's legal fees to date.'

Then the blow really fell:

'For these reasons, both Mr Spencer and I feel – with considerable regret – that the matter should not be pursued'

Probably to emphasise the extent of the cost to me, Mr Marshal warned me that legal aid would not be an issue, because if I was to pursue my application for legal aid, Mr Spencer would have to state to the Legal Aid Board that my chances of success would be in the order of 30%. Then it

would be certain that legal aid would not be granted. Mr Marshal ended his letter with what was almost an ultimation:
'The matter does, I am afraid, need a fairly early decision
on your part.'
I was totally bewildered by this change of attitude. I could not understand why my chances of success were suddenly reduced to 30% and the costs to greatly exceed the first estimate. As far as I was concerned, I could not see how the coroner's affidavit could seriously demolish my case against him. Granted that Dr Chan had been expected to try to do so, but I had been led into believing that I had a case strong enough to stand up against any arguments Dr Chan would present. Needless to say I lost no time in arranging a meeting.

I did not receive much of an explanation for the change in Mr Spencer's assessment of my chance of success and his obvious reluctance to pursue the case further. Mr Marshal repeated what Mr Spencer had said in his further advice:

'We have now received the affidavit of the coroner, Dr Chan. It contains, inter alia, a number of findings/concessions which – it seems to me – are much more satisfactory from Mrs. Barrack's point of view than anything we have heard or seen from this coroner so far...'

I questioned how Mr Spencer could say that anything in the coroner's affidavit was satisfactory to me, when he hadn't asked for my point of view. I had understood that the affidavit was merely presenting the argument that Dr Chan was planning to use, in justifying his inquest conduct to the High Court. It was not a question of satisfying me, but for Mr Spencer to argue my case against Dr Chan's, irrespective of how forcefully he apposed my application. As far as I was concerned, as I had been granted leave to appeal, then the case should go forward and just as forcibly be argued on my behalf. This was more or less how I argued with Mr Marshal against withdrawing my case from the list. I could not, from that conversation, figure out whether or not Mr Marshal was totally in agreement with Mr Spencer. All I can say on that point is that the previous enthusiasm seemed to be absent.

I won't go into the details of Mr Spencer advice as I have already covered the points raised in part one, and have given my reasons why I do not agree that my case should have been withdrawn. In any event, all the points I made in my application when put together are constitute 'an insufficiency of enquiry', which under Rule 13–(2) of the Coroners Act 1988, are grounds for making an application for a second inquest.

Mr Spencer though, considered that Dr Chan had made sufficient concessions in accepting some of the inconsistencies in his inquisition, particularly in relation Mr Simpson's evidence not being consistent with the medical evidence, and the reasons for conducting the inquest in the way that he did:

> '...His affidavit contains superficially attractive explanations as to the way he conducted the inquest and, in particular, as to why he did not pursue Mr Simpson's evidence. I think that the combination of these explanations and the concessions make it highly likely that the High Court would conclude, whatever the force of our conclusions as to the lack of questions to Mr Simpson, that no court of inquiry is perfect in the sense that it cannot think of every question which might occur, and that the coroner discharged his legal duties more than adequately.'

Mr Spencer continued. What I found was muddled explanation, that the coroner had put his finger on the principal difficulty, that realistically he could not have returned any other verdict than accidental death. Also, that the coroner had come some considerable way towards a more satisfactory conclusion as to how Alexander Barrack met his death. To me those concessions were more of an admission of Dr Chan's mismanagement and I had learned nothing about the real circumstances and cause of my son's death...

My counsel concludes his advice by saying that 'adopting the same reasoning' he regretfully concludes that in the light of the coroner's affidavit there was only a 30% chance of successfully seeking a judicial review. Therefore in view of the very substantial risk in terms of costs, his considered advice, unpalatable as it may be, was for me not to take the case forward. Unpalatable?, I almost choked on it, and although I did my best, I floundered in trying to convince Mr Marshal that my case should go on, and was very conscious that my ignorance of the law was a huge drawback in the argument; however, Mr Marshal again stressed the fact that if I lost, the costs could wipe out all my savings. I reminded Mr Marshal that I had already accepted that possibility, but I would have my pensions, which were adequate for my needs and so I thought the final decision should be mine. It was also my opinion we should wait for the Legal Aid Board's decision'

Mr Marshal then said that he thought Mr Spencer would continue the case if I insisted, but he could not press my case for legal funding as my chances of winning were less that 30%. Therefore neither he nor Mr Spencer recommended that I should continue to take the case through the Court, as the penalties to me, if I lost, could be excessive. The worst scenario but the most likely, was that I would also have to pay the coroner's costs, then the total costs would be so high that I would be forced to sell my home to cover them.

I was devastated, losing my home had never entered my head, nor had either the solicitor or the counsel mentioned such a possibility. I was seventy two, and the thought of being made homeless at that age appalled me, yet I could not bring myself to agree to withdraw my application, not then.

I told Mr Marshall I needed to think things over. He reminded me that as my case was pending; he had to have an early decision but agreed to give me four days to decide. He also told me that if I withdrew my case, he would ask the coroner to pay his own costs, and there was a reasonable chance he would agree.

It was a nightmarish situation to be in. I did so want to take my son's case to the High Court but the prospect of being homeless and penniless was frightening. Perhaps I was foolish in not asking my family or others for advice, but I knew of no one who could help me financially. However, as Mr Marshal had twice told me, the final decision was mine alone. He also told me that once I had withdrawn from the list, I would not be allowed to re-apply to the Crown Office.

For the full four days I struggled with the problem, but in the end, the fear of being homeless won the day and on the 9th February 1998 I wrote the withdrawal letter to Mr Marshal:

'It is with the deepest regret and reluctance that I have to accept that the financial penalties (in the absence of legal aid) of loosing the case are potentially too severe for a person in my situation to risk. I therefore withdraw my application.

I handed Mr Marshal the letter personally and I felt like crying from sheer frustration, but, once Mr Marshal had had accepted it and said I was doing the wise thing, I left his office, dry eyed but seething against the injustice. I didn't feel wise at all; just a sense of deep resentment against the coroner who had outwitted me again.

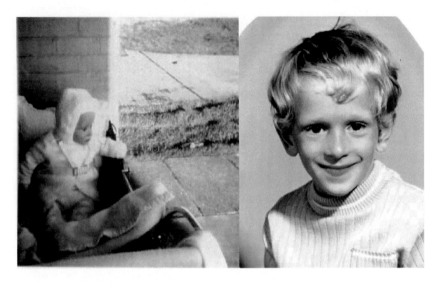

Alex at eighteen months          Alex at eight

Alex at eighteen          Alex at twenty-eight

*Alec the gourmet enjoying his Christmas Dinner 1986*

*"The Nan who loved me"*

*Alex's ashes, in his new casket for the last night he spent in his mother's house before leaving for his final resting place in Wormley & Nut Wood in Hertfordshire.*

*His father Bill carefully carried his son's ashes to the grove now called Barrack Grove, where after a short ceremony in the company of a small group of his friends, Alex was left to peace and tranquillity he had earned.*

Celebration of Alex's life

DEDICATED TO
WILLIAM ALEXANDER BARRACK
REMEMBERED WITH LOVE BY HIS FAMILY
Also dedicated to his friends, with thanks.
THIS AREA IS CARED FOR BY
THE WOODLAND TRUST

The commemorative plaque

The grove in spring

The grove in summer

*The Grove in winter*

*93B Caledonian Rd, Kings Cross – the first home that Alec could call his own.*

*His flat was on the first floor flat with the window to the right of the front door, over looking the very busy road. The area was rather rough, but this flat had the advantage of inside window shutters, which offered both privacy and protection.*

*The Apprentice Club London E*
*Where Alex had his ill-fated meeting with Simpson*

*This is the back view of the flats where Alex died. Flat 12 is*
*probably situated on the second floor*

This is the Police Station where we were interviewed by the
Investigation Team and where the saga of false information which was
to last fourteen years and where collusion started

Poplar Coroner's Court and the attached mortuary where Alex's body lay for five months, still labelled as 'unknown male', after two post-mortem examinations and identification.

# CHAPTER SEVENTEEN

*Any failure seems so total. Later you realise you can have another go*

**Part 1 – Another beginning – the interview with the CPS – John Smith appears.**

Failure is something I don't accept easily but for a few days after I handed in the withdrawal letter, I felt ill and very low in spirits. Fortunately I had a dissertation to prepare for my Masters Degree and settled on giving my studies first priority but the injustice still rankled. Then in the local newspaper I saw that Mr Edward Leigh, my constituency Member of Parliament, was due to hold a surgery in Gainsborough and I immediately perked up. This was because, although I knew I couldn't go back to the High Court with my case again, I saw this as chance to use the services of a highly respected politician to at least, have some explanations for the extraordinary conduct of the police and the coroner. I contacted Mr Leigh's agent and explained my reasons for wanting to see the MP, but he thought, that under the circumstances, it would be more fitting to arrange a private meeting without a time limit. This was arranged for the 19th February, ten days after I had agreed to withdraw my case.

Before this meeting took place I received a letter from the Legal Aid Board in Nottingham rejecting my application for legal funding. It would appear this decision was taken even before Mr Spencer could have had been asked for his opinion on my chances of success, because the letter was dated 3rd February 1998. I did not receive this until 16th/17th February, as it was sent to Mrs Doris Scorer and neither Mr Marshal nor the Retirement Park Office knew of such an individual. However, my Christian name eventually established my identity.

The letter was formal and quite abruptly worded, as were the reasons given:

"You have not shown that you have reasonable grounds for, taking, defending, or being party to proceedings.

It is considered that on the information available, you would derive insufficient benefit from the action.

It appears that the cost of the action would be out of proportion to any benefit likely to be obtained.'

The letter seemed to indicate that I would have had a better chance of funding if I had been claiming compensation, from which the Board could claim reimbursement. There would be no recovered money for the Board, when the case merely involved the High Court remedying an unjust inquest verdict.

This information was included in the documents handed to Mr Leigh at our meeting, which he carefully studied in relation to our long discussion over Alex's case. Mr Leigh was obviously convinced by my argument, as he promised he would take some action. True to his word, within a few days, Mr Leigh had contacted the Lord Chancellor and requested that he launch an inquiry into the shortcomings of the inquest, and that of the subordinate authorities.

At the end of March Mr Leigh received a quite helpful letter from the Under Secretary of State Lord Williams of Mostyn. Mr Leigh's letter had been passed from the Lord Chancellor's Office to the Home Office, as it was the Home Secretary who had responsibilities for coroner's law. However, as coroners are independent judicial officers, the Home Secretary had no authority to re-open the inquest or enquire into any other matters Mr Leigh had raised. Lord Mostyn commented on my withdrawing my case from the High Court and that as the issues raised, also concerned investigations into a suspected crime, advised that they should be taken up with the Metropolitan Commissioner of Police. He also said that on the questions of decisions taken by the Crown Prosecutions Service, I should seek comments from the Director of Public Prosecutions (DPP). Lord Mostyn very considerately supplied the addresses of both of these authorities.

After considering Lord Mostyn's letter to Mr Leigh very carefully, I decided that as the DPP - Dame Barbara Mills had made the decision against strong police evidence, that the CPS was not to prosecute a man arrested and charged with manslaughter, then she should be requested to provide reasons for her judgment. I again met Mr Leigh and he agreed to contact her on my behalf. He wrote to her on 23rd April.

While waiting for her to reply I continued writing my dissertation for a Masters Degree which I gained in June 1998[106] .The graduation ceremony was held in July and after that I was ready to take up my campaign again. I don't know of course, what was in the letter Mr Leigh sent to Mrs Mills but from the reply, sent three months later, it is almost certain that Mr Leigh passed on to her, my critical comments of her inaccurate analysis of the evidence, along with the documents dealing with the inconsistencies in Robert Simpson's evidence, particularly in relation to the forensic medical evidence, which has already been fully discussed throughout the previous chapters.

In her reply, the DPP stated that she had received a full report from the Chief Crown Prosecutor for CPS Central Casework, who had instructed a Senior Crown Prosecutor to consider in detail all the papers sent to the CPS by Mr Leigh. The Crown Prosecutor had noted in particular, Dr Heath's evidence at the inquest that Mr Barrack's body had been laying on its trunk "for a minimum of two hours. Something in that order" and that this fact had prompted the Senior Prosecutor to meet Dr Heath and to consider two main aspects of the case:

1.   Whether there is sufficient evidence for a charge of manslaughter.

2.   Whether there is sufficient evidence for a charge of perjury in relation to the evidence Mr Simpson gave to the inquest.'

Mr Leigh also received an explanation on how a Crown Prosecutor applies the tests for prosecuting, set out in the CPS Code[107] which must be applied to each case. There are two stages in the decision to prosecute. Very simply they are:

---

[106] The dissertation was accepted and gained me a Masters degree in Modern History in June 1998.
[107] Prosecution of Offences Act 1985 (Section10)

**The Evidential Test**

The Crown Prosecutor must be satisfied that there is sufficient evidence to provide:

1. A realistic prospect of conviction. He must consider objectively how the defence case may go and how it is likely to affect the prosecution case.

2. A realistic prospect of conviction means that a jury or bench magistrate is more likely than not to convict the defendant of the charge alleged.

If the case does not pass the evidential test, no matter how serious or important a case may be, it will not proceed to the second test, which is to decide if a prosecution is needed in the public interest. The CPS required a 60% surety of a conviction.

**The Public Interest Test.** – 'In cases of any seriousness a prosecution will precede, unless, there are public interest factors tending against prosecution, which clearly outweigh those in favour.'

The public interest test condition was a clause which would be continually used against me in the future. Although at that time the criteria used for deciding Alex's case was apparently limited to it only passing the evidential test. This same limit in testing a case was also applied to the charges of manslaughter and perjury and for the CPS to decide that there was insufficient evidence to afford a realistic prospect of prosecuting Robert Simpson for either crime.

As a point of information, the term 'public interest' was one I was to have used against me over and over again, but I found it extremely difficult to have the term defined in clear precise terms. Perhaps the only one which made any real sense, certainly to me, was the definition given to me in a letter from a MPS Information Access Department, in which it was stated the public interest test was applied when the evidence obtained, if made public, could seriously damage the Nations major interests, such as National security and the countries economy, and it was important for the common good, to conceal the facts from the public. I can't imagine anything about Alex's death or his status, threatening either national security, or the economy, therefore, any publicity could only have damaged high profile reputations.

However, the term public interest was not applied on this occasion. The patently paltry excuse given by Mrs Mills for not proceeding with a prosecution for manslaughter, appeared from the letter, to be based only on **Dr Heath being unable to rule out the possibility that death was caused by a number of factors, including vomiting and choking.** In consequence a barrister has advised a prosecution for manslaughter would be bound to fail.

On the question of a prosecution for perjury, it would rely on proof that Mr Simpson was lying about the time that death took place, bearing in mind that the body was lying on its trunk for two hours, **"Dr Heath cannot rule out the possibility that hypostasis occurred after the arrival at the hospital but before the post-mortem was conducted."** I don't believe that was the case, it is more likely that those remarks of Dr Heath were made during a longer discourse, taken out of context and used to suit the purpose of the CPS. Dr Heath had decidedly ruled out both factors at the inquest.

While I was in the process of considering my next move, in early August I had an unexpected phone call from a gentleman, an independent journalist, whom I only ever knew as John Smith. The purpose of his call, he told me, was to offer his help in furthering my case. I will give more details of this call later, which was important to the direction of my future action was to take. Initially we discussed the DPP's letter and I told John that what I found particularly remarkable, and also disquieting, was the lack of independent medical input into these discussions. He suggested that I should take up all the points she had made, particularly the medical forensic evidence, and challenge them. He also recommended that it would add more weight to my letters if I used my titles in the letter heading, MA, BA (Hon) SRN.

In November 1998, taking John's advice I wrote to the DPP, and in no uncertain terms expressed my dissatisfaction with the inadequacies of her explanations. Here I quote extracts from my letter, which express my antipathy to her argument:

"The number of legal minds employed in conducting the inquiry, is impressive but I would have been more convinced that they were working in the interest of justice on my son's behalf, if the group had included independent medical experts who agreed with the conclusions of the legal experts. There are many anomalies contained in the inquest report relating to the circumstances and cause of death and the behaviour of Mr Simpson, which needed to be discussed with an impartial pathologist and a hospital practitioner."

It is extraordinary that hypostasis was used to deny perjury; when all pathologists are aware that on its own, it is the least reliable change in estimating the time of death.[108] However, when taken in combination with the stiffness (rigor mortis) of the body and the degree of the coldness, an acceptable and reasonably accurate estimation of the time of death can be obtained. We know that in Alex's case, there were three experts in different medical fields, who noted and certified that the advanced stage of all three changes on his body, which positively indicated a much earlier time of death that the one Simpson had given to several officials, some given under oath.

On the manner in which Mrs Mills dealt with the question of perjury, my reply to her was couched in terms, which I hoped would make her realise that I was aware of her ignorance of forensic medical facts, Also the inappropriateness of her using hypostasis as sound evidence, in order to justify the non-prosecution decision, in a case which involved very serious offences, manslaughter and perjury (and others):

"All three signs when considered together as they should be will provide conclusively that death took place at least two hours, and probably more, before the emergency call was made. The combination of signs is positive proof that Mr Simpson did commit perjury. Knowing that my son had been dead for some time, Mr Simpson should have called the police. His motive for not doing so is quite obvious."

---

[108] Simpson's Forensic Medicine. p

I also told her that as retired nurse with thirty years experience in handling the bodies of the dead, I totally refuted the claim that the hypostasis took place in the hospital. This death after all, was reported to the coroner as being suspicious by the Hospital Registrar, and therefore it is absolutely certain, and this was confirmed by the Senior Consultant of the A/E Department, that the body was treated with the greatest respect while in the hospital and the mortuary an covered with a shroud, (It was after a suspicious death and there can be no doubt that extra care was taken.) I concluded my letter by saying that I was determined to continue my efforts to obtain justice for my son; I considered it was my right and my duty to do so.

Making the DPP aware of my being an MA and a qualified and experienced nurse, and not an uninformed civilian, seemed to have been affective, as she referred the case back to CPS Central Casework in London, who in turn passed it on to an outside third party, Mr Ensor, the York Branch Crown Prosecutor. Letters were passed between us, but really all he did was reiterate the points already made by Mrs Mills. Naturally I rejected his attempts to change my opinions, and eventually, he offered to meet me for a face to face discussion. I accepted this offer on behalf of Alex's father, Bill Barrack, and myself, and arranged a meeting in York for January 18th 1999.

We found Mr Ensor to be a very considerate and gentlemanly person and, from this impression, Bill and I had hoped that this meeting would satisfy our demands to know the truth and give us the full facts of our son's untimely death, and therefore, bring an end to the distressing uncertainty about the nature and cause of his death. This then, would make it unnecessary to take any further action to bring about the closure which could help in reconciling us to his loss.

It was a hope which quickly dissipated, because during the long discussion with Mr Ensor and his advisor, we were made aware that there were even more differences in the interpretations of the evidence by the three authorities, than we had realised. This strengthened our suspicion that a covert conspiracy had indeed been set in motion, not only to obscure Alex's identity but to deceive his family as to the cause of death. This was solely for the purpose of protecting a senior member of the CPS from the consequences of a sexually related death activity, and to avoid further embarrassment to the

211

department, which had already been beleaguered by the press for its exceptionally high rate of decisions favouring non-prosecutions.

What was extremely disturbing to me was the admission of Mr Ensor that the CPS was not in possession of all the facts when the decision not to prosecute was taken. Mr Ensor himself said that he had learned many of them from the inquest report and my personal record of events, my notes and the letters I sent to him. These had made him 'think hard', even though the CPS had previously called upon the opinion of several legal experts to e-examine my son's case. He had also been impressed by the fact that our well-informed argument was based on sound medical backgrounds, Bill Barrack being an ex-RAMC Staff Sergeant and was then a senior manager with a pharmaceutical company. I was retired Nursing Officer, with experience in both Army and civilian hospitals and very familiar with the changes in a body after death. I told Mr Ensor, in view of the DPP's claim that Dr Heath had reinterpreted his evidence; I had a right to a second forensic medical examination by an independent pathologist

Realising that I was steadfast in refusing to accept any of the decisions taken without a second opinion, Mr Ensor did arrange one, but not the medical opinion that I wanted. He called upon the services of another legal mind, a Treasury Counsel, a lawyer who was deemed to act independently of any department. He had apparently subjected Dr Heath to a "defence type" examination on what was termed medical issues and that as a result of "deficiencies" in Dr Heath's replies to questions put to him, the counsel's opinion was that there was insufficient evidence for prosecution.

What a one sided argument that must have been, no prosecutor to defend and argue Alex's case, and no jury present to hear the evidence, and no independent legal prosecutor to question witnesses or to challenge 'the defence type' evidence put to Dr Heath. Incidentally it did not say much for Dr Heath's expertise if he could not sustain his own professional opinion. He certainly did so successfully at the inquest against the coroner. Of course my case was never allowed to reach the stage where we parents could participate in some way. In fact Bill Barrack and I were excluded from all debate over our son's death and I told Mr Ensor that we considered this exclusion to be an outrageous infringement of our parental rights, above all others, were entitled to the truth. I also told him indignantly, that the CPS was acting as judge and jury but without a trial. At this he looked at me thoughtfully, and then said 'I suppose we are.'

Then, in very decisive terms Mr Ensor was told by me that the conduct of the CPS was unacceptable and a violation of Alex's rights. The refusal to even consider my request to have a second medical opinion was proof enough to us parents, that justice was being denied our son. I also told him that the CPS was not following its own code of practice which is *'to serve the cause of justice'*. At that point grief seemed to overtake me and the meeting was quickly terminated. Mr Barrack and I were served tea while I recovered, after which we left the building, but still fuming.

In October 1998 I had written to Mr Absalom of the London Ambulance Service asking him to verify some points with the paramedic Miss Lee on her observations and findings when she attended to Alex. These I have already covered in an earlier chapter but I also asked him about the taped recording of the dialogue between the Call Taker and Mr Simpson. Mr Absalom told me he did have the original and the police had been given a copy. When I had previously contacted DI Bathie, he had refused to comment on the tape. But Mr Absalom was more co-operative and told me, that although legally he could not give me a copy of the tape, he could instead invite Alex's father and me to his Headquarters to listen to the actual tape. This invitation we accepted.

On the 22nd of January 1999 Bill and I met Mr Absalom at the London Ambulance Headquarters and listened intently to the recording. Although it was very distressing, it began to dawn on me that Simpson's demeanour throughout the so called resuscitation efforts did not tally with my own experience of carrying out sustained CPR. In my personal experience, it is very hard work physically and mentally, and most certainly during such a long resuscitation, the inexperienced Mr Simpson should been gasping when talking and very breathless when it was over, he was thirty nine at the time. In fact he was quite unmoved by his experience, and there was absolutely no evidence of Simpson exerting himself during the whole of the call. It was Mr Absalom who provided me with a transcript of the whole procedure which was to prove invaluable in my future analysing of the forensic and medical evidence. It was at this meeting that we learned that in his opinion the coroner had been very remiss in not calling the paramedics to give their vital evidence to the coroner's court, when it involved a suspicious death.

A few weeks later Mr Ensor wrote to say that the CPS had gone as far as it could and therefore considered the matter ended. My reply to him and the CPS was that it wasn't the end for me and I intended to continue my attempts to access the truth. In fairness to Mr Ensor I have to say, that I had realised that throughout the interview that he was trying to be helpful, but also became conscious of the fact that he was restricted by his superiors' instructions and hindered by incomplete information.

I contacted John the journalist, and told him what had resulted from the York meeting, and told him that not having any joy from complaining to any of these authorities, the Attorney General, the coroner and the DPP, still rankled but those failed attempts plus the little information I had on the police at that time, made me reluctant to tackle the MPS. Yet, it wasn't too long before John Smith provided the advice and documentation, which dictated my next step.

# CHAPTER EIGHTEEN

*The object of the Convention is the protection of human rights against infringements by the State; the UK recognised the right of individual petition in 1996.*

## Introduction - The European Convention on Human Rights

When John Smith first contacted me over the phone, in view of my experience with Mr Hepburn, I was very chary about answering his questions and queried his intentions. He assured me he was not interested in writing articles for the press, but that his main aim was to help me right an injustice. He had seen Mr Hepburn's report in the Sun Newspaper, and considered that Alex's case had similarities to other cases, in which he had helped uncover CPS and police 'cover-ups' which had also deprived other victim's of justice. I was still not convinced of his sincerity and said I needed time to think things over, and would only work with him, if, he was able to show me that his interest in my case was genuine. John accepted this condition that said he would write to me and give me more details of his work, and then, I could decide whether or not to accept his offer of assistance.

It didn't take him long to convince me; within two days I had received a letter in which he described his mission in life to be that of exposing injustices, an interest which had developed as a result of his investigative journalistic experiences in mismanagement of criminal investigations, particularly those of the police and CPS. He said that despite what I had been told by the MPS and the CPS, he was certain that they would not have wanted Robert Simpson prosecuted. His familiarity with the methods of both public bodies had convinced him that both police and CPS often coalesce in cover-ups and fit-ups. For a number of years he had been involved in monitoring police and CPS activities, and had carried out private investigations and forensic photography for defence cases, and had helped to destroy a number of attempted police fit-ups. As a result he had become very unpopular with the MPS and it had become expedient to move from London to the South East and assume the *nom de plume* of John Smith.

To support his letter he enclosed a large number of news cuttings whose contents shocked me, especially the disturbing number which had occurred in the London Metropolitan area, and featured police officers, CPS lawyers and other individuals belonging to the privileged classes. I had always suspected that there would be a certain amount of corruption amongst the members of the political and justice systems, but it was an unpleasant revelation to me to find just how extensively corruption had spread. What was worse, even when positive the police had uncovered evidence, many perpetrators were dealt with more leniently than the ordinary citizen or allowed to escape punishment entirely. One particularly heinous case was reported on in 1989 from Hong Kong, by Ian Hepburn, in a lengthy report published in the News of the World. It covered the investigation into the very serious sexual offences of a CPS lawyer, a known paedophile, who had been allowed to escape any penalty in England and to move to Hong Kong, where he apparently carried on with his evil depravity, and at that time, was still a practising lawyer. Reading this article made me realise why Mr Hepburn had been so interested in the circumstances and the CPS personnel involved in Alex's death or the aftermath.

It was rapidly coming home to me that I was in conflict with the Establishment as a whole and not just certain departments and officials. I told John that I was beginning to feel that the task was too monumental and that these Government officials for they own ends, would obstruct my every effort to obtain justice from the British Courts., but knew of no other course I could take, John replied, 'Ah but I do, you can take your case to the European Court on Human Rights'. This was an organisation I had not heard of before, but John explained briefly why it had come into existence and its purpose, he suggested that I research the internet to obtain more information on the purpose and procedures of the European Convention on Human Rights, before I took any action. John Smith had opened the gate to hope again, just a little though, but enough to encourage me to take another step towards the justice I so wanted to achieve for Alex

**Part 1- ECHR – the right to challenge the state**

Before I begin any discourse on the ECHR I would like to remind you that this was an entirely new area of law that I now had to tackle. Both International and European laws were very complex constituents of the ECHR process. I took the task on without any guidance or instruction from legal representation, or legal funding, and only with John Smith's

216

background help. Therefore, the interpretations of the Convention articles and procedures used in my petition to The European Court, are from my own common sense reasoning, and by using as a guide, the useful information provided in a text book dealing with previous cases and commentary, entitled, *'The UK before the European Court of Human Rights'*.[109] Other sources of helpful information were provided by articles published on the websites of organisations interested in human rights, such as LIBERTY and INQUEST.

Before I purchased the text book I brought up the internet website of the ECHR, I then discovered that the full title of the Convention on Human Rights is, 'The Convention for the Protection of Human Rights and Fundamental Freedom' (ECHR). This Convention was based on the Articles defining human rights, and was influenced by the United Nations Declaration of Human Rights in 1948. This was a treaty between European States which came from the reaction to the horrors and atrocities of the Second World War. Its objective was to seek to protect the human rights of the people of Europe and prevent any infringement of those rights by States. The ECHR treaty was drafted in 1950 which was when the United Kingdom became a signatory of the Convention; and it came into force in 1953. The important point to be made is that the Convention is binding in international law on all signatories. Previously the purpose of the Court was to prevent large scale infringements by States but its scope was enlarged to include individual petitions.

The right of individual petition became effective in July 1955, (but was not recognised by the UK until 1966). This meant that anyone who believed that a public body[110] had breached their Convention Rights, or were proposing to, could bring proceedings against that public authority as an agent of the State. A person could also raise a breach of their Convention rights as a defence against any court proceedings against them. Unfortunately the Convention does not allow proceedings to be brought against a private individual; otherwise I would have made such action against Robert Simpson my priority. It is interesting to note, that in 1996, the right of individual petitions meant the bulk of complaints were on specific infringements of the articles,

---

[109] Author Sue Farran – published 1996
[110] Public Bodies – agents - acting on behalf of the UK Government, such as Police, CPS, Coroner etc.

and the UK had the highest number of individual petitions against such violations, than any of the other State signatories to the Convention.

It was quite easy to locate the listed Convention articles, but I was dismayed when I saw the formidable number displayed, about 66, which were divided into four sections. In addition there was a very disconcertingly large section on 'Rules of the Court', and another on 'Organisation & Working of the Court'. It was a great relief on consulting John Smith to learn that initially I need only really concern myself with Section One and a few other articles dealing with procedural information. He advised me, before making any preparation, to also familiarise myself with the key requirements laid down for an individual petition to the European Court and the procedure for taking a case to Strasbourg.[111]

It is quite a performance taking a case to the European Court; in the first place three key requirements, i.e. conditions have to be met which are:

1.  You must be a victim of a violation of one or more of the articles of the Convention. Generally, this means you must be directly affected by a breach of the Convention.

2.  Before you make an application to the ECHR, you must pursue any proceedings that you could take in the UK, that are capable of providing you with an adequate remedy for the breach of your Convention rights.

3.  You must make your application to the ECHR within six months of the conclusion of any court proceedings that you have taken in the UK, that could have provided you with a remedy, or, if there were no proceedings that it was reasonable to expect you to take, within six months of the event which gives rise to your application

**Condition 1.** meant, of course, that I had to identify which of those fourteen articles I considered the public authorities had specifically violated, and who were the public authorities who had carried out the infringements. Public

---

[111] The city in which the Court is situated.

Authorities are departments who carry out public functions on behalf of the UK Government. Examples of these are the police, the courts and local government bodies. Also included associations who are agents of departments, such as Local Councils A recent example is a recent High Court ruling that Housing Authorities, who administer housing benefits on behalf of their local councils, are subject to the Articles of the European Convention.

I also had to show how the actions of these officials had damaged my case and prevented my access to the true facts and in doing so had interfered with the course of justice.

I considered each of the fourteen articles carefully before deciding that Articles 1. 2. 3. 6. 13 & 14 had been infringed by the UK Government through the actions of the Metropolitan Police Service, the Crown Prosecution Service and the coroner.

## Part 2 - The Articles selected - official or simplified explanations
### Article 1.
*The High Contracting Parties shall secure to everyone within their jurisdiction, the rights and freedoms defined in section 1 of this Convention.*

This Article specifically places upon the UK government the duty to secure the rights and freedoms of its citizens as defined in the ECHR, and where, if a Contracting Party fails to do this, an external enforcement process can be applied. I took this to mean that if a State ignored a European Court decision then measures would be taken to compel it to do so.

### Article 2.
*Everyone's right to life shall be protected by law. No one should be deprived of his life intentionally.*

This means that, generally, the taking of life must be illegal under a state's law. This includes contravening legislation intended to protect life such as Health and Safety regulations and Road Traffic Acts. Murder and manslaughter under UK domestic law are also considered to breach Article 2 of the Convention. This also gives relatives the right to a full police investigation when a family member dies under suspicious circumstances.

### Article 3.
*No one shall be subjected to torture or inhuman or degrading treatment or punishment.*

I considered that the perverted circumstances under which Alex had died were degrading and humiliating. Sadomasochism in 1996 was condemned as such by both the British Court of Appeal and the European Court, who ruled that even consenting to the acts was not a viable defence.

### Article 6.
*In the determination of his civil rights and obligations, (or of any criminal charges against him), everyone is entitled to a fair and public hearing within a reasonable time by an independent and impartial tribunal established by law.*

This means that any person accused of offences, or persons with causes that involve court action have the right to a fair trial. This is a key feature of a democratic society, and includes:

1. the right to a *fair* hearing; the right to a *public* hearing

2. the right to a hearing before an *independent and impartial tribunal*

3. The right to a hearing *within a reasonable time.*

Therefore in law, everyone is entitled in full equality to a fair and public hearing and this should include legal representation before an independent and impartial tribunal, in the determination of his rights and obligations...

Article 6 does *not* give an absolute right to legal aid. But the European Court had ruled in some cases that where the applicants could not afford to bring proceedings, the denial of legal aid to the applicants had deprived them of the opportunity to present their case effectively. I thought that this ruling was applicable to my case

**Articles 13 &14.**

*Everyone whose rights and freedoms, as set forth in this Convention, are violated shall have an effective remedy before a national authority notwithstanding, that the violation has been committed by persons acting in an official capacity.*

Under Article 13 the State has duty to ensure that everyone has the right to an effective remedy by the courts or tribunals where his/ her rights have been abused.

Under Article 14 everyone is equal before the law and is entitled to be protected against discrimination of any kind.

In my opinion I had not received and effective remedy under Article 13 because of status discrimination being applied by the authorities to protect the interests of departmental and high profile individuals' reputations, contrary to Article 14 which stipulates:

*'The enjoyment rights and freedoms set forth in this Convention shall be secured without any discrimination on any grounds...or any status.'*

Under Article 14 it was obvious to me that discrimination in more than on area of justice and more than one department had been practised against Alex.

**Condition 2.** necessitated identifying to the Court which authorities had committed the infringements and to describe the actions by which I considered they had violated those articles. These authorities, were of course the police, by conducting investigations kept secret from the family, the CPS, who had failed to prosecute an obviously guilty suspect. In particular, the conduct of the coroner, whose inadequate management of the inquest and his inappropriate verdict of 'accidental killing' had resulted in all official enquiries being halted and the truth remaining concealed. I did not anticipate much difficulty in that respect; I felt I had ample material at hand to prove my case against all three agents of the State.

**Condition 3.** however, presented me with a serious problem. It was based on Article 25 of the ECHR which stated, *'The Commission can only deal* *with the matter after all domestic remedies have been exhausted ...'* My problem was that the my sole purpose in taking legal action in the first place, was to have the original inquest verdict quashed and a new one ordered. However, that decision had to come from a higher court, but through my own naïve acceptance of what I now believe was ill-conceived advice to abandon my appeal, I had succeeded in barring myself from making any further direct appeal to the High Court to grant or refuse a domestic remedy for the same case. The only remaining way for me to access the High Court was through an application by or under the authority of the Attorney General and that fiat I intended to apply for quite soon.

But I needed further evidence to support my right to apply to the Attorney General under Section 13 (1) (b) of the Coroners Act that the coroner had carried out an 'insufficiency of inquiry' and of his failure to observe several rules and procedures governing an inquest. I attempted to do this by writing to Dr Chan asking him to explain why he had disregarded so many rules and procedures during his inquest and asking him to provide copies of **all** the documents and report he had referred to during the inquest, but had withheld from Alex's family. His reply was quite polite and included a long explanation of a coroner's duties at an inquest and claimed he had scrupulously observed them. For the first time he expressed condolences to me over Alex's death. I thought a three year delay in doing so was a bit extreme.

I sent him a second letter in the same vein as the first, rejecting his explanation and insisting that he issue the copies of papers I had requested. His reply to this letter was not so polite, and his comments in refuting my claim of irregularities, came via the court clerk. In it he accused me of spurious statements and untruths, which I thought such accusations, coming from him, were hypocritical to say the least. Furthermore he refused to accept any further communication from me. That was OK by me, because then I could cite this refusal in my application when I applied for the Attorney General's fiat.

Before I started my correspondence with the coroner, I had began a series of letters in late 1999 addressed to the Limehouse Superintendent of Police, asking him to explain the extraordinary manner in which the Investigating Team had conducted investigations into Alex's unlawful killing. In later letters I invoked the Articles of the ECHR which I considered the police had infringed. Copies of these letters were sent to the Metropolitan Commissioner of Police, with the result that all my requests for explanations were passed to the Legal Secretariat to the Commissioner, Mr David Hamilton. Mr Hamilton evaded answering any of my questions and refused to release any documents related to police inquiries. Instead he referred to the coroner's verdict and described it as being the final outcome of the case and therefore no further action would be taken. As a result the correspondence became somewhat acrimonious especially when in January 2000, Mr Hamilton advised me that the time had come when the police could no longer devote any further resources to answering my questions and that in future I was required to 'fully explain my purpose' and unless he considered my requests were reasonable he would not respond them in future.

Throughout all this correspondence the Articles of the ECHR frequently quoted by me where disregarded by Mr Hamilton. I began to wonder if he had ever studied the Articles. After sending Mr Hamilton a letter in which I was highly critical of his and the police behaviour, I broke off the correspondence. It would, I thought, be useful in demonstrating to the European Court how the police had violated Articles 2, 'the right to life' and Article Six 'the right to a fair hearing', but had blatantly ignored their purpose.

## Part 3 – Second application - for the Attorney General's Fiat.

By June when my preparation was well advanced, I felt it was time to apply again for the Attorney General's fiat. It was registered as a formal complaint against the coroner's conduct, using the wording in Section 13 of the Coroner's Act1988 as the grounds for requesting his authorization that the High Court should grant me leave to appeal to have the original inquest verdict quashed, and for a new inquest to be held:

> (1) (b) ...*where an inquest has been held by him (the coroner), and there has been insufficiency of enquiry, the discovery of new evidence, or is desirable in the interests of justice, that another inquest should be held.*

I began my letter by reminding him of the public directive to his subordinate authorities to obey the laws of the European Convention and that the European Commission had stressed the importance of Article 6 in relation to the principle 'equality of arms' in legal process, where the ordinary individual is pitted against the power of the State. I also drew his attention to his duty to protect the individual's life under Article 2.

From that I went on to detail the manner in which Dr Chan had 'totally and grossly' breached the Coroners Rules and the Coroners Act, contrary to the Articles of ECHR and by his irregular inquiry had deprived the unlawfully killed Alex of a just verdict and his family of their rights. Briefly describing how the coroner and his officer had denied the victim and family their rights, by disregarding the Rules governing the conduct of an inquest. I explained how this denial had left the family ignorant of the right to have legal representation and to question and challenge the evidence, and had failed to disclose some of the most important statements and forensic medical reports at the inquest, which would have established Alex's death as an unlawful killing. Furthermore, Dr Chan had also offended the principle of 'equality of arms' by refusing to provide documentation to be used in supporting a petition to The European Court. All the information I referred to has been discussed in detail in previous chapters. It was quite a strongly worded letter which I hoped would at least, convince the Attorney General to re-examine my case.

While waiting for the reply to my application, some doubts began to arise about the wisdom of petitioning the European Court. Actually, it was the lack of legal funding that caused me to hesitate to start proceedings in the European Court. John Smith came to my rescue again when he told me that although legal representation was recommended; I did not need any funding to make an application to submit a petition. The Court would decide the question of eligibility for legal aid if and when the case was accepted for a hearing. This view was confirmed by a ruling I found in a textbook'. This recorded the fact that the court had, in one case, held that '...*Applicants should not encounter undue financial difficulties in bringing complaints under the Convention*'[112]. Then I found this paragraph which further resolved my doubts:

---

[112] Verdict – Young ,James & Webster Series A, Vol44, para 15.

224

*"... the opportunity to request an authority to reconsider a decision it has taken does not constitute a sufficient remedy for the purposes of Article 26. For example, failure to reapply to the Legal Aid Board, which has already refused an initial application, does not amount to a failure to exhaust domestic remedies."*

The problem of legal funding appeared to be solved, so I continued to work out what was the best way to present a convincing petition to the court based on the material I held. This was in anticipation of a refusal of a fiat by the Attorney General which would then allow only six months for me to make the first application to the European Commission. In the next chapter I will explain how I later conducted my pursuit of justice after receiving the reply to my application for the Attorney General's fiat.

But first I had to prepare my application for the Attorney General's fiat and by June it was ready. I made it in the form of complaint against the coroner using the wording in Section 13 of the Coroner's Act1988 as the grounds for requesting his authorization for the High Court to examine my request for quashing the inquest, and for a new inquest to be held on the grounds that:

> b) *...where an inquest has been held by him (the coroner) and there has been...insufficiency of enquiry, the discovery of new evidence, or is desirable in the interests of justice that another inquest should be held.*

I began my letter by reminding him of the public directive to his subordinate authorities to obey the laws of the European Convention and that the European Commission had stressed the importance of Article 6 in relation to the principle 'equality of arms' in legal process, where the ordinary individual is pitted against the power of the State. I also drew his attention to his duty to protect the individual's life under Article 2.

From that I went on to detail the manner in which Dr Chan had 'totally and grossly' breached the Coroners Rules and the Coroners Act, contrary to the Articles of ECHR and by his irregular inquiry had deprived the unlawfully killed Alex of a just verdict and his family their rights. Briefly, the coroner and his officer had denied the victim and family their rights by

225

disregarding the Rules governing the conduct of an inquest. This left the family ignorant of the right to have legal representation and to question and challenge the evidence, and by failing to disclose important statements and forensic medical reports at the inquest which indicated an unlawful death. Dr Chan had also offended the principle of 'equality of arms' by refusing to provide documentation to be used in supporting a petition to The European Court. All the information mentioned has been discussed in previous chapters. It was quite a strongly worded letter which I hoped would at least, convince the Attorney General to re-examine my case.

In the next chapter I will explain how I continued my quest for justice after receiving the reply to my application for the Attorney General's fiat.

# CHAPTER NINETEEN

## Part 1 – Knowing what to do is one thing – knowing how to do it is another.

I had grown used to dealing with officials whose policy, when dealing with complaints, was to delay taking action as long as possible, in the hope that the complainant would vanish into thin air, therefore I suppose it was unrealistic of me to hope for prompt action from the Attorney General. I did have a quick acknowledgement of my letter in early June which informed me that my case was to be handled by Mr Philip Geering the Legal Secretariat to the Law Offices. After that response, I waited, and I waited, but by October I was loosing patience, and on the 7th I wrote a sharp letter to Mr Geering complaining about the undue delay. Another month passed before he replied apologising for the delay and saying that he was seeking counsel's advice on the issues raised, and he hoped to provide me with a substantive reply as soon as possible.

So I waited over Christmas and New Year, but nothing happened. Altogether, I had to wait seven months before, on March 8th 2000; I finally received Mr Geering's substantive reply:

> *'Having considered your application the Solicitor General has decided that he should not grant his authority. Your application is therefore denied.'*

This refusal was accompanied by an apology for the delay in resolving the matter, for which Mr Geering, said he was entirely responsible. He assured me that the matter had been considered with great care under advice on matters of law from counsel, and he said he realised that I would be disappointed

He was wrong; I was not disappointed, and even through the refusal was expected, I was actually disgusted with the whole processes of the legal system which had allowed decision after decision to be made against my interests. This was especially so, when it was obvious to me, that I was quite was justified in my accusation that there was something very sinister about the circumstances of Alex's death. My investigations had entailed

227

every authority who had been contacted by me over the years, and for them to have long discussions under advice from several counsels before rejecting my demand for a fair and impartial resolution. The consultations which had taken place were quite disproportionate in time and cost, certainly a great deal more extensive that would be expected for the 'accidental death' verdict given by the coroner. Obviously it was not expedient for the authorities to bring the facts of the case into open court. It was another thirteen years before my suspicions of murder were confirmed as facts.[113] At that time though, this particular refusal did at least give me the go-ahead to apply for permission to petition the European Commission.

First though, Ken, his children and I had to face a very sad situation. On May 16th 2000 our beloved Maureen died after a very long and courageous battle with cancer. She died in the wonderful care of The North London Hospice. Over the previous year, the staff at the hospice had helped this family to come to terms with the inevitability of loosing a loving wife and mother. The Sunday before she died, Ken, Maureen and their children Rachel and Simon, spent a last happy and fun day together in the Hospice, a lovely last memory to console them in the days ahead. Maureen passed away on the Tuesday morning at about 9am. She now rests in peace.

Then it was back to duty. During the long wait for the fiat result from Mr Geering, I had started to prepare a document I intended to present to either the British Court or the European Court, which ever was appropriate. It was a lengthy comparative analysis of all the events that had taken place from the day I first heard Alex was missing, right up to the inquest and the coroner's iniquitous verdict. Had I left writing until after the decision, it would not have been ready to meet the deadline, and writing thirty thousand words, for the benefit of the Court, would have been a waste of time and effort. I already had an outline of what would be the substance of my petition, from study of the conditions laid down in Court procedures but was uncertain how I should apply to the European Court itself.

This is where the internet proved to be useful, especially as it gave me speedy access to information. By keying into the Court website, I found a

---

[113] MRG Report 2000

printable ECHR guide which immediately provided very clear instructions on the procedure, and saved a great deal of time in letter writing and in the cost of postage. The instructions made it quite clear that for a case to go forward to the first stage in the procedure, the Section Registrar had to accept the application.,

> *'If it appears from your correspondence with the Registrar that your complaint is one which could be registered as an application and you wish this to be done, you will be sent the necessary document on which to submit your formal application.'*

Obviously, my first letter had to convince the Registrar that I had an acceptable case, and so I followed the guidelines carefully. The first stage was fairly simple; I had to write a letter addressed to the Registrar[114] at the European Court of Human Rights and ask permission to make an application to petition the Court. I wrote this letter immediately and in it I made my objective in approaching the European Court as clear as possible, that it was to request the Court to intervene with the UK Government, and rule, that it should provide a domestic remedy for violations of the Convention Articles by its agents.

With the letter I was also required to include:

1.  a brief summary of my complaints,

2.  indicate which of the Commission rights I thought had been violated;

---

[114] European Court Registry employs many lawyers and administrative staff, to provide legal and administrative support, and draft decisions and judgements. It is divided into five sections, each with its own Registrar and Deputy Registrar, and cases were assigned on the basis of knowledge and the legal system concerned with each section. I took this to mean a section dealt with particular countries with a common language, and the section handling my case would therefore have staff with a UK legal background.

3.   state what remedies I had used;

4.   list the official decisions in my case, the date and the authority/court and the details of the decisions;

5.   Also needed were copies of the decisions.

This last item gave me yet another problem, because the official decisions on paper were meagre and vague, providing next to nothing which I could claim to be refusals of domestic remedies. There was really only one official decision which actually fitted the 'a domestic remedy' required by the Court, that was the brief refusal of the Attorney General to grant fiat. All other decisions were really a series of written refusals by the involved authorities to provide information which would have helped me to gain access to Higher Courts, in order to ask for a remedy.  Lesser formal decisions, had to be included though, to support to my contention of wilful mismanagement of the entire series of processes carried out over Alex's death, which had then culminated in an inappropriate inquest verdict. A selection of these papers was included with my letter of application, and the bundle was despatched to the Court Registry at the end of February 2000, almost fours years after Alex's death.

The principal function of the Registry is to process and prepare for adjudication applications lodged by individuals with the Court, and are assisted in this by Section Registrars.  Cases are assigned to the different sections on the basis of knowledge of the language and legal system concerned and therefore, I assumed my case would be dealt with by an official fully qualified in the UK legal systems, and who would advise the Section Registrar on English law, if he were not a British National.

I had been very impressed with the principles of the ECHR and its defence of the 'individuals' rights. After studying some of the recorded cases, I was further uplifted by the number of rulings which very often favoured the 'little man's interests' against that of the State. I began to feel quite confident and saw the door to achieving justice begin to open

Why on earth I was so confident that things would go smoothly for me with the European Court, I really do not know. Experience with the various

British authorities should have taught me to be wary of dealing with any official legal body without legal representation. Yet, at that stage I was still very green in matters of law, and had every confidence of receiving a fair and impartial hearing from the European Court. It wasn't too long before a letter, sent to me from the Registrar of Section III of the Registry, shook my confidence in the European Court the section to which my case had been allocated.

This letter signed by AM Austin for the Registrar and dated 15 May 2000, first acknowledged my application, and then continued to inform me, that under the case-law and practice for admissibility my attention had to be drawn to shortcomings in my application. The shortcomings were as follows:

> *'From your submissions it appears you wish to complain about your son's death and subsequent events.*
>
> *However insofar as you complain that you son died as a result of a hazardous homosexual event and that he died in cruel circumstances, you should note that the Court is not competent to hear complaints against private individuals.*
>
> *There is no right under Article 6 of the Convention to have criminal proceedings instituted against someone.'*

My reaction was one of dismay and disbelief, which demonstrates just how far my treatment at the hands of the British justice officials had undermined my trust in any justice system, because I immediately took this to be a repeat of British tactics to keep me out of court. Especially as I had at no time indicated to the Court that my objective was to obtain a private prosecution.

A copy of the letter was faxed to my friend John Smith with a note expressing my fear that my application was to be refused. He rang back almost at once, and assured me that the letter was probably only a formal way of requesting information, so as to clarify what was most likely a weakness in my submission, and his advice was to restate my intention in clearer more concise terms. I carried out this level-headed advice, and

231

wrote a more comprehensive letter explaining my position, and stressing two main points:

> 'In the opening of my application I informed the Registrar that I was necessarily acting as my own representative, having been denied legal aid and therefore legal guidance. Therefore, although my application may not have been in exact legal terms... it does however make it quite clear my complaints are against violations of Articles 1. 2. 3. 6. and 13, by the subordinates of the UK Government, and not against any private individual.
>
> Obviously my son's death is the crux of the whole matter, but the culpability and prosecution of an individual is a matter for the authorities and would have been resolved one way or another, had the authorities conducted their investigations to have accorded with the directives of the European Convention on Human Rights'.

In the hope that it might excuse any weaknesses in my presentation, I thought it was important to remind him in my reply, that from my very first approach to the British Courts, I had been forced by UK agents to act without legal funding which had successfully blocked any access to domestic remedies. With the letter I enclosed the post-mortem report and the inquest report which had been requested by the Registrar. Then once again I waited, this time in trepidation in case my application was rejected as it appeared to have been in the first letter from Ms Austin, and justice would once more elude me.

A.M.Austin, rank unknown, on behalf of the Registrar replied more quickly than I expected. My explanation had been acceptable and on the 16th June 2000, I received an application form and instructions on how to proceed. It stressed that the form had to be fully and accurately completed, because the Court would examine my petition on the basis of the completed form, but I was allowed to refer to other submissions made in previous correspondence. I was further advised to return the completed form promptly, as any delay could put my application outside the time limit, which was given in the letter as due to run out in six weeks. But this, according to my calculations, was two months short of the six months limit, and therefore did not give me sufficient time to send a well presented case. I wrote to the Registrar and pointed this out and asked for an extension, and this was granted. The final date for the Registry to receive and accept my application and full documentation was set as 17th September 2000.

Then followed one of the most hectic periods in my life, it was even more intensive than researching and writing a dissertation. However, by the beginning of September, I had completed a comprehensive account of all the circumstances of Alex's death and the events which followed, and all related to the MPS investigations, the CPS decisions and the coroner's inquest and verdict. This comprised a document consisting of approximately 30,000 words, and was professionally bound and labelled 'A Comprehensive Analysis'. The analysis file and a total of 60 documents, ranging from one to twenty pages in length, and bound into five separate files, were very carefully parcelled up and made ready for posting on the 5th September.

To ensure that the parcel arrived on time it was sent by the Post Office Courier Service at a cost of £33.55p, for guaranteed next day delivery, (6th). On my return home I immediately faxed AM Austin (who I now knew was M/s) and described in detail the contents of the parcel she was to expect next day. I then prepared to wait, in a mood of contented achievement, for a letter giving me the case registration number and an approximate date for the first hearing.

## Part 2 – When one door begins to opens...

It was an unexpected an unpleasant surprise to receive a reply from the Registry after only twelve days of posting the parcel. It was a very brief letter from M/s Austin but what she had to say, left me in a state of shocked disbelief:

> 'I acknowledge receipt of your telefaxed letter dated 5th September 2000. To date we have not received any documentation or application form referred to in your letter.

The letter was dated the 15th September but was not in my hands until the 18th, but it took a while for it to register that if the Registrar had not received my parcel, it was then too late for it to be accepted. It was already a day past the deadline of 17th September the last day, on which I had been warned, my application had to be in the hands of the Section III Registrar.

My first coherent thought when I was over the shock, was to contact John Smith for advice but he wasn't available. It was an hour or so before I realised that the obvious thing to do was to find out if my parcel had been despatched by the Post Office, but as it was actually situated in a village shop, it was half day closing. By nine o'clock next morning I drove the six miles to the village to check on the parcel, and fortunately the Post Master was able to confirm, that it been collected by the Courier in the afternoon of the day it was posted, and should have been delivered to Strasbourg Court the next morning. This gentleman, who knew how important the documents were, contacted PARCELFORCE-Worldwide enquiries for me and asked them to trace the parcel and requested that I should be contacted directly by phone when they had information.

The following morning, the export manager Nacem Din, rang me to say she had traced the parcel to Cologne and it had been despatched to Strasbourg on the morning of the 6th but although she had made several attempts to obtain delivery details from their agent, she had failed. The Strasbourg Registry had been contacted but claimed there no record of my parcel being delivered. M/s Din told me that she found this totally unacceptable and intended to contact Section III and speak to M/s Austin personally. By this time it was the 22nd of September, five days past the time limit and I had almost resigned myself to another failure in my justice quest.

Later, I think it was the same day; I had a second call from Nacem Din to tell me the result of her call to M/s Austin whom she found to be 'somewhat reluctant' to co-operate. The Courier manager had insisted that a careful search be made for my parcel, and eventually, it was located somewhere within the Court Registry, but it was not known how long it had been there, but it was immediately passed to the Section III Registrar. M/s Din had advised M/.s Austin that the Registry would be held responsible for holding up my application, as it was obvious that it had

234

arrived at the Registry on the guaranteed date (6th) and had been misplaced by the registry staff.[115] This news was reassuring but I still needed to have confirmation from the Registrar that my application had been accepted.

Where my parcel had been during the time it was posted until located in the Registry after the time limit expired, was never explained. Indeed when M/s Austin did eventually contact me, the matter was ignored, even though she confirmed its late receipt. Just one more very odd event to add to the long list in the chronicle of Alex's death, but which none of the various authorities involved deigned to explain.

I continued to be worried about the fate of my petition, but as the Registrar did not seemed to be in any hurry to put my mind at ease, I faxed M/s Austin on the 4th October 2000 and asked for a progress report. I received a letter dated 11th October in which she acknowledged the receipt of my application and documentation 'which arrived on the 18th September 2000. I noted that there was no reference to it either the misplacement of the parcel or the expiration of the deadline. But that didn't matter. The only thing that concerned me was the fact that my application had been registered and given a file number. The letter explained that my application was considered to have been introduced on the 18th April 2000, and a warning that it may take up to a year from the registration in April 2000 to have a decision.

I was thankful to be over the first hurdle but the next very important stage, would decide on the admissibility of my petition.

**Part three ... someone slams it in your face.**

This stage in petitioning is of vital importance to any applicant, because it is then that the decision is made, whether the petition will be deemed admissible, or not. The admissibility procedure appears to be fairly simple. Each application is assigned to a section, which in my case was Section III,

---

[115] Most details confirmed in letter from M/.s Din. Also received was a full refund of the postage from Parcel post as kind gesture for the distress caused, even though the Service was not responsible.

and the Section President assigns a judge rapporteur[116], who examines the case, and decides whether a three member Committee, as in my case, or a Chamber of the Court, should deal with the case. If the Committee decides that a complaint is admissible (that is, if it accepts an application) the complaint can be examined. However, the Court can reject any application which it considers inadmissible under Article 34[117] at any stage of the proceedings.

You can see then, that any prolonged wait for that decision can be very wearing on the nerves. That is why I wrote to the Registrar on April 15th 2001 asking for a progress report, on the grounds of my age and the five year period of Alex's death. This could have been a mistake as I may have drawn undue attention, and too close a scrutiny to my case. I should have remembered, that two unusual attempts to nullify my application had already been made by the Registrars advisors, which I had managed to rebut. One lesson which I have slowly, but surely, learned in my encounters with officialdom, is that the 'lesser' citizen, can incur the antagonism of Senior Government officials when they question or challenge their decisions, even when these officials known they are in the wrong.

There was no reply received to that query from M/s Austin, instead I was sent a very disturbing letter advising (or warning) me of an unexpected development, signed by the Section Registrar, S. Dolle:

> *'Further to Ms Austin's letter of May 15th 2000, I would inform*
> *you that in preparing your file for presentation to a single*
> *member of the Court acting as rapporteur, that has come to our*

---

[116] A judge rapporteur prepares a preliminary account of proceedings for committee, or a Chamber

[117] Article 34. The Court shall reject any application which it considers is incompatible with the provisions of the Convention or the protocols thereto, manifestly ill-founded, or an abuse of the right of application.

*attention that there may be further shortcomings in you application'.*

These alleged shortcomings given were quite short and there was no attempt to soften the blow:

*'My submission was out of time, because the final domestic remedy was given in 1997 by the Legal Aid Board when it refused me legal aid.*

*My efforts to obtain domestic remedies from the concerned authorities were merely attempts to keep the case open'*

The letter ended:

*'The Court may therefore decide to reject your case as being out of time.*

When I had recovered a little from the shock of receiving this letter, which appeared to me to be a third attempt from the Registrar to keep my case from the Court, I wrote a strong letter to S. Dolle (who I understood was not a British National) on the 31st July and I protested at the assumption that my attempts to gain other remedies were merely a strategy to keep the case open. Stating that my efforts were genuine attempts to obtain a second inquest which only a High Court had the power to grant, and that I thought I had acted well within the conditions of Article 35. I pointed out, that the granting or refusal of legal aid did not constitute a domestic remedy, in fact, the regulations of the Legal Aid Board made that quite clear. Its role was merely to provide legal aid to enable lower income applicants to have the benefit of qualified legal assistance in obtaining Court decisions. The Board had not the power to grant effective domestic remedies; therefore, being denied legal aid was not a legitimate reason for declaring my application inadmissible.

On the 2nd of August I wrote a similar letter addressed to Ms Austin, whose status was unclear, but who always appeared to be acting for the Registrar. My reason for writing was that, I felt certain it was at that level of Section III the Judge Rapporteur would have received advice on the admissibility of my application. It would then be on his advice that the three-man Committee would base their decision.

On the 8<sup>th</sup> of August M/s Austin replied to both letters, in a tone which I thought was unnecessarily confrontational, telling me that the jurisprudence of the Court did not recognise the additional steps I had taken as effective domestic remedies. In particular, the request under section 13 of the Coroner's Act 1988 was an **extraordinary** remedy and, further, the unsuccessful application for fiat did not start the time limit of six months. That sentence infuriated me because obtaining the Attorney General's fiat was the only course open to me. I was even more infuriated when she stated that it was insufficient for me to say I was not aware of the six months rule set out in Article 35, when I said no such thing. I had worked hard to stay within the time limit.

By now I could see failure looming ahead of me, but I wrote another letter and enclosed a copy of the Legal Aid Board policy and underlined the relevant sections which defined the limits of its powers. On the 30<sup>th</sup> of August Ms Austin acknowledged my letter and enclosures, and informed me that I would hear from the Court shortly. In fact the Court had made its decision on the 28<sup>th</sup> August 2001. The decision came into my hands on the 6<sup>th</sup> September 2001:

THE EUROPEAN COURT OF HUMAN RIGHTS (THIRD SECTION) *Sitting as a Committee composed of three judges:*

- *Mr W. FUHRMANN, President*
- *Mr .H. S. GREVE (Norwegian)*
- *Mr M. UGREKHELIDZE (Georgian)*
- *And Mr T .L EARLY (Deputy Section Registrar)*

The decision as I had feared was based only on the Legal Aid Board's decision; all other attempts were dismissed as not being required for the purpose of Article 35:

> *'It follows that the application has been submitted to late and must be rejected.' The Court declared the application inadmissible'.*

238

Even though I had been warned to expect rejection, I found it hard to accept, I felt physically sick. All I could think of was all that work, all those words, all those hours, all for nothing. I really did feel cheated out of justice, and it was very difficult to accept that it was the European Court which had let me down so badly on such a flimsy excuse; I had expected justice from the Convention.

From that moment I lost all faith in all Courts, British or European because I sensed that the hand of the UK government had reached into both these Courts and manipulated justice to suit its own ends. Sometime later I when I read several articles on how it had been revealed that National Governments were able to influence decisions through their nationals working in the Registry Sections, I felt justified in my suspicions of UK Government influence over the European Court decision in my case.

With the Court decision I received a brief letter from Mr T L Early advising me of the rejection and also that

> *'This decision is final and is not subject to any appeal to the Court or any other body'*

I may not have been able to appeal, but that did not stop me writing strong letter protesting at the conduct of the Section III officials and the misinterpretation of Article 35 to both the President of the Court and the Commissioner for Human Rights. It was a waste of paper and postage, because both of these Presidents replied to the effect it was not in their 'remit' to interfere in European Court affairs.

I gave up then. Someone had indeed slammed the door to justice in my face - and it had hurt.

# CHAPTER TWENTY

## The UK Government - The ECHR - Sadomasochism and Article 8

I have a theory why the strange course of action was taken by the authorities over Alex's death, and of the steps taken to prevent my appealing to the High Court to have the inquest verdict quashed, and why it is quite possible that the UK Government interfered with the course of justice in the European Court. It all stems back from the sadomasochistic circumstances of Alex's death and the status of those who were implicated in his death, and the reason why those unidentified high profile officials decreed that in the public interest', **"a murder such as this, needed to be conducted in strict secrecy".**[118]

My theory is this. During 1996, around the same time that Alex's death was being investigated, the UK Government was before the European Court as a defendant answering the charge of violation of Articles of the ECHR, but the one I am concerned with is the violation of Article 8 'the right to respect for private life'.

The case centred on a video, which had accidentally come into the possession of the police in 1990 during a routine search. It depicted these men indulging in extreme sadomasochistic practices, which involved deliberately inflicting severe pain on each other. As a result, all three were charged under 'The Offences against the Persons Act of 1861, Section 20 & 47:

> **Section 20** *"Whosoever shall unlawfully and maliciously wound or inflict grievous bodily harm upon another person... shall be liable to imprisonment..."*

> **Section 47** *"Whosoever shall be convicted on indictment of any assault occasioning actual bodily harm shall be liable to imprisonment..."*

---

[118] Letter from MPS Information Access Department.

The full case was actually a very complex and distressingly sordid affair, and resulted in all three men being sent for trial, found guilty and given prison sentences. They appealed against their convictions to the High Court on the grounds that consent to the practices should provide a defence, because they had inflicted harm on willing victims, and, that every person had the right to deal with his own body as he chooses. The Judges did not agree with this defence and on February 19th 1992 dismissed the appeal against their conviction. A year later, the case suffered the same fate when on appeal, to the House of Lords; it was dismissed on a majority vote.

The important point I am making is, that the convictions of the three men stood, because it had been established in English law, sadomasochism which involves cruelty and degradation of the victim, was under the Offences against the Persons Act 1861, a criminal act. Therefore, the three participants had been lawfully judged and convicted of a criminal offence; furthermore, it could not be argued that their consent to these practices was a viable defence against prosecution.

However, in an attempt to have their convictions overturned, the three men petitioned the European Court against the violation of their privacy under of Article 8 of the Human Rights Convention, by the UK Government. Unlike my own application, this one was considered admissible, and was preliminarily examined by a Chamber on 21st October 1996. In accordance with the President of the Court's decision; the hearing took place in public.

Singularly, the ECHR preparatory examinations would have proceeded concurrently with the secret investigations into Alex's death and the DPP's decision in September, not to prosecute the suspect charged with an unlawful death. The ECHR actual hearing was underway when at the end of November, the coroner decided to discontinue his own enquiries into Alex's case and to no longer contest the CPS non-prosecution decision, and very suddenly, released the body to the family for cremation.

I think that the decisions of both the DPP and the coroner were the result of the three convicted men's petition being sent to the European Court Chamber for examination. The petition was subsequently passed and put before the European Court in February 1997. Very briefly, the appellants argued that their case was one involving sexual expression rather than violence. Therefore, their prosecution and conviction amounted to interference with their 'private life' and was a violation of their Convention rights under Article 8. However, by then the coroner had successfully halted all further investigations in the circumstances of Alex's death, by giving a verdict of 'accidental death. He avoided making any reference to Simpson's interest in sadomasochism or related paraphernalia found at the scene of crime

The European Court dismissed the case. The Court upheld the UK Government' right to prosecute and convict the applicants under English law on the following grounds:

> *The court finds that the national authority were entitled to consider that prosecution and conviction of the applicants was necessary in a domestic society for the protection of health within the meaning of Article 8 -2*

The verdict was:

*THERE WAS NO VIOLATION OF ARTICLE 8 OF THE CONVENTION.*

One of the most important points I wish to stress was made by Judge Pettiti of the Court in order to demonstrate how seriously both the British Courts and the European Court viewed the offence of sadomasochism:

> *"The dangers of unrestrained permissiveness which can lead to debauchery, paedophilia or the torture of others have been highlighted. (At the Stockholm World Conference).*

> *The protection of private life means the protection of a person's intimacy and dignity, not the protection of his baseness or the promotion of criminal immoralism".*

There it is, both the British and the European Court had established that sadomasochism under English law was a criminal offence, and that consent was not a viable defence. It had also been established that the men had not been witnessed committing the offences, but videos and physical artefacts found on their premises were sufficient evidence for them to be charged and brought to trial and convicted.

There are similarities between the two cases but great differences in the ways the authorities dealt with them. Three men had quite properly been charged and convicted under the law, so why then, irrespective of whether Simpson had unlawfully killed Alex or not, were he and his associates never charged under the Offences against the Persons Act? The MRG Review recorded that physical artefacts associated with sadomasochism were found in Simpson's flat and he owned the camera containing a film, which when developed by the police, produced photographic evidence that such practices had taken place. One photograph showed the body of a man wearing a head device which the pathologist considered had been the cause of Alex's death. Furthermore Simpson had admitted to having an interest in bondage and sadomasochism. In one aspect though, the two cases differed greatly, in the first there was no unwilling victim, no dead body. But in Simpson's incident, there was. Death had been the result of a sexual practice which he and the others involved, must have known, was potentially lethal, and there is no doubt in my mind it had been inflicted on an unwilling victim, and it killed him.

The UK Government had gone through very expensive Court legal actions to defend its agents' actions in charging and successfully convicting three men under the Offences against the Person Act, yet had allowed another person and his unnamed associates, who had committed the same criminal offences to escape any penalty. More seriously, the UK Government had allowed its agents to protect the same persons who were responsible for a more serious criminal offence arising from sadomasochism, that of an unlawful killing. In effect, the UK Government had prosecuted one group for breaching the Offences against the Persons Act, a course which had the approval of the European Court, but had allowed another group to escape any penalty for the same crime by hiding the actual facts behind covert operations.

That is why I feel quite certain, that UK Government agents had interfered with the European Court of Justice in my case to prevent exposing the Government's double standards to the Court judges and possibly adversely affecting the admissibility of UK's case. The actions of its agents would not have stood up to full public and press scrutiny. Most certainly though such exposure of double standards would have been detrimental to the UK Government's standing within the European Community.

I think it also justifies my conviction that status and influence can, and has in Alex's case, perverted the course of Justice.

# CHAPTER TWENTY ONE

*Actions are what they are, and the consequences of them will be what they will be; why then should I desire to be deceived?[119]*

## Part one – Another source of help

I had no desire to remain deceived, but shortly after the European Court had declared my case inadmissible I found myself in a position where I had to remain temporarily deceived. For a month or two I felt very low over the entire situation and was beginning worry because thought I was sinking into a state of depression. Then, very suddenly, I found myself almost crippled by a blocked leg artery and had to seek my GPs advice. He diagnosed that I had developed two stress related conditions, an unacceptably high blood pressure and an under active thyroid. After following his treatment and his good advice, I put Alex's case to one side until such time that I was I was ready to cope with normal activities again. The treatment I had for the deficient thyroid and the blood pressure worked wonders. After a year of treatment, the depression had disappeared, so I started to resume my usual routines, including re-examining Alex's case.

I spent sometime going over the papers relating to all my legal actions hoping to find some loophole which would help me restart legal action, but it was a forlorn hope. It seemed the only possible action was a private prosecution and apart from knowing that it could be an expensive course of action, I had no idea what it entailed or how to proceed. I decided that it would be worth my while to pay for a solicitor's advice on the matter. The solicitor I choose, who was highly recommended, was based in Lincoln, Mr David John.

Although I am very grateful for the help given to me by Mr John and his associate Mr Bescoby, I won't spend too much time on this because it was another failure. Both solicitors were extremely interested in my case and willing to look at the possibility of a private prosecution or try to find an alternative. It was decided by Mr Johns that it would be advisable for me

---

[119] Paraphrase of a Rolls Chapel sermon, (1736)

to first obtain a barrister's opinion on my situation. He further suggested that I should apply for legal funding to cover the QC's expenses, and I did so.

It was refused on virtually the same grounds used by the then Legal Aid Board, mainly; it was not in the 'public interest'. This time I appealed against the decision and in due time I was granted a personal hearing. Mr John was absent at the time but for some reason his associate Mr Bescoby, decided I could cope with the interview on my own. That was grave mistake. For a start I arrived at the venue much too early and was very nervous and I became even more unnerved by being kept waiting to be called. When the chairman of the Appeal Board did appear he asked me where my solicitor was, and when I told him I was on my own, he looked piercingly at my white hair, and then said 'Oh dear me! That is unfortunate.' It certainly was for me, I sensed at that moment I had already lost the appeal, and the interview that followed was an ordeal. Presenting a comprehensive case in writing was one thing, but facing an interrogation from four men, who sat opposite me at the far end of a very long refectory table, was another. I felt so intimidated and it was all I could do to answer their questions, let alone give a convincing argument against a group of experts who continually used the coroner's inquest and verdict in framing their questions.

When they dismissed me and told me I would have their decision soon, it was obvious to me I was not to be given a grant and I told them so. I did my best muster an air of disdain and indifference towards them as I went through the door, but in fact I could hardly see through the tears of disappointment and frustration. Once again legal aid had obstructed my path to justice for my son.

It wasn't quite the end though; Mr John spent time and effort and obtained a free, time limited, barrister's opinion for me. Unhappily I had to précis my whole case into a hundred and fifty words. I felt this brevity weakened my argument but Mr John must have given quite an amount of information over the phone to the barrister. I think this gentleman did a thorough examination of that information, and his advice to me covered 1-3 pages. Unfortunately I seem to have lost the written report, but basically his advice was that it would be very difficult to overturn the coroner's verdict and that I should let the matter rest there. He also said that in his opinion, I would have been better served if the first solicitor had tried for a private prosecution against Simpson. Mr John regretfully could do no more for me, and had to withdraw his assistance, but I will always very grateful for all his understanding and his help. Incidentally he made no charge.

After that, I suppose I fretted over my failures and continually hunted through my files trying to find some solution which would bring a satisfactory closure to Alex's death. Eventually, the stress pulled down my health again. In May 2003 I had a stroke and that put me into hospital. I was paralysed down one side and my speech was affected. I actually made a very good recovery but it took time and a compulsory, prolonged abstinence from stressful physical and mental activities. It was due to excellent physiotherapy and scrupulously following the routines laid down for me that I was eventually restored to about eighty percent of my previous standard of health. By the middle of 2004 I was ready to take up the battle for justice once more.

Ready yes! But ready to do WHAT? I seemed to have done everything possible and had failed at every thing I had tried. Even so, I was not prepared to accept complete failure just yet, and again I closely searched through all the information I held but could find no new approach. Then quite unexpectedly I saw on BBC news a small item on the pending retirement of Sir John Stevens the Metropolitan Commissioner of Police. It occurred to me that with his elevated rank he might not always be fully aware of the direction of lower rank officers' *modus operandi*. I believe that in general, the higher the rank the more reliance is placed on investigation reports supplied by subordinates, especially if cases are deemed to be low profile.

### Part 2 -The door begins to open – again!  The Metropolitan Commission & the Murder Review Group

It took me several days to plan out my letter, which was intended to describe in full detail an account of all police investigations and conduct from May 4th 1996 onward. I did not want that letter to be taken as only a complaint but also as a strong, convincing argument for a case of mismanagement by the police into an unlawful killing, which would persuade the Commissioner into ordering a further investigation into Alex's suspicious death. I included with the six page letter a number of selected documents and letters relating to the police, the CPS and the coroner whom I thought would help validate my request for his intervention. I posted the bulky parcel about the middle of November 2004. I expected there would be the usual long delay before I would receive an answer. I braced myself for another disappointment.

There was to be no disappointment this time, instead I had an unexpectedly speedy reply, my letter had worked. About month later by e-mail, I had this response sent in eye catching, blue print, and because of its importance and the revelation, I quote the e-mail in full:

**14 December 2004**

"Dear Mrs Barrack,

Your letter and correspondence sent to the Commissioner has been passed to Commander Baker who is Head of Homicide for London. I am sorry to learn of the death of William.

Thank you for providing such a comprehensive report; I am tasked into researching the matter further in the first instance. This means drawing all the police files and coroner's reports. Once this is completed I will present all documentation to Commander Baker for review.

I expect this will carry over into the New Year. I shall update you with what progress I have made, in any event by 24th January 2005.

I trust you will have a pleasant Christmas and happy New Year although I am sure William's passing will never make these times easy."

Keith Giannoni DCI
Staff Officer to Commander Baker.

The tears flowed and this time I let them flow, because they were tears of release, at last someone had responded to my appeals with sympathy, understanding and above all had accepted that my account of events could be true.

I did not have to wait until the New Year. I barely had time to absorb this new development fully, before I had another e-mail, however, not a rejection this time:

**22 December 2005**

Dear Mrs Barrack,

Commander Baker has reviewed the original police file together with the papers you have submitted. As a result he has asked our Murder Review Group (MRG) to carry out a review of the matter.

An officer from the MRG will be in contact with you. (Most likely now, in the New Year) This officer will explain the procedure and depth of the review planned.

Kind regards
Keith.

Although this news was an uplifting message to have for Christmas, it was also a poignant reminder that Alex had died an unnatural death, had died in fact by criminal action.

Criminal Homicide is defined as the killing of a human being by another and includes murder and manslaughter.[120] After eight and a half years of official denial, the MPS had admitted Alex's death was investigated as a homicide from the first day. But the question remained. Why had it been conducted in such secrecy? I hoped to learn the real reason from the MRG team.

---

[120] Legal Glossary, Webster's New World College Dictionary

I had up until then, never heard of the Murder Review Group but it was in fact, a comparatively new body, set up in 2000 in response to the management irregularities and their aftermath, in the Stephen Lawrence case investigations. Its function is the re-examination of unresolved murder cases and serious crimes, whose non-resolution are raising public and relatives concern and the calling for further action. The Group is composed of retired police officers of good standing and reputation, who work independently of the police and CPS. The cases are referred to the Group by Senior Police authorities for their independent and impartial assessments.

The MRG review officers examine only one case at a time and the two officers assigned to Alex's case were Review Officer Mr John Ahern and Research Officer Mr Rowlands. They contacted me by phone very quickly after the New Year and arranged a meeting in my home for 12th January 2005. I decided it would be a good policy to meet the team with a witness present and called upon a very good, level headed friend to be with me, Mrs Valerie Whiteman.

I must say from our first meeting the team, both Valerie and I considered these two gentlemen had been well chosen for the work, and we accepted their assurance that they were completely independent of any authority, and that their examination of the facts and their conclusions would be honest and impartial. Neither Valerie nor I had any reason to change that good opinion any time later.

Mr Ahern began the talks by giving us two warnings. One was that it was a time taking procedure but that he would keep in regular contact over the progress of the investigations. The second warning, very tactfully worded, was that some of their findings might reflect upon Alex himself, as present day advanced forensic evidence might show he had some responsibility for his own death. My reply was that I had always been ready to accept that possibility, even though I had believed it to be unlikely. The mention of forensic examinations gave me the opportunity to introduce some discrepancies in the inquest forensic evidence particularly relating to finger printing analysis, when so much importance had been attached to the handling of the head device. Val pointed out that it could have shown whether Alex had concurred to or had resisted wearing the head device.

Mr Ahern replied that they had noted this omitted evidence and that was one of the first items in his agenda.

Although I have referred to this in earlier chapters, Mr Ahern gave us a complete description of the obstructive head device and how it was operated. According to his information, the device consisted of two head shaped plastic bags, sealed together at the base and forming a cuff. There was a small valve into the inner lining, and larger outer valve in the cuff, by which air was pumped between the two bags. This air pressure sealed the smaller valve, so cutting off further air supply to the inner bag, and eventually reduced the oxygen supply to the brain. This dreadful apparatus was intended to promote the condition of hypoxia and increase sexual gratification. Then Mr Ahern added a very significant fact, which had not been mentioned by any official before, that the head device needed **two** people to operate it.

I listened with horror to this graphic description of what to me was an extremely nasty form of torture, and if I had any previous doubts about Alex wearing the bag, which I had not, they would have vanished then and there. But, I already knew with absolute certainty that my son, a chronic asthmatic and with a fear of confined spaces, would never, never, have voluntarily worn such an evil device. I could see more surely at that point, why this information on a two man operation had been deliberately withheld from both Alex's father and I, when we questioned Mr Ensor of York CPS about the bag in 1998. It was because of Simpson's status in the CPS and revealed why Simpson, against all the evidence, had maintained that Alex had not worn the head bag. To have admitted it would have incriminated himself or others present because one of them must have inflated the bag. And just as surely someone had to take the bag off after he died.

I asked Mr Ahern why this important fact had not been revealed at the inquest, he replied that he was not authorised to comment on the coroner's conduct, (or on the decision of the  CPS) but could only examine the inquest report in relation to the other evidence and witness statements. Perhaps I was a bit obtuse, but I couldn't see how that could be done, without also querying the coroner's conduct in relation to omitting essential evidence.

251

This was quite a short meeting, which had been arranged originally to advise me on the purpose of the review and the procedure to be followed. I may have jumped the gun a little on my questions, but I felt I have gained more information than ever before. Both Mr Ahern and Mr Rowlands told me they would do their best to bring about a satisfactory resolution for me, and if they should unearth incriminating evidence they would not hesitate to place it in the hands of the CPS for a prosecution. This would be done even if such action was against my wishes. Valerie and I assumed that that meant, even if I considered it would be detrimental to Alex's character and ask that it be withheld. After promising to keep in regular touch with me, they left for London

As soon as I was on my own I placed a careful account of this conversation on the computer, which Valerie later the same afternoon, confirmed was a reliable record. This practice I continued with telephone calls, until the Review Team made the final visit.

Mr Ahern telephoned me on the 17th January 2005 and it was a brief call. I was first asked to verify Valerie's full name and address 'for the record' but the main reason for the call was to assure me that an examination of official papers had commenced, and that an independent assessment of the forensic evidence had been requested. He promised to keep me informed of his progress at regular intervals, especially if there were important developments.

His next phone call came after an impressively short period, on the 28th January, only eleven days later. Mr Ahern had already commenced examining the papers; files were still being requested and drawn. He confirmed that a fingerprinting officer had been present at the scene of crime and that MRG had requested that the forensic file be drawn for examination by the team. He was pleased to say that that a forensic expert had already been engaged and within the week would start to examine the files as they became available. He then added, 'I will be in touch again, but I have to advise you that it would appear that the procedure would be prolonged.'

I didn't care to much for the rider, but as things seemed to be shaping well, I decided my misgiving were probably a reaction to previously disappointing experiences, and that on the whole everything was going quite well.

# CHAPTER TWENTY TWO

*It is folly to expect (police) men to do all that they may be reasonably expected to do.*[121]

## Part 1 – The MRG reinvestigation of Alex' case

It was another month before I heard from Mr Ahern again, when he phoned and asked if Mr Rowlands and he could call, weather permitting, on the following Thursday, 3rd March, to update me on the situation as it stood at present. I thought that it was much too early for him to have achieved any positive results, and so I asked him to give me an explanation for the visit. 'There was, he told me, no resolution and they had not drawn any definite conclusions, but he would rather outline all that had been done, when he came. When he added 'I will explain to you, why there is to be a delay.' I could hear the warning bell in the distance. I asked him if this meant there was to be a setback for me. He replied 'By no means, but it is necessary for us to explain things to you in person'. I asked no more questions and agreed to the Thursday meeting in my home.

This scenario was becoming so familiar, build my hopes up, and then knock them down, and I began mentally to brace myself to receive the inevitable bad news at the next meeting. However on the 2nd March a message was left on the answering phone that the meeting had to be cancelled due to atrocious weather, but Mr Ahern would ring me next day and give me as much information over the phone that he deemed possible.

When I told Valerie about the postponed meeting and expressed my fears that things were not going the way I had expected, she commented 'I think perhaps you are over reacting, just wait and see'. I said 'may be' but some how I knew I would be proved right in the end.

I don't know why my affairs are never straight forward and this is true of my dealings with the Murder Review Group (MRG). In all, I have three accounts of progress at different stages in the investigation by the MRG Investigation Officer Mr Ahern, all basically the same with similar contents

---

[121] Paraphrase of quotation – Richard Whately. 1787-1863

but introducing slightly different points relating to the same event, but for the sake of brevity I will analyse them together, but utilising the lengthy verbal report given by Mr Ahern at our final meeting, as the main source of reference, but using the sequence of events listed in the official document, including the variations I noted between the verbal reports and the official document.

First though I need to say a little about the long telephone Mr Ahern made the 3$^{rd}$ March, as he had promised, but which strongly signalled that the review was not going too well. He started the conversation with the cautionary warning, "…**that there was certain evidence that could not be changed, although hindsight indicated that investigations could have been handled in a different way, and I certainly would have done so.**" I found this confusing and very alarming, and so requested he explain further and was told, **that forensic evidence, fingerprinting and DNA analysis, were now the main lines of investigation and they were pushing on with this.**

With regard to the fingerprints the MRG Team were still waiting for the report and Mr Ahern would request more urgent action. However, there was a report on the DNA swabs taken in 1996 from the small inflation tube of the mask which contained a mixture of DNA, and certain numbers of the DNA belonging to Alex had been identified, but were not strong enough evidence to prove he had worn the mask. However, breakdown techniques in 2005 had vastly improved and more numbers were being identified from DNA models, therefore Mr Ahern had requested a further break down of Alex's DNA.

DNA is a very complicated scientific subject but I did a simple breakdown of the subject to help me understand the importance of DNA testing, but I do not guarantee that it is accurate.

DNA (Deoxyribonucleic acid) is a chemical found primarily in the nucleus of cells. DNA carries the instructions for making all the structures and materials the body needs to function. An individual's DNA is unique. It is virtually a 'blueprint for life. DNA is found in the nuclei of every cell of the body, and the chromosomes carry the coded information. DNA is arranged into groups called genes that are inherited. They in turn are arranged into two entwined ribbons of DNA arranged into four building blocks called bases, known by their initials ACGT. The ribbons have been compared to a zip fastener, but in order to fasten the teeth, that is the ACGT bases, two initials must pair in a particular sequence. These bases are numerous and it is a complicated process identifying the numbers in an individual's particular DNA, which I do not fully understand, although, only a tiny sample is required for analysis. Eventually, when the processing of the sample is completed, an x-ray film will reveal the DNA as patterns of dark bands, not unlike supermarket bar codes, and with the exception of identical twins, every individual's DNA has unique a pattern.[122]

This very simplified version of DNA testing, compiled after Mr Ahern's call, helped me to understand the great importance of DNA testing in forensic investigations and also raised my expectations that it would prove my conviction that Alex had worn the head device. After all, only a tiny sample was needed for a successful analysis, and at the very least, they had that. I should have known better than to expect such convincing proof, because, what emerged from that last meeting with Mr Ahern and Mr Rowlands left me wondering who the victim was, Alex or Simpson and which of the two was entitled to the protection of the law?

The last meeting with The MRG Team took place on Wednesday 27th April 2005 with Valerie Whiteman as my witness. Mr Ahern had brought a large file of documents with him to which he constantly referred. He began his verbal report by telling me that he had been instructed to conduct a review into the Police investigations into the death of William Alexander Barrack. However, according to the official redacted[123] document created June 1st 2005, and obtained several months later, it was referred to as a review of the investigations into the **murder** of William Alexander Barrack; this was the very first time the term murder had been used by any justice official.

Part two of the review briefly covered the circumstances of Simpson's version of his taxi journey to the London Apprentice club, the meeting with Alex and the journey back to the flat. These events has already been discussed and dissected by me in previous chapters. There were, however,

---

[122] Taken from Brian Lane's - The Encyclopaedia of Forensic Medicine (1991)
[123] All names of witnesses and officials, with the exception of the Investigation team were marked by series of X's

several entries, which were of particular interest, and some were disquieting. One of the most disquieting statements made by Mr Ahern was to the effect, that although an investigation was set up by DI Baff and DS Bathie – the review was unable to establish that they had created a policy document in relation to the investigation. I asked him, not without good reason, if the absence of any policy explained the many anomalies in the case that don't fit together? Mr Ahern was unable to say that it could. I told him that in my opinion it was more than likely than not that there was such a document and that it was to the advantage of the Metropolitan Police that it should not be traced. No comment was made on that.

Mr. Ahern continued his verbal report, saying that after interviewing the Hospital Registrar; the police went to Simpson's flat, while he was taken straight to Limehouse police station where he made a statement giving his account of the events. He was then released on bail until September. Mr Ahern could not say whether the release was before the autopsy and the natural death report, or later in the day, after Alex's missing persons data was entered on the computer. It seems possible to me that it was before the autopsy; otherwise he would have been released without bail after the pathologist had reported that the death was from natural causes.

### Part 2 - MRG review - DNA & fingerprint analysis

Several of the anomalies listed below are taken from Mr Ahern's verbal discussions or are contained in the MRG Report. They mainly concern Simpson's statements made during the interview following his arrest on suspicion of manslaughter on 12 July 1996, the Review Report on investigations carried out by the Police.

- The autopsy conclusions of Dr Heath on the manner and time of Alex's death were put to Simpson, but he insisted that his previous account of a sudden death was the correct one.

- Several items of clothing were found strewn about floor, but as Alex's clothing was taken to the hospital, and Simpson was fully dressed, it was not known who owned the clothing. *Or was this a carefully arranged scene to fit in with Simpson's account of acting speedily in an emergency? If this was so, then the advanced stages of death would give the lie to that statement, which was only one among many false statements made by Simpson, yet the CPS saw no reason to charge him with perjury.*[124] *Or for the coroner to give the more fitting open verdict.*

- As previously stated, the police took possession of several items, which were found in the bathroom, and the lounge relating to extreme sexual activities, including the string with four red balls attached. *Mr Ahern could not say why this item was not seized .or forensically examined, even though it may have been cut from Alex's legs.*[125]

- Singularly the obstructive head device was not among the items, found in those two rooms; the police had found it a drawer in the bedroom. *(This could be taken as a deliberate attempt to hide the bag. No mention of the location of the device was mentioned at the inquest.)*

- 'No report was available of exactly on which date Alex's clothing came into police possession, but a police constable, name obliterated, thought it might have been the 16th of May when he found only one piece of evidence in the pockets, and that was a tablet which he identified as an ecstasy tablet.' *This tablet was not sent for a toxicology analysis to confirm this amateur opinion.* Mr Ahern could not say why none of Alex's effects were ever returned, especially the small amount of currency found in his clothing'

- 'It was not known when it was established where Alex lived or whether a search was made of his flat'. *I know when they had the address, because I gave it to the police myself, on the 14th May, and I can confirm that the flat was never searched even for drugs before I cleared it on the 17th May. I did not find a second inhaler.*

---

[124] Inquest report – Mr Martins letter
[125] Dr Heath's statement at the inquest.

This lack of investigations into the drug situation I found extraordinary. It was known from day one, that Alex had taken ecstasy and I would have expected a search to have made of his flat, and certainly, that enquires would be made at The London Apprentice for a possible supplier. Also, very significantly, Simpson was in possession of three bottles of amyl nitrate which is a prescription only drug, yet there is no record of any enquiries being into his illegal possession of the drug. Nor were there any investigations made into how he had acquired it, or to discover who his supplier was.[126] Simpson did voluntarily admit to the coroner that he would use it on other persons. No doubt he made similar statement to the police, but not until days after, when it became known that Alex had been a chronic asthmatic. This drug possession was another offence of Simpson's which the CPS chose to ignore.

Although Alex's blood was tested for other drugs it was not tested for amyl nitrate, and the reason given was that it evaporates very quickly. That may be so if there is along delay in performing the autopsy, and if the first PM was performed only a matter of hours after death, as Dr Heath had claimed, then I would have expected him to have asked for an urgent analysis in case there were still traces of amyl nitrate in Alex's blood. Although there certainly would not be, if as I suspect, the bloods were taken twelve days later.

One other point in relation to drugs and other substances is that although Simpson was actually arrested, he refused to give any samples, yet the drug review does not specify the type of samples requested from him; blood or intimate body samples. Had this case gone to trial, as I believe it should have done, then, according to the Police Manual, inferences from such a refusal could have been drawn by the court.[127]

- At the time of his arrest, Simpson was questioned on the differences between Dr Heath's autopsy findings and his account of events, Simpson insisted that his account of the time and manner of Alex's death was as he had previously stated.

---

[126] Amyl nitrate – increases sex arousal and reduces inhibitions
[127] Blackstone's EVIDENCE AND PROCEDURE 2001. p277

Although Simpson had given different accounts to several medical personnel and the police, the report does not specify which account he was referring to. Oddly though, although there were many inconsistencies in Simpson's account given in his inquest evidence to those given in two statements to the police, the coroner appeared not to have noticed them. He even preferred Simpson's version over Dr Heath's factual, but belated medical conclusions. The coroner even excluded the Scene of Crime Officer (SCO) from giving evidence at the inquest and important forensic evidence was never revealed. Mr Ahern had noticed these omissions.

During the long verbal report Mr Ahern made to me, I raised the subject of the Police individual note books, which he had said previously, could provide important evidence and interpretations of the evidence noted 'on the spot' by each police officer concerned. However, when he requested these notebooks they could not be traced. On page 85 of the Police Manual a reference is made to cases where police notebooks could be used as points of reference in court, and have on occasions provided evidence of collusion between officers. That really makes me wonder why in this case, the notebooks are missing?

It is my practice, which I had developed as a nurse, to closely observe the mannerisms and facial expressions of patients, and staff, which helped me to assess the integrity of information or reports I was receiving. I retained the habit for many years and from habit observed Mr Ahern and Mr Rowlands carefully during the long meeting and his lengthy oral report. Mr Ahern, I thought, was not as comfortable with me or as confident in manner as at our first meeting. Mr Rowlands contributed very little to the conversation, only glancing at me occasionally.

As the report continued I had a growing impression that both review officers were unhappy about the way the investigation had progressed. Mrs Valerie Whiteman, my friend and witness, on the other hand, told me later, that she thought the report covered the facts satisfactorily. In a way she was right because in as far as he could go, Mr Ahern had done his best to prove that the original investigation was faulty, but I could see that he was handicapped by the very restricted information he had been able to draw from the files. This became even more apparent when the finger printing and DNA analysis came under discussion.

In respect of other evidence, excluding fingerprinting and DNA, Mr Ahern told me that there were areas where he was unable to say whether or not the police had made adequate enquiries, particularly those weak areas concerning the pre-death results. Here I think he meant that time and inefficiencies in investigations had undermined the value of such evidence. These were the reasons he had to concentrate on the other forensic evidence, the fingerprinting and DNA.

**Finger printing and DNA – the results**

Mr Ahern, at the March meeting, had explained to me that his review was handicapped by the deficiencies in the original investigations, and the way the evidence had been handled. Therefore, his obtaining a satisfactory result from the reinvestigation would depend on the improved methods of analysing fingerprinting and DNA samples. I fervently hoped that the tests from both would provide conclusive results that Alex death was an unlawful killing, and resulted from asphyxiation when the obstructive device was forcibly applied to his head. Even then I began to have doubts as it was becoming almost a habit to expect adverse results from any investigations. Unfortunately future events would once again I had anticipated correctly.

At the first meeting in December I had referred to the absence of fingerprint analysis at the inquest and Valerie who was present, had pointed out it would have shown whether or not Alex had worn the mask. The review officers had both noted this absence of such important evidence. Unfortunately they were unable to say how it could have affected the verdict as their writ did cover the coroner's conduct of the inquest.

In April, when Mr Ahern had told me that because of incomplete or missing forensic evidence, and that as the forensic evidence of fingerprinting and DNA analysis, were now the main lines of investigation, they were pushing with them. It was felt that as the techniques for testing in both these areas had vastly improved since 1996, more positive results would be produced to improve the case, and increase the likelihood of CPS action, by reinforcing the opinions of the three medical experts against the misleading evidence of Roberts Simpson.

# Fingerprinting - Analysis.

On the phone, before the final meeting, Mr Ahern said that police had confirmed that a fingerprinting officer was present at the scene of crime and that MRG had requested the Forensic fingerprint file for examination. The forensic report had been recovered and there were fingerprints and markings on the surface, but there was no conclusive evidence that some were Alex's.

I found this unacceptable and asked what was meant by inconclusive evidence but his explanation I found even more unacceptable. He said that Alex's fingerprints had been taken at the mortuary. **Please note this – "They had only been taken for identification purpose for the Missing Person Bureau and had been disposed of soon after identification."** Therefore, as Alex had no criminal record there was no police record of his prints. When I asked why the post mortem finger prints had been destroyed or why new ones had not been taken when death was known to be suspicious, and the body had been available for seven months, Mr Ahern stated 'no explanation was available.' This raises the question - how then did the CPS accept and consider a case when no fingerprint report was available?

Mr Ahern continued by saying that some of the fingerprints found on the bag had not been identified, but even by using the new techniques on the fingerprints, there was no way of comparing Alex's against them. Therefore, unless new evidence on Alex's finger printing could be found, this forensic line had to be set aside. I still had had several glossy birthdays and Christmas cards Alex had sent to me stored in a protective box, which I offered to Mr Ahern as I thought they might still retain Alex's prints. However Mr Ahern rejected my offer saying he did not think they would help. Frankly, I don't accept this or any other of these explanations, not when this was a suspicious death, which was investigated as a murder.

To me, the whole fingerprint business savoured of being a contrived situation to assist the guilty rather than give justice to the victim. Therefore to have located a source of fingerprints would have been an embarrassment to the department. So then I asked if Simpson had wiped or interfered with the head device in any way, the reply was 'it appears not' as the police had taken immediate possession of the device and they reported no interference. If Simpson didn't, then someone else either interfered with the evidence or Mr Ahern was not given the complete report, which should have covered other areas of the bag. I will explain this when the DNA findings are considered.

All the above comments made orally to me during the telephone calls and the verbal discussions on the MRG report, were inexplicitly omitted from the MRG document, which surprisingly were, not covered in the MRG official report. What was entered into the report on fingerprinting was brief and extremely inadequate for an important official record.

> "The mask was fingerprinted at the time and two palm marks and one fingerprint were obtained. A number of other marks were found on plastic bags and correspondence from within XXXXXx's flat. None of the marks was identified as belonging to Alex. A further request was made in March 2005 for the outstanding marks to be checked against NAFIS but with negative results. It is not possible at this time to search 'Palm prints' against any data base." The review has not identified further forensic opportunities in this case."

All that left me wondering what was the point of checking these 'marks' against any data base if they had none of Alex's 'marks' to compare. That however cannot be correct, because Alex was said to have drank vodka and tonic at the flat, and surely he would use a glass and have left both fingerprints and DNA evidence on the surface. If, as it has been stated, the SCO attended the scene to collect forensic evidence, he most certainly would have carried out this task and also he would have found Alex's prints on other items in the flat. In my opinion, it can be taken as certain that the SOC would obtain a copy of Alex's fingerprints, taken at the mortuary, for analysis and comparison of evidence by forensic experts. What then, became of this copy?

Nevertheless, even in the face of all these inconsistencies, the conclusion of the review team was that they were certain that the palm marks did not belong to Alex and therefore there was little point in trying to identify them when a data base became available. How the Review Team could be so certain of anything in the face of so many conflicting statements and inconsistencies in the evidence, is beyond my comprehension. No one seems to have considered that Alex's prints were not on the bag because he didn't handle it enough. On the other hand, the smudged palm marks could have been his, and most likely were, if someone else pushed the bag on to his unsuspecting head, then instinctively he would  raised his hands and try to remove it, smearing his  own palm prints in the process. I faired no better when the DNA analysis was discussed in the MRG Review.

## DNA - Analysis.

Although we had a long discussion on the question of Alex's  DNA at the last meeting, and although he gave details on the fingerprint report, the written review on DNA sampling didn't match up to all that was discussed verbally. Nor did it fully answer the questions I had asked of Mr Ahern.

The MRG preliminary examination of the earlier report on the DNA analysis, showed it to have some elements of Alex's DNA, Mr Ahern therefore called on the services of a Special Advisor from the Forensic Science Services at Huntingdon, to carry out a further analysis, who carried out further examination from the extracts taken from the mouthpiece of the hood and a sample of Alex's blood. According to the Review:

> "A mixed profile was obtained from the DNA relating to the mouthpiece of the hood at least four contributors to the profile. It was the opinion of the scientist that there was nothing to suggest that Alex contributed any significant amount of the DNA to the mixed profile.
>
> There was no support for the proposition that Alex was the last to wear the hood and use the mouthpiece"

At the inquest it had been recorded that four elements of Alex's DNA had been isolated but not enough to establish that he had worn the mask. I had noted at that time that only the 'tube' had been examined, but did not fully realise the significance of that until that last meeting with Mr Ahern. I questioned why it had been impossible when DNA experts had claimed that only tiny sample was needed for analysis, Mr Ahern explained that the tube was so small the DNA profiles were 'so scrambled' that it was impossible to separate them.

I found the whole explanation very difficult to accept, what was more difficult to understand was that so much significance had been given to the DNA in the tiny air tube but there was no mention of any DNA analysis of the much larger area of the inner surface of the head bag. That was why I asked if the bag had been wiped, but the police had insisted it had not. I can't accept the police denial, I am absolutely certain that any wearer would have deposited large quantities of specific DNA from his nose and mouth, unless of course steps were taken:

1. To have been very carefully washed out, to remove any DNA trace

2. DNA was present but purposely not reported on to protect the identity of other wearers.

3. A report was made but deliberately mislaid.

4. The bag examined was not the one Alex was wearing that night.

There is an entry in the MRG report that several plastic bags were examined for fingerprints, but nothing was said about their purpose. I hardly think though, that entry would refer to plastic bags used merely for storage.

So ended my high hopes for conclusive DNA evidence.

### Part 3 – The MRG Review conclusions – exit the team
*'The rule of evidence 1745...its general principle to produce the best possible evidence from the best possible source, still holds good today*

The conclusions of the Review team in the written report make interesting reading but in general they fail to live up to the above principle. These are given in less positive terms that were given in the final oral report. Some or the conclusions I consider to be inaccurate, some less enlightening but others are simply infuriating. My impression is that my own conclusions on the improper conduct of the case were confirmed, but the time that had elapsed and the absence of many documents and items of physical evidence had proved greater obstacles to reopening the case that Mr Ahern, Mr Rowlands and Commander Baker of the London Homicide had anticipated. Instead of action, the Review offered me only a mixture of facts, excuses, misinterpretations, inadequate explanation or no explanation at all.

The review conclusion did agree with me that there was little doubt that Simpson had lied when giving his account of what happened in his flat that night. *(Yet there was no prosecution for perjury.)* However, the police investigation had failed to establish what happened to Alex and the Review fared no better. All efforts to establish that Alex had worn the mask were unsuccessful. The MRG Report stated "But it seems unlikely that **if** he was wearing the mask he was forced to do so" I totally disagree with all that, the police knew perfectly well what had happened to Alex, why and how he died, and who was responsible.

In conclusion number 1 of the Review agreed that the evidence of the Paramedics, the Consultant at the Royal London and the evidence of the Pathologist as to the condition of the body gave strength to the argument that Alex died some considerable time prior to the 999 call, and therefore Simpson was lying. *(More perjury, and yet, still no prosecution).*

Number 3 is meaningless, when it states "At the inquest the coroner heard all that evidence, but there is no indication within the court papers that he wished the matter to be referred back to the CPS". because, as Dr Chan gave an inquest verdict of accidental death, he would not have been expected to do so. Here someone is confused, as it was **before** the inquest, that the then coroner twice referred the case back to the CPS when they refused to prosecute Simpson. *(I will explain why 'then. is underlined later).*

Number 4 conclusion states that "...the worst scenario is that Alex did put on the mask and in doing so restricted his breathing, which resulted in his death". I reject that scenario, but even if it was true it does not justify Simpson's criminal offences in failing to call immediately for help or his obstructing the course of justice. I find it insulting for the Review team to defend that callous behaviour by saying, "Simpson, either in panic or for reasons of self preservations, bearing in mind his position in the CPS

266

removed the mask and time elapse which allowed *rigor mortis* to set in." That objectionable excuse though, actually endorses my view that status and influence does work against cause of justice, it certainly worked in favour of Simpson.

Number 5 conclusion dealt with Alex's property and the fact that it was missing and prevented him being identified, and lists two reasons: One, that as a homosexual it was the normal practice for him not to carry any identification *(But that would not explain his missing keys or money.)* Two, it may be Simpson removed the identification in order to delay the process. In my opinion the second is the most likely reason, as I am reasonably certain that Alex's key tab bore the name of the Housing Association which rented him the flat.

Number 6 conclusion simply states that when first seen Simpson agreed to a medical examination, but refused to provide samples, but the officers did not pursue this. The Review fails to explain why when Simpson was arrested, no samples were obtained? I believe that intimate samples need the suspect's consent, but what about his fingerprints, surly they were taken. However it seems that throughout the investigation, the Senior Crown Prosecutor suspect was the one in charge, well supported by the DPP and his CPS colleagues, and they were not the only supporters. Notably, even Simpson's drug and alcohol levels seem to have been omitted.

Number 7 is a reference to my 'contention' that the 'lack of investigation and prosecution' was the result of a conspiracy between the police, the CPS and the coroner. "Her belief was, in part, due to a lack of information from the investigating officer and the investigation in general".

This point is not actually dismissed because even though the Review found no evidence of a conspiracy it did agree that there was a lack of information, but, offered as an excuse that "This may have been in an attempt to protect Mrs Barrack from the true facts of her son's sexual activities. That is utter rubbish. DS Bathie at our meeting on the 14th May 1996 went out of his way to stress the fact that Alex was engaged in a homosexual act when he died, and also that he was naked. What was denied me was the fact that the police were investigating Alex's death as a suspected unlawful killing and not one from natural causes.

Number 8, really stunned me." when in an attempt to excuse the behaviour of the Limehouse Investigating Team the following explanation was given. This incident occurred in 1996 and since that time the MPS ethos on the supply of in formation to the relatives has been greatly changed. It is felt that with the current practices a similar situation would not be allowed to arise in the future. Well I have to say, that I doubt very much that even in the less advanced culture of 1996, that the ethos, the spirit, the culture governing police policy, would have allowed any scientific or medical forensic evidence to be reshaped and distorted, and statements, oral or written, to be falsified, and stay within the accepted rules of law and justice.

At the end of the very long discussion of the Review Team's report on the reinvestigation into the police *modus operandi* Mr Ahern apologised that the review had not achieved the reopening of the case that I had hoped for, and asked if I now accepted their findings. I had received far too much information for me to give a decisive answer so I merely said I could not say whether I did or did not, and needed time to think it over.

Before the Review Team left for London, Mr Ahern promised me that the case would not be closed. If at any time in the future, he came into possession of concrete evidence to reinforce the very convincing circumstantial already held, and which would give the CPS a 60% possibility of a successful prosecution, then the case would be reopened. That promise, to some extent, mitigated the keen disappointment and the realisation that I had another failure to record. Yet I still retained some hope of succeeding in the future, in that Mr Ahern would find the concrete evidence to review the case again and give Alex his justice.

Months later when I received the Review document, I was not so sure of Mr Ahern's intentions and was infuriated at the contents of the last conclusion:

> "Mrs Barrack is now fully aware of all the details of the investigation, which she has been pursuing over the years. She has accepted that in the light of there being no other evidence, the death of her son must be treated as a tragic accident."

That statement could not be further from the truth. I have never accepted that Alex's death was an accident and I never will.

## CHAPTER TWENTY THREE

*'Let justice roll down like the waters, and righteousness like an ever
lasting stream'[128]* - (until someone dams the waters.[129])

**Part – 1 - the difficulties faced in applying for the Review Report**

So, in the end the verbal report signified another failure for me, and the
success I had hoped for never materialised; had Mr Ahern succceded in
gaining a new investigation for me, whatever its later outcome, then this
book need never have been written. As it is, I still have several chapters
and an epilogue to write before my legal advocacy on behalf of my
murdered son ceases. With the publication of this book, members of the
public and unbiased authorities who read it can make their own judgement
on the facts of my case.

These facts that I give, to the best of my knowledge, are true and have
been obtained only through fourteen years of patient efforts on my part
and the encouragement of understanding supporters against all the efforts
of the police, the CPS and the coroner to persuade me that Alex's death
was accidental and not murder. I know that the circumstances of Alex's
death were unseemly and that was the reason the authorities expected I
would stay silent and not delve too deeply into the truth. However, Alex,
as do other unfortunate victims who died in unseemly circumstances,
deserves justice and should have it. If this narrative can help any of the
families of such victims to remedy or prevent injustices, and to gain the
support and understanding from the public they need in their quests, then
writing this book will have been well worth the commitment and I will
have fulfilled to the best of my ability, my duty to Alex.

I have to admit though, at the time when I heard Mr Ahern's
disappointing report, I no longer felt like a campaigner, and I was a very
quiet and down hearted when Mr Ahern and Mr Rowlands returned to
London. Valerie Whiteman, my staunch friend stayed with me a while,
and did her best to encourage me to take a positive look at what I **had**
achieved. It was difficult for me to see that I had achieved anything

---

[128]Quoted in DVD – Nemesis – Agatha Christi
[129] Added – by D Barrack

whatsoever, because on that day I felt only a strong sense of failure coupled with the deepest regret that my campaign for justice had to come to an end. For the first time I was on the point of conceding defeat.

Not the next morning though, because when I read over the notes I had made the previous night, I found the verbal report contained too many irregularities and gaps in the events for me to accept that the review was final, it wasn't even complete. It was after all supposed to be a full reinvestigation into a murder case, but the more I read, the surer I became that it lacked adequate research and therefore, was not the in-depth inquiry promised. Actually, when I finally obtained the official MRG document, I compared its content with that of a dissertation required to gain a BA degree. In my opinion, had it been submitted to a university examiner for grading, it would have received only 40% at the most, and marked 'inadequately researched'. That comment is not intended as a criticism of Mr Ahern's investigation because I am certain that in compiling his report, he had been seriously handicapped in his research by lack of official co-operation and strangely missing evidence, and, that he would sincerely have preferred to have given me a more positive result.

That being so, I still felt obligated to go forward with my enquiries, but before I could do so, thought it was necessary for me to have the MRG Review in a documentation form. Any points I planned to challenge in the Review needed to be officially documented and signed. Yet, even though I wanted to make that challenge, it was some weeks before I could bring myself to ask for the MRG document, the thought of possibly adding to the already long list of previous failures, was very was daunting.

Eventually though, I overcame the reluctance and in early September I contacted Mr Ahern by telephone. I told him that I would not come to any firm decision over his report, until I could study it in document form. I half expected him to be offended at my request, but he was surprisingly co-operative. He told me he quite understood my reasons for wanting a written document but that the request must be in writing and I was to make it to him. Then he said in effect 'When you write, say that you are making your request under the Freedom of Information Act 2000, this will ensure that it will receive very serious consideration'.

271

I thanked him and rang off, but without telling him I knew nothing about the Freedom of Information Act. However, I lost no time in finding out why it was important for me to invoke that Act, and I found the answer by going to the Internet. It took a while to find a guide on the internet which described in simple terms the purpose of the Act itself: This is my simplified understanding of the FOI Act.

The Freedom of Information Act (FOI ACT) was passed on November 30th 2000 and came into force in January 2005.

It gives the public a right of access to all types of recorded information held by public authorities. Public authorities as defined in the Act, includes all public bodies and Government Departments in the UK.

The Public Authorities from which information was requested in my case are: The police and Police Authorities, the CPS and the Coroner's Unit.

This was all very encouraging, particularly when I read that the Act encourages an organisation to be open and transparent.

My confidence in openness and getting the information I required was a little shaken when I read the section on 'EXEMPTIONS' but then I did not really understand the official term or exactly when exemption could be applied, or if they could be applied to me.:

> " Exemptions deal with instances where a public authority may withhold information under the Freedom of Information Act Exemptions mainly apply where releasing the information would not be in the public interest, for example, because it would affect law enforcement, harm commercial interests. "

Nevertheless, at the time I quickly acted on Mr Ahern's advice and on the 19th September 2005, sent a written request directly to him, asking to be issued with a copy of the documented Review, under the Freedom of Information Act. I then waited for my request to be processed in accordance with the direction laid down in the Act "... the organisation must provide the information within 20 days"

272

Considering the long wait I had in the past for replies to other requests, I was very surprised to receive a reply within three days by e-mail from Detective Inspector Highley, who advised me:

> *"I am writing in connection with your application for a copy of the Murder Review, regarding the **murder** of your son, (victim)".*

This was the first openly expressed admission by the Metropolitan Police, that <u>Alex was the victim of a murder</u>. However, the purpose of the letter was to inform me that the deadline of 20 days may not be met if the information was subject to the exemption rules of the Act, or contained a reference to a third party. If this applied then I would be given a revised timetable.

I was taken aback by the reason given for the extension, that the information might not be met because of exemptions especially in particular if it contained a reference to a third party. To my mind there would of course be a third party, the case after all was a homicide and there is no secrecy in a murder case. The paragraph which stunned me most though, stated that I may have to pay for the retrieval, collation and provision of the information requested, and if that was the case, the twenty days limit would be suspended until I paid the required fee. The statement concluded," **If you choose not to make payment then your request will go unanswered".**

This to me was tantamount to blackmail in reverse, 'keep quiet or else you will have to pay', and so I immediately phoned Mr Ahern and demanded to know why I should be expected to pay for information that the police should have provided from the beginning, and most of all, why the information could be withheld in document form, when I had already had it verbally from him.

He explained that it was a payment policy laid down, for the functioning process of the FOI Act, for a charge to be made for expenses incurred over the time and work involved in the processing of information, which would mean the withdrawal of personnel from other duties. The cost, he said, varied, and I may find that I **would** have to meet any cost, unless the authorities chose to waive it. But, if I remember rightly, he mentioned that it could not exceed £500. I was dumbfounded that I was expected to pay the expenses of trying to remedy a situation created by the MPS themselves.

I asked again, how could there be any question of withholding information in document form, when they couldn't deny I'd already had it in a lengthy verbal report, and a witness to prove it. Mr Ahern explained that it was government policy, that when documented information had to be tested in the public interest against the exemptions clauses of the Act, a charge was raised against the expenses incurred. It was apparent the MPS authorities had decided that my request needed to be tested against the exemption rules. Mr Ahern stressed, that he himself had no involvement in that decision to allow me the Report, because that rested with the legal department's judgment. All that he said to me that day, did not in any way appease my dissatisfaction with the MPS procedures, and did nothing to ease the growing apprehension that there was more failure ahead.

The next e-mail communication reached me on the 18th November 2005 and it reiterated the exemption clause policy, and confirmed that my request for the Review Report was being considered under 'qualified exemption'[130] clauses, and that the amended date for their response was the 20th December 2005. There was also a reminder that there may be a cost involved.

The FOI Act states that exemptions deal with instances where a public authority may withhold information under the Freedom of Information Act. Exemptions mainly apply where releasing the information would not be in the public interest, for example, because it would affect law enforcement. There are several other types of exemptions, but only one was used in my case as was confirmed in the next e-mail from DI Highley, which arrived on the 21st of December:

---

[130] Qualified exemptions – Information requested which must be tested to see if disclosure would be against public interest. I never found out exactly who makes the decision.

**"We are currently considering whether 'qualified exemptions' apply to the Information you have requested"**

So it was back to the FOI guide to find out why there was this delay in processing my application.

It seems that **Qualified exemptions** in this instance could be applied, because the information requested falls into the category 'investigations and proceedings conducted by public authorities' and even though in general they are exempt, the information may still have to be released if it is considered that it is in the 'public interest'. I was still left wondering just why my request had to be subject to the public' interest, the explanation is given later.

In the meantime, as the date for the response was amended to 10$^{th}$ January 2006 I could, I thought, forget the whole affair until after the New Year.

Not so! Because the day after Boxing Day, I received a package, which unbelievably contained a Redacted copy [131]of: **A Review of the Investigation into the Death of William Alexander BARRACK. This** was a demonstration of the serious lack of communications between various MPS Departments dealing with the same matter, as was shown by the date on the accompanying letter from Mr Rowlands dated December 18$^{th}$, which was three days before DI Highley informed that the decision to issue the Report to was postponed until January 10$^{th}$.

**Part 2. -** *I find that I am not alone - only one of three parents seeking justice for their murdered sons.*

Early in 2006 while I was still studying the MRG Review Report, I had an unexpected letter from a solicitor, Mr Tony Bennett. It concerned a letter that I had written in September 2002, following a BBC news report on an inquest held on a young man Stuart Lubbock, who had died under suspicious circumstances at the home of a well-known TV celebrity. My

---

[131] Redaction – meaning edited for publication. In this instant names obliteration by XXXs

letter had been written to his father because both John Smith and I were struck by the incredible similarities relating to the same pathologists autopsies of the two victims, the delayed investigations and the almost identical cover-up procedures in Alex's case and that of Stuart Lubbock's. It was John who had suggested that I contact Mr Lubbock, to advise him of the similarities in the cases, with the prospect in mind that we could help each other. John managed to locate a Mr Terence Lubbock's Harlow address for me, and I duly wrote to him, hoping that he was the right one, outlined my case and experiences, and offered to assist his legal representative in anyway I could. As I did not receive an answer, after a time, I simply forgot about the letter.

Mr Bennett, as I was to discover, was a solicitor who was zealously interested in remedying injustices, and as the Lubbock case reeked of injustice, he had taken on the task of assisting Mr Lubbock, in his fight to expose the truth and have justice for his son. After I had contacted Mr Bennett, he visited me in my home, which was then in Torksey, near Lincoln, and during our discussion it became obvious that the parallel between the two cases was even more marked than I realised, especially so, when I was given the opportunity to study some of Mr Lubbock's documentary evidence and compare it with mine. I understand that some of my comparisons of the evidence were useful in a small way to the book Mr Bennett and Mr Lubbock were in the process of writing.

The reason I introduce the book, its launch and its outcome at this stage, is because although it was not ready for publishing until 2007, in the conversations with Mr Bennett there was revealed an unbelievable number of coincidences in the flawed autopsies undertaken by the same pathologist, and delayed police investigations, but carried out by different police forces in different years. These revealing conversations were instrumental in my delving more deeply into the MRG Review when it was in my hands, and identifying the areas I was to challenge in my first FOI requests.

During the period that the MPS was considering my application for information, the book launch of Mr Bennett and Mr Lubbock's book entitled 'Not Alwight' took place on July 13th 2007 and I was happy to accept an invitation to the launching, at Mr Lubbock's Harlow home. I was accompanied by Ken Amphlett, who, as I have described in the first chapters, together with his late wife Maureen, my niece, played a very supportive role in the first two years after Alex's death. Now that that his children Rachel and Simon were more independent, Ken had been able to resume his supportive and greatly appreciated role. He has encouraged me to write this book and has given me invaluable assistance by checking facts and correcting my mistakes (His grammar is better than mine) and acting as my literary critic.

At the launch we met Mr Terry Lubbock, Mr Bennett's co-writer and heard first hand, not only of Terry's remarkable struggle to expose the truth of his son's horrific death, but also how Mr Bennett had worked tirelessly to support him. Ken and I also had the opportunity to meet Mr Lee Balkwell, the father of another victim of injustice, stemming from another of Dr Heath's flawed autopsies and who was another parent being assisted by Mr Bennett. During our discussions, we three parents realised that the similarities between the three cases were more extensive that we thought possible. Also it was very clear, that in trying to prove that our sons' deaths were murders, we were opposed in our struggles by the same government bodies of the Establishment, the police, the CPS and coroners, who all seemed intent on concealing, or obscuring the truth behind our sons' deaths.

It is not necessary for me to discuss the actual circumstances of either of the other two cases, as they have already been well recounted by the fathers themselves. The details of Stuart Lubbock's cruel death in 2001, at the home of TV celebrity Michael Barrymore, are excellently presented in the book by co-authors Mr Terry Lubbock and Tony Bennett entitled - 'Not Alwight". While the full account of Lee Balkwell's horrific death in a cement mixer, in 2002, can be read on Les Balkwell's website,' www.leebalkwell-the-truth.co.uk." Les regularly updates his website.

Nor do I intend to go over all the material listed in the MRG Review Report, which dealt with matters relating to the reinvestigation of the original police inquiry into Alex's death, as this has already been closely analysed in Chapter twenty two. I shall concentrate on some of the items in the Review which provided grounds for requesting further information on important points of evidence, whose significance had either been ignored, or only briefly referred to when discussed at the inquest by the police, Dr Heath the pathologist, and by Dr Chan the coroner. None of these servants of the justice system elected to reveal their significance in establishing that Alex's death was a criminal act.

It was hoped, that by obtaining information under the FOI Act, I could use it as evidence that the case warranted a fuller in-depth independent police inquiry. In fact to give Mr Ahern the 'concrete evidence' he required to convince the CPS, that there was sufficient **real evidence** for them to take the case forward to a prosecution and trial. But before I reached this stage I needed to do some research on the legal definitions of evidence. In particular, the meanings of the terms used by Mr Ahern and others, to justify the CPS non-prosecution of those persons, I hold responsible for Alex's murder.

**Part 3 - Concrete evidence versus circumstantial evidence - the CPS decides the winner.**

Mr Ahern had told me that if he found **concrete evidence** to prove that Alex's death was murder, he would definitely push for a prosecution. In the end he decided that there was not sufficient <u>concrete</u> evidence for him to do so, and that the circumstantial evidence was not strong enough to persuade the DPP & CPS,[132] that it warranted a prosecution.

I should imagine, like myself, not many lay persons understand the difference between the two types of evidence, I certainly did not then, so as was my usual practice, it was back to the reference books to search for more simple definitions. But, as with most legal terms, there was no such thing as a simple definition for either type of evidence, as I found when I consulted a police reference book, *'Blackstone's* **Police Manual – Evidence and Procedures**. (2001), but after reading the relevant chapter, I wondered if the ordinary police constable could understand their meanings entirely. This manual contained a thirty three-page chapter devoted to explaining types of evidence, in which they are categorised into eleven distinct types. Quite notably, the term 'concrete evidence' was not included, but circumstantial evidence was. These two types of

---

[132] Director of Public Prosecutions & Crown prosecution Service.

evidence were the ones I wanted to understand most, because their presence in, or absence, from the police files seemed to affect the outcome of all types of investigations into Alex's death.

The term concrete evidence, used by Mr Ahern and others had been used in such a way, to suggest to me, that it was solid, physical, irrefutable evidence of a crime, which could be interpreted only one way. However, it is not a legal term used in the Police Manual and legal glossaries, instead they refer to **"real evidence (sometimes called direct evidence),"** and that actually covers a much wider range of materials that can be classed as such evidence. I also learned that 'oral evidence', a feature of Alex's inquest, was of extreme importance in a court of law, in that it can be considered as proof of a crime, which could be challenged in court.

I would be out of my depth if I tried to define any of these types of evidence with any accuracy, because I found the subject so difficult to understand, mainly due to compilers of the glossaries using different slants in explaining oral, real and circumstantial evidence to the general public. Eventually though, I began to make enough sense of the differences between types of evidence to understand how they are applied to criminal investigations which can possibly lead to prosecutions and a trials.

Evidence, I learned, is essential in convincing the judge and jury of the facts, as the judge is expected to start off with a blank slate with no preconceived idea or knowledge of the facts. So it is up to the opposing parties to prove, to the satisfaction of the judge and jury, the facts in evidence used to support their case, whether prosecuting or defending an accused.

**Original Evidence**
Proof of fact(s) presented at a trial. The best and most common method is by **oral testimony**; where you have an eye-witness swear to tell the truth and to then relate to the court (and jury) their experience. This personal or first hand knowledge can then be challenged on its truth in cross-examination.

## Evidence

Besides oral testimony, an object can be deposited with the court (e.g. a signed statement). This is sometimes called "real or direct evidence." The rules of evidence are strict in criminal cases, little or no weight can be attached to real evidence unless it is accompanied by **documented evidence**, identifying the object and connecting it with the facts in issue. This consists of <u>all</u> types of documents produced for inspection and assessment by the court. Documents can be either real evidence or as hearsay or original evidence. Documents produced for the court are usually accompanied by some testimony and identified by a witness.

## Circumstantial evidence

This is evidence, which may allow a judge or jury, to deduce a certain fact from other facts, which have been proven. In some cases, there can be some evidence that cannot be proven directly as with an eyewitness, yet that evidence may be essential to prove a case.

The following example of circumstantial evidence which follows and is one of special interest to me, as it revealed to me just how importance the finger print report was to Alex's case:

> *"Fingerprints are an example of circumstantial evidence: while there may be no witness to a person's presence in a certain place, or contact with a certain object, but the scientific evidence of someone's fingerprints is persuasive proof of a person's presence or contact with an object."*

The fact that the report was missing when requested by Mr Ahern was of great advantage to the police and the CPS. I will give reasons for arriving at this opinion on the absence of finger printing a little later, when I discuss the measures taken to persuade officials of the MPS Access Office, under the FOI Act, to release withheld evidence, which I thought would have provided the "concrete evidence" needed for Mr Ahern to push the DPP into ordering a prosecution and trial, previously denied in 1996 by the then DPP.

It was only when I realised that I had reached my limit in understanding the very difficult concept of identifying forensic evidence, that I closed the text books and, being only a little more enlightened, started planning the next stage of my action for justice under the Freedom of Information Act 2000.

Earlier in this chapter I recorded that there were many irregularities and omissions in the evidence set out in the MRG Report and it was now more than ever obvious to me, that coroner Dr Chan, under rule 37 of the Coroner Rules 1984, should have, but did not, make available to the family all copies of the **Documentary Evidence** he had used that was relevant to the inquest and, **"upon which he seeks to rely on for any purpose"**[133]. Although he had used this evidence during his inquisitions, he had in fact not only failed to call essential witnesses and withheld statements, but also made certain that there was no jury present to question the witnesses or his manner of conducting the inquest, which did not conform to the standards expected at coroner's inquest. These normal standards of a fair and impartial inquest if applied, could have achieved a more fitting verdict, considering that the clear evidence should have established that Alex's death was an unlawful killing.

It was most of this withheld Documentary Evidence real and circumstantial, that I intended to request under the Freedom of Information Act, to convince the CPS that there was sufficient strong evidence in order to achieve the 60% proof the CPS needed. Mr Bennett, although heavily committed to the Balkwell cause, was able to advise me on the most suitable action to take.

**Part 4 - *The Freedom** of Information Act 2000 - becomes The Restriction of Information Act 2006*

By March 2006 I was ready, under Mr Bennett's guidance, to make my second formal application to Mr Ahern for information under the FOI Act. I had noticed, that although it was mentioned in both oral and written MRG reports, the full  important Police Schedule of Evidence had been redacted, i.e., edited out of the documented report altogether. This

---

[133] Coroners Courts – Levi, 16-11 p92

schedule should have contained a list of the evidence related to the police investigation into my son's death, which included:

1. All exhibits
2. All physical artefacts
3. All documentation
4. Forensic reports
5. Pathology reports
6. Histology reports
7. Toxicology Reports

I must admit it was a quite ambitious to request almost the entire list, but while I didn't expect to get everything listed, I was fairly certain that I would receive some items. My letter received by Mr Ahern on the 15th of March was passed to DI Highley for his attention. In a staggeringly short time of nine days, my request had been passed to and examined by Access Office officials, and a decision made. On the 24th March 2006 at 11.36 am, DI Highley sent me a very sensitively worded e-mail and I was at first favourably impressed this and by his understanding of my position and also the speed of the reply to my letter.

Little did I realise at the time, that in opening the e-mail I was about to find just how little benefit the Freedom of Information Act was to the ordinary citizen such as me, in trying to obtain legitimate information about public bodies mistakes, in my case, the MPS irregular investigations

It proved to be of no benefit to me at all, because from the decision received on 26th March 2006, I learned just how effectively the exemptions can be used to favour, not the public interests, but the interests of the police.

## THE DECISION

**Having located and considered the relevant information, I am afraid that I am not required by statute to release the information requested. This letter serves as a Refusal Notice under Section 17 of the Freedom of Information Act.**

Section 17 of the Act was something I was to become very familiar with, it was to be used other requests I made for information about police activity in Alex's case. The wording of the section was as obscure as officialdom could make it. I did understand that applying Section 17 to a request allowed other exemptions to be used against disclosure of information, providing the following conditions were complied with:

(a) States the fact- *I took this to mean make it clear that it is a refusal.*
(b) Specify the exemption in question. *Clearly identify the exemption/s being used.*
(c) States (if that would not be otherwise apparent) why the exemption applies. *To this particular request.*

The exemption clause in my case was Section 12 (1) which had three subsections. It was the first of these three subsections used to justify refusing to disclose the information I had asked for:

**"(1) Section 1(1) does not oblige a public authority to comply with a request for information if the authority estimates that the cost of complying with the request would exceed the appropriate limit".**

The reason for applying Section 12 1(1) to my request was:

**"The case file is made up of two sizable dockets and further extraction of the relevant information coupled with the processing of suitable response to your application, would exceed the 18 hour (£450.00) limit, therefore these are exempt"**

DI Highley attached a complaints form entitled 'Complaints Rights' for me to complete if I was dissatisfied with the response.

Dissatisfaction didn't describe the rage and frustration I felt at hat moment; I could not believe that such a paltry reason and such a meagre cost limit could be applied to refuse access to information on such a serious matter, as a legitimate attempt to have an unresolved murder reinvestigated. I telephoned the MPS Access Office and belligerently demanded a full explanation. I was told by the official I spoke to that the limit to the cost of complying with such requests was not the main reason for refusal; it was the concern over requiring the withdrawal of valuable man-power from other duties. He didn't actually say, 'from more important duties' but I am sure that is what he was implying. This official was not prepared to give further explanation and his ears should have blazed, as I expressed my opinion of him and his department when I replaced the phone.

My opinion of the Freedom of Information Act is that it can be used as a Restriction of Information; it does not give a general right of public access to all types of recorded information held by public authorities. On the contrary, to me, it was designed to deter the ordinary citizen from enquiring too deeply into instances of questionable conduct by public bodies.

> *"However, organisations covered by the FOI Act are entitled to withhold information when an appropriate exemption can be applied."*

That clause allows stringent application of exemption clauses to requests for information, particularly used in criminal cases, when disclosure of inappropriate conduct would offend the general public and there would be calls for public inquiries. This clause allowing unsound exemptions can make a mockery of law enforcement. My opinion of the Freedom of information act is that it can be used as a Restriction of Information, it does not give a general right of public access to all types of recorded information held by public authorities. On the contrary, to me, it was designed to deter the ordinary citizen from enquiring too deeply into instances of questionable conduct by public bodies.

> *"However, organisations covered by the FOI Act are entitled to withhold information when an appropriate exemption can be applied."*

That clause allows stringent application of exemption clauses to requests for information, particularly used in criminal cases, when disclosure of inappropriate conduct would offend the general public and there would be calls for public inquiries. This clause allowing unsound exemptions can make a mockery of law enforcement. The next three years were to prove me right.

# CHAPTER TWENTY FOUR

## *Police accountability*

**Part one - "The police have a duty to enforce the law, but in enforcing the law they must act within the law, and this enables the court to regulate police conduct."[134]**

A fine sentiment indeed, but the courts can only regulate police conduct, or the conduct of any other public body, if the matter can reach the court for adjudication. I hope that I have demonstrated fully that the extensive restrictive measures taken against me were taken solely to prevent my case gaining access to **any type of court.** I have no doubt that had the case been scrutinised by a judge and jury, then all the irregularities I have claimed, would have been publicly exposed. Then, which ever side the verdict favoured, defence or prosecution, the press would have had a field day with the coverage of the case. However, like many other murder victims' parents, I've never had my day in court.

Alex had been dead almost ten years when I started invoking the Freedom of Information Act. In January 2006 I had written to Commander Baker of the MPS Homicide Division, when I wrote to say that although I appreciated his role in implementing the MRG Review, I was in no way satisfied with the outcome, and that I intended to keep up my campaign for justice. I don't remember every receiving a reply to this letter

Although for some time after I made no further attempts to contact the MRG officials, I had every intention of doing so as soon as Mr Bennett was in a position to assist me further. In the meantime I carefully studied the MRG Report and did a fair amount of work in comparing the pathology reports on Stuart Lubbock and Alex's autopsies. The flaws in both were remarkably similar, but hardly surprising when the same pathologist performed both autopsies, and who was also responsible for the flawed post-mortem that had been carried out on Lee Balkwell.[135]

---

[134] Quote from Dear and Saunders – Politics & Economics
[135] The full details of my conclusions can be found on my article on Les Balkwell's website *'Three grieving fathers and a mother'*

I also became aware that there was another very interesting aspect to this saga. During my study of the role of MPS police officers (and other officials), I realised that not only had vital items of evidence disappeared from the scene, so had all the personnel involved in processing the case in the early stages. They had died, or were transferred, had resigned from or were removed from post.

## In order of disappearance

- Detective Constable Hardy – the third and most junior member of the Investigation Team – Transferred in early 1997 – his whereabouts were withheld.
- Detective Chief Inspector Bathe – committed suicide on May 4th 1997, the first anniversary of Alex's death.
- Detective Inspector Bathie – about that time, off duty on long term sick leave and resigned on sick grounds after a year.
- Commander in charge of Limehouse Police Station – moved, reason and whereabouts not known.
- Police Sergeant Martin also of Limehouse Police, who was helpful in trying to locate Alex's effects - in 1998, apparently not known at Limehouse.
- Mr Martin CPS – Letter to police read at inquest, some input into decision not to prosecute over Alex's death, died some time before 1999.
- Dr Heath - Pathologist resigned 2002, removed from Home Office Top Pathologists List – over flawed autopsies
- Dr Chan – Coroner resigned 2001– reports of questionable inquests.

Whatever the cause of their disappearance I could not contact any member of the Limehouse Investigation Team, my letters went unanswered. I did wonder if this was just a series of coincidences that not one police officer from Limehouse could be called to account for his conduct? I eventually decided that given the history of the case, it seems very unlikely.

During the spring and summer of 2006 I concentrated more on my neglected house and garden, but by the beginning of the Autumn, I reluctantly had to accept that age was beginning to take its toll and I could not longer cope with the extensive work that my own home and garden required. In addition I lived nine miles from the nearest town, and the time was also coming nearer when I would have to give up driving my car, to Gainsborough and back to Torksey, especially on dark nights. I would then, due to restricted local public transport services, become isolated from all the church friends and activities that were so important to me, when inevitably, whether due to success or failure, I have to draw a line under the justice for Alex campaign, and that closure would create quite a vacuum in my life should I stay in Torksey where there were few facilities to occupy my time. Within a matter of weeks I began to look around for accommodation in Gainsborough.

In October 2006, before becoming actively engaged in contacting suitable agencies, I wrote once more to Mr Ahern pointing out the inadequacies of the DNA report and requesting the police to re-examine the DNA material in Alex's case. The request was made on the grounds that DNA testing had recently become more advanced and had been used successfully in the Damilola Taylor case. Mr Ahern acknowledged my request and said he would reply in due course. However he did not, nor did anyone else from the Murder Review Group. I forgot about the letter for a time because sooner than expected, my domestic affairs had to take priority.

Just a few days after my eighty-first birthday in November, I obtained the tenancy of a Housing Agency flat in Gainsborough, which suited all my housing needs admirably, and also put me right into the centre of shopping and transport facilities. From then until February 2007, I made preparations to move with the generous assistance of my sister Joan and her husband Brian. Between them they completely redecorated the flat, helped me choose new furniture, carpets and curtains and supported me through all the trauma of moving home. On the seventh of February they installed me in my new home and when they left me about 6pm, I was standing in a flat that had the hallmark of a long established home, with everything unpacked and in its right place. Even my computer was in position and ready to operate, because they had called in our nephew David to move it from the Torksey house and install it in my new home. It was a comforting day for me and it could have been so depressing and unsettling.

By February I was well settled in Gainsborough and had revised my interest in developments in forensic medicine. The most recent reports, which immediately gained my attention, were those discussing the advances in DNA testing. Yet, I postponed taking any action on bringing this matter to Mr Ahern's attention until April, because in March I had started to correspond with the MPS Access office, therefore I will leave the contents of the letter dealing with DNA until later.

In late March Mr Bennett was in a position to give me some of his time and assistance, which he gave pro-bono[136]. Following on from the refusal of the second FOI information application in 2006, Mr Bennett had contacted DI Highley by phone, questioning why requests for every item had been refused. DI Highley had at that time suggested to Mr Bennett that I should apply again, but this time for each document to be listed separately. In this way, the police would be able to respond more positively and consider the requests which <u>could</u> be met within the imposed limits.

On March 22nd 2007, Mr Bennett sent a carefully worded letter to a contact he had recently made, Mr Mark Pleece, a Freedom of Information Officer of the Specialist Crime Review Group. He advised Mr Pleece that I was seeking a limited reinvestigation by adopting the approach suggested by DI Highley, and breaking down the list into separate items. A copy of this letter was sent to Mr Ahern.

In brief Mr Bennett advised Mr Preece that he was listing the items of information required in priority order, and that he would like to receive as many as could be fulfilled within the approved 18-hour limit. If for example - extracting 1, 2 and 3 items from the files would take up the 18 hours allowed, and then those three should be issued. However, if only 1 & 2 would take the 18 hours, then those two should be issued. And so on.

In this way, Mr Bennett hoped to avoid a repetition of the en bloc refusal of all information requested, as had happened to the first application, when the police applied sub section (1) of Section 12(1) which restricted the time and cost allowed to extract any information from the files.

---

[136] used to describe work that someone, especially a lawyer, does without getting paid

In brief, the list requested the issue of the following seven items:

1. All photographs in the case- including details of those found on the Pentax camera.
2. Items found on Mr Simpson' property.
3. All statements made by Simpson and non-medical witnesses.
4. All statements made by paramedics and hospital doctors.
5. All hospital notes and X-rays
6. All forensic and toxicology reports and statements – including DNA findings.
7. A list of all other auricles and documents in the case.

A very rapid reply was received by Mr Bennett and me on March 30th, containing the usual acknowledgement and a promise of a response, if possible, within the statutory 20 days. It was a little over the twenty days, the 21$^{st}$ of April  when Mr Bennett and I received the letter informing us of the decision, which I expect will have been anticipated by the reader:

> *"Having considered the relevant information, I am afraid that I am not required by statute to release the information required"*

And here we go again, Section 17 and its three conditions, what these public bodies would do without it?

> *"The letter serves as a Refusal Notice under Section 17of the Freedom of Information Act 2000 (The Act)".*

> *"Unfortunately the information requested cannot be released due to the status of the investigation and the type of material requested."*

Although Section 12 (1), with its time and cost limits was not used this time, Mr Young had excelled himself in finding many others ways to fully exempt him from providing the relevant information: Sections 30, 31, 38, 40 and 41. It took eight pages to explain why this information was '**fully exempted**'. I am not going to attempt to explain the legal jargon used to explain the sections to a lay person like myself, who had difficulty in translating the language into understandable, commonsense English. Happily though, when I wrote an irate letter of protest to Mr Young, I seemed to have made the right construal of the exemptions applied, when I used the BBC list of exemptions they applied to requests for information.

> 30. On-going investigations - planned or relating to confidential sources

> 31. Law enforcement – if disclosure would prejudice the detection or prevention of crime

> 38. Health & safety - protecting the health and safety of any person

> 40. Personal information – if disclosure would breach the Data Protection Act

> 41. Confidential information – where disclosure would be a breach of common law.

The above is a very simplified version of those exemptions used in order to justify the refusal of the information I asked for, which were made more complex by the plenitude of subsections attached to them. It took eight pages for Mr Young to explain why these particular exemptions and subsections had been used to refuse me all the information requested.

Actually I could not fathom out why they had been applied to Alex's murder and I certainly did not accept the reason that disclosing information on the routine investigations into Alex's murder would harm other similar investigation and allow others to use the information to gain an advantage over the police in other cases.

It was as clear as daylight to me that the police would certainly not want the peculiarities of their investigations and line of enquiry into Alex's case to become public knowledge, but the FOI Act 2000, (in theory) does not allow improper use of exemptions in order to conceal excessive irregularities in this 'type of investigation', (or of the misconduct of any official).

It had never been clearly expressed what this type of investigation was, until Mr Young in justifying the use of the Public interest test under Section 40, and possibly inadvertently, named and described the type and nature of the crime against Alex and how the police conducted the investigation:

> **"Murder cases such as this one , are highly emotive and the manner in which they are conducted are usually kept in strict secrecy, so that the tactics and processes that the Investigation Team follow, do not become public knowledge thereby rendering them use useless".[137]**

Then having explained that non-disclosure of this type of investigation is covered by the conditions of Section 40, in the next paragraph he endorses my right to have the police account for their actions.

### Accountability

> *"When information relates to the efficiency and effectiveness of the Service and its officers, the purpose of the Act is to make public authorities more accountable and this factor therefore, may be applied to the MPS's conduct in this* **specific investigation.**

This specific investigation is referring indisputably to Alex's murder and Mr Young has, in writing the above, provided real evidence, which can be attested in court, that the police did investigate Alex's death as murder and I believe that he has sanctioned my right to have the police account for their secrecy and irregular conduct, 'in the interest of the efficiency and effectiveness of the service'. Even though the failure to have the case taken through to a prosecution and trial rests with the CPS, the secrecy of the early investigations, inadequate collection of 'real' (concrete) evidence and the failure to preserve vital evidence of many kinds in 1996, I believe, rests with the police. It is certain that their mismanagement was to be instrumental in preventing an effective and satisfactory outcome of the Murder Review Group's reinvestigation into the Alex Barrack case in 2005. In my view, the FOI ACT, Section 40; allows me to ask the police to account for their actions but I cannot do so, if the MPS refuse to disclose the evidence I need.

---

[137] Letter from My Young Room, 114 MPS New Scotland Yard, 20.2007 - para 4 page 3

Not that Mr Young would agree because 'having weighed up the competing interests' when applying the balancing test to my application, he then undermines the case for making the police accountable, because the public interest would not be served if releasing the information relating to this murder case would compromise this or any future policing investigation

I hadn't realised that my interests were in competition with those of the MPS, all I was trying to do was right a wrong. When, as Mr Young had actually stated,[138] the police had a case to answer, in my opinion, it was in the public interest for MPS officers concerned to be held to account for the unprofessional conduct of the case, even if it meant airing their mistakes in court. Such exposure would be desirable, in that it could act as a deterrent to other misguided officials, and therefore would definitely be for the good of the people.

He ended this missive by saying that the Specialist Crime Directive was anxious to maintain a healthy relationship with FOI applicants. I found that hard to believe, and most certainly, I thought it was a bit tactless of him to add:

*"I hope my decision does not adversely impact on this honestly held viewpoint".*

If he was expecting this to placate me for the refusal, he was wrong, I was angry, as such a sentiment savoured more of hypocrisy than honesty. Perhaps here I am being a little unfair, because in his review of my application, he will have done no more than any other official; he has concentrated principally on that part of the case which affected his own department, and its interests, and incorporated only negative decisions, namely, the CPS non-prosecution decision and the coroner's verdict to support his conclusions. Whereas, any fair and impartial reinvestigation, demanded a complete analysis of every department's aspect and input into the case, when from the beginning it had been investigated as a murder and yet, for eight months the family were deceived into believing it was a death from natural causes.

---

It was some time before I could bring myself to respond to this upsetting open homicide disclosure, but this does not mean I was idle because there were two issues in the MRG Review I had already been tackling and intended to pursue. They were the issue of DNA in the mask and photographs taken with a Pentax camera, both of which had been documented and therefore could be classed as real evidence.

## Part 2 – DNA testing
*"The voice of one crying in the wilderness"*[139]
– or the voice of one, falling on deaf ears

I said earlier that ahead of Mr Bennett's preparation and composing his letter to Mr Young, I had on the 20th October written an informal letter to Mr Ahern in connection with recent advances in DNA techniques, and which had been extensively reported in the media. The advanced techniques of 2007 could now distinguish between multiple profiles from the smallest samples of DNA. I have mentioned earlier, that at the inquest DCI Baff had stated that the techniques of 1996 were not advanced enough to 'unscramble' the mixture of DNA found in the small tube of the head device, for it to be possible to identify individual profiles. I suggested to Mr Ahern that this was an opportunity to re-examine that DNA mixture using the new techniques, and to establish once and for all, that the head device mask was or was not the cause of Alex's death.

A reply was not received until 1st April after Mr Bennett had submitted his formal application. The reply was not from Mr Ahern, but from Detective Superintendent Sweeting. It was also sent from a new office, that of the Specialist Crime Review Group. These changes were due to a move to new accommodation, in which I understood, the MRG Group had been reorganised, At this point, Mr Ahern disappeared from the scene. I regretted this, as I felt I had lost an advocate and someone with extensive knowledge and understanding of the policies of the MPS, especially those applied to my case

Mr Sweeting after explaining the reason for the delayed answer, continued by saying that he had studied the MRG Review and that he considered it to

---

[139] Matthew

be 'a very thorough review, I found his view barely credible, considering the deficiencies and obstacles encountered by Mr Ahern, and admitted by him, to have been a hindrance in his attempts to take the case forward to a prosecution.

In the next paragraph he dismissed the media reports by saying that that it had made much of the advances in DNA techniques, but in reality this technique was only in the assessment stage and not ratified for general use. Well, it may not have been generally ratified, but it had been, according to many reports, used successfully on the controversial Damilola Taylor case. This point it seemed, was ignored.

The letter continued, that having read the MRG report Mr Sweeting had made the decision, that this technique would not progress the matter to a conclusion that would satisfy me. Even if a profile of Alex was found, it would not 'advance whether or not the mask was worn voluntarily'. He was sorry he could not be of further assistance to me. I took exception to this, I thought it arrogant that someone who was not an expert in DNA science, should make such sweeping decisions apparently without an expert's opinion. Within days he had my response written on 10th April.

In plain terms I told him I would not accept his decision as I did not consider that he was qualified to make one on the difficult science of DNA testing, it was a process which required a qualified scientists opinion. I insisted on my right to have such an opinion on my son's case, as had been promised by Mr Ahern

A month later, on the 14th of May 2007, Mr Sweeting wrote again to me. It was a brief letter and a copy was also sent to Mr Bennett. The letter informed me:

> "To clarify the situation and to ensure the advice I give you is correct I have asked an independent scientist to review the DNA issues in this case."

The scientist was not named and her qualifications were not listed, and certainly no written report was included. Instead Mr Sweeting summarised her conclusions, quoting almost exactly those in the first DNA analysis given at the inquest. Mr Sweeting then stated that there were no control samples available which would enable the scientist to progress the matter and establish the **contributors' profiles.**

He concluded with apologies for not being able to progress the matter further and the assurance that he would not close the inquiry, and that my son's case would be brought forward for re-examination in two years time or as new techniques became available.

This was most unsatisfactory, and once again it was claimed that the only sample of DNA available for testing was in that minute tube on the head device. As I had done so before I questioned why was there no record of any tests on the larger inner surface of the bag, particularly when Mr Ahern had said to me that the inside of the device 'did not appear to have been wiped'. I sent another letter to Mr Sweeting on the 18th June with a detailed question on that point, and insisted on an explanation, and also, queried why no other control samples were available, when Alex must have deposited his DNA on other physical artefacts.

I also questioned his stating there were no control samples[140] available for comparative analysis with those elements found in the tube, and his claim that there were none specific to Alex's DNA, when the first test had established that four had been identified. I also pointed out that even further advances on DNA testing had recently been reported and it was claimed they had successfully tested even smaller samples of fragmented DNA, by using the DNA of close family members. Also I wrote that Alex had close family members who could provide control samples, two parents and a half brother, even if only used for purposes of elimination.

Mr Sweeting had referred to Mr Ahern's MRG Review which he considered to be 'very thorough', but I drew his attention to the fact that missing items of very important evidence would prevent the review being classed as 'thorough'. Mr Sweeting acknowledged receipt of my letter on 23rd July 2007 and said he would look into the points I had raised.

I heard no more from Detective Superintendent Sweeting on that subject.

---

[140] Control samples – understood to be obtained from other sources i.e. physical contact with other objects or family DNA

I waited throughout August and September for a reply and then on advice from Mr Bennett took up the Specialist Crime Directorate refusal to supply information requested under the FOI Act. This letter has already been mentioned and had been received in September from Mr Young and contained an exceptional number of exemptions.

I began my letter by expressing my strong objection to his use of so many exceptions to refuse a legitimate request for information. Most of all though, I attacked the way in which the secret investigation into and the nature of Alex's murder had been used to exempt the issue of information under the Public Interest Test. I demanded an explanation of why the fact that the death was a murder had been concealed from the family for so many years. I condemned the MPS authority's infringement of Alex's rights under the ECHR and the Human Rights Act, and the denial of my right to a fair, impartial hearing. I concluded my letter by demanding that they review my request. I did not hear anything further on the matter from Mr Young. My letter was passed to yet another officer and another office.

Earlier, I had commented on the disappearing act of the MPS officers who quietly disappeared after the crime investigations, but now I had a situation where different officers kept appearing and disappearing from the scene as my letters for remedies were passed from one official to another. The majority failed to give their rank or status so I did not know whether I was being passed up or down the chain of command.

A Mr Nigel Shankster of the Public Access Office took over from Mr Young, and the first paragraph contained two apologies for the terminology used by Mr Young, as unfortunate in his referring to *'your son's untimely death as 'murder'.'* Mr Shankster did not say that the term murder was right or wrong. He merely 'remarked' that **this aspect fell outside his remit** and that the death was still considered by the police to be unexplained. He managed to throw in two mentions that the coroner's verdict was 'Accidental Death and then, after quite a long justification of Mr Young's exemption clauses, Mr Shankster *'suggested that the decision taken by Mr Young still stands'*. That was it, no further mention of the murder or which official did have a remit to deal with the matter.

My response to this attitude of Mr Shankster was more belligerent than previously, as his casual dismissal of the important information  that my son's death was a murder, together  with his references to the coroner's verdict and the en bloc refusal of information, had really angered me. I refused his apology for the use of the terminology 'emotive murder' used by Mr Young, and said I considered he had used that expression with integrity. I suggested that in view of the excessive exemptions used, the FOI ACT 2000 should be referred to as 'THE RESTRICTION OF INFORMATION ACT 2008'.

I dismissed any suggestion that refusing me information had anything to do with the good of the people and reminded him of a phrase often quoted by the police, 'There is no confidentiality in a murder inquiry, citing also a rule from the FOI Act which should be adhered to when applying exemptions to requests for information, but which they had flagrantly ignored:

- *Authorities must **not** take into consideration the possible embarrassment of government or any other public official;*

- *Or the seniority of persons involved  in the matter.*

When this letter was completed and posted the next day, I turned my attention to the second matter I mentioned above, that of the Pentax Photographs. This was vital evidence which had been first raised at the inquest by Dr Heath, but dismissed brusquely from his inquisition by Dr Chan.  Mr Ahern in both his verbal and written MRG, had only lightly touched on the subject, but I could see great significance in the photographs.
.

At the inquest the photographs had been important to Dr Heath in identifying the apparatus used to kill Alex, but I saw them as being of greater importance, a last chance perhaps for me to prove that Alex's death was not an accident but an unlawful killing. In the hope of setting the wheels of justice in motion again it was essential for me to be given the opportunity to try to identify a masked man in one of the photographs.

298

# CHAPTER TWENTY FIVE

## *Justice denied*

### The Pentax Photographs - Whose was the body in the photographs - and why did they disappear?

At the inquest Dr Heath had told the coroner that he had examined the head device and been shown some photographs

> *"...and in his opinion if the apparatus that we see there had been applied to this gentleman, it could have produced the changes I have described and his death"*

At that time the significance of photographs escaped me, they could have been of anyone and shown merely to demonstrate the type of bag used on Alex. It was when Mr Ahern referred to a Pentax camera with a film which had been developed, that I became concerned and had asked if the photographs could have been of Alex. Mr Ahern had, with some hesitation replied he didn't think so. Later when I received the MRG document, I became aware that the Pentax camera and the photographs were indeed vital evidence, but at the inquest and in the MRG Review Report, their importance had been played down.

Until I read the documented MRG Review I had not realised that the camera and the film were actually the property of Robert Simpson that had been found at the scene and were taken in as evidence by the police. When the film was developed by the police there were seven photographs, apparently taken in the flat, of a man in various poses. One photograph was quite graphically described, and this one really disturbed me, and I include its official description, although it is not easy for me to do so:

> *"One photograph showed a man who was naked other than a pair of rubber waders, wearing an* **inflated** *blow up balloon head bag. The identity of this man was not established"*

The photographs, apparently, were of only one man whom the police claimed was not identified. I can't accept this failure to identify him, because

299

in only one photograph was the head covered, therefore the police should not have had a problem in identifying the man posing in the other six, but it seems to me they had chosen not to do so. When I read that the camera was Simpson's and he was probably the photographer, then I began to question Mr Ahern on saying that he didn't think they were of Alex and he was in fact quite wrong and they were photographs of Alex, and it was him wearing the inflated head bag.

There is very little doubt in my mind that whoever the man was, he must have been dead when that picture was taken. I believe it is quite illogical to think that someone would willingly have, worn such a potentially lethal device over his head, have it inflated and to risk his life to pose long enough for a photograph to be taken. That device would need to be removed by an assistant in matter of minutes; otherwise the wearer would be at great risk of a speedy death or irreversible brain damage from hypoxia. As unpleasant as it was to me, I had to consider that the body was Alex's and that taking the photograph had been the perverted conclusion to the sadomasochistic ritual in which he died.[141]

I discussed this with Mr Bennett and he asked if I had ever been shown the photographs to help identify if it was Alex, and had refused. I said no, and that I was not aware that that the pictures even existed, until the inquest. Mr Bennett's opinion was that if secrecy had not been applied to the investigations, that irrespective of their unpleasant nature, either I, or more probably Alex's father, should have been shown the photographs to confirm or rule out that they were of our son. He advised me that in view of the evidence of serious mismanagement of the investigations which my enquiries were revealing, it was even more important for me to inspect the photographs, because if they were of Alex, then that was real evidence that he had worn the bag - and - it was the cause of death. Mr Bennett had it in mind to take the case to the Criminal Injuries Compensation Authority (CICA) and the Independent Police Complaints Commission (IPCC), but before deciding to do so, he suggested that I should try to gain access to the photographic evidence. I will return to the CICA and the IPCC later

---

[141] If this conjecture was correct, then, as a routine, a police investigation would have been underway immediately. If the body was Alex's then there was such an investigation, albeit undercover.

The problem was of course, that copies the photographs and relevant documents had already been requested under the FOI Act, but Mr Young in his enthusiastic application of exemptions had refused the request, and that avenue to the evidence was now closed to me. There was though, one other possibility of having access to the photographs, and that was to ask that I be allowed to personally inspect them.

On the 2nd March 2008, I requested Mr Shankster under the FOI Act to allow me to view the photographs, preferably in my home, but said if it was necessary I would be prepared to travel to London. I made it quite clear that it would not be possible for them to argue that "disclosure to me meant disclosure to the world" since viewing rather than obtaining copies, prevented any disclosure on my part. I also in insisted that any consideration of my sensitivity should be disregarded.

In the first week of April I had my reply, not the usual response letter but one containing a decision and it was from Mr Young. In brief he informed me that searches within three sections of the MPS had failed to locate any information relating to my request. Therefore he, Mr Young, had decided that access could not be given. The reason for this was that

> "...due to the CPS decision not to prosecute and the coroner's verdict, **all personal property which would have included the camera, negatives and photographs, would have been returned to the owner in the course of normal police practice"**

My reply to Mr Young was very short and speedy. It said I was not satisfied with the statement that there were no copies of the photographs available for me to view, it did not tally with information that I had already held, and that I intended to challenge his decision.

Mr Young acknowledged my letter on 8th May 2008 and noting that I intended to challenge his decision, he had forward my letter to the Reviewing Officer at the Public Access Office for it to be reviewed. This was quite surprising really, as I was still in the process of completing the complaints form.

This Reviewing Officer was Mr Shankster, who informed me that my complaint was being reviewed and the MPS hoped to respond by the 29th July 2008. In addition, he was handing the case over to an independent member of staff, Miss Sarah Pallen as due to his previous involvement and correspondence with me he would not carry out the internal review. It puzzled me that a member of the MPS could be regarded as being independent.

However, just to make sure that Miss Pallen was in possession of the full facts behind my request to view the photographs, I wrote her a long letter of explanation. I stressed as strongly as possible that I was not prepared to accept that all copies of the photographs had been returned to Mr Simpson in September 1996. The coroner and Dr Heath had referred to them at the inquest and his opinion on the cause of the victim's death being asphyxiation by the application of an inflated obstructive device to his head, was endorsed by the evidence of the photographs. I reminded her that as they were important forensic evidence, those copies shown at the inquest, together with those held by the police and the CPS should according to law have been retained in all these case files.

During July 2008, although Miss Pallen did contact me, I was unable to respond due to the death of my brother and family matters had to take priority over other concerns. Therefore I will deal only with the letter she sent to me on the 30th July which contained the MPS decision on my request. That decision was given in very few words:

> "The Metropolitan police Service has completed its review and has decided to: **_Uphold the original decision_**"

The reasons given were a little more detailed:

- Searches were conducted at the Central Property Store within the Specialist Crime Directorate.

- Searches were conducted within the original case file and the MRG file – to no avail.

As a result she was able to confirm that Mr Young's original response was correct and the information is not held by the Metropolitan Police Service.

For this reason she was unable to answer the questions I had put in my follow-up complaint. I had asked - 1. Was the wearer Alex? 2. Was the wearer dead or alive at the time?

One very significant point I had made was that in a letter I thought came from Mr Young but was actually from Mr Shankster. I was informed that the photographs were still held on file and Mr Shankster had said "there is information in the files which would be highly likely to cause distress, namely photographs". However, according to him, these were not the seven Pentax Photographs, but of others related to the scene of the incident and could not be issued to me. Really though, I found the explanation very odd, because Alex's body had been taken to hospital before any Forensic investigations were even started, therefore I cannot believe that pictures recording views of lighted candles and scattered clothing would cause distress to anyone.

In my letter written 26th August 2008, I rejected the explanation that all the original photographs taken on the Pentax camera together with all copies were returned to Mr Simpson because they were his personal property. If that was the case, as I informed Miss Pallen:

**"I would be very interested to learn if the murder weapon, the restrictive head device, also the property of Mr Robert Simpson, was returned to him at the same time."**

On 3rd of October 2008 I received an e-mail with the decision:

> *"I have today decided that access cannot be provided to the information you requested as it is not held by the MPS.*
>
> *As standard procedure all property for this investigation has been returned or destroyed."*

That last reason is not true, not one item of Alex's personal property was returned to me, not even the five pound notes and the small coins found in his possession; and it has never been explained why they were not handed to me as the next of kin. Certainly, there was no reason for any of these items to be destroyed.

It seems quite remarkable to me that following Mr Young's disclosure of 'an emotive murder, no one questioned or refuted my referring openly to Alex's death as **murder.** In fact, several officials had themselves freely used the term.

During the course of this correspondence I attended to two other matters; the first dealt with the unfinished business of the improved techniques in DNA. On 28th July 2008, I wrote to Mr Sweeting, the Detective Superintendent dealing with my request, who had a year before promised to further respond to my insistence that the, most recent advances in DNA should be applied to Alex's case.

His reply was received on the 19th September and of course it was another refusal:

> *"Further to my previous correspondence I am sorry to say that all the advice we have taken and have advised you to date, has not altered since our last communication."*

He did offer to arrange a meeting for me with a scientist who would explain the current techniques to me and explain why they could not be taken in this case. I did not take up his offer, as I could have obtained that information from the internet, and also it would have been very expensive to travel to London only to receive negative information. It was obvious to me that all MPS investigations into DNA would still be centred on that tiny tube. All my enquiries about tests on other possible sources of Alex's DNA had been repeatedly ignored.

So there I had it, no further investigations because the importance of the very important items of evidence, the fingerprints, the DNA and the photographs had been reduced to insignificance, quite simply by the convenient mislaying of the real evidence, the documented reports which could have in attested in court before a judge and jury, **if** they had been allowed to reach the Courts. The second matter, very surprisingly had partial success and it was given by the CPS. It was decided by Mr Bennett and I that in the event of me making progress in my enquiries, it would be as well to find out what had happened to Mr Simpson in the interim. I therefore wrote to Mr Ken Mc Donald QC, the Director of Public Prosecutions (DPP) on the 20th March 2008 and using the FOI Act, I asked the following questions:

1. Is Mr Simpson still employed by the CPS? If he is please provide the location of his present office. I am aware that in 1999 he was so employed

2. If he has left the CPS please state whether he is still employed within the Civil Service or with some other public body and give date and details of present employment.

Also - In relation to his involvement with the death of Mr Barrack:

3. Were there any investigations or disciplinary proceedings undertaken into his role in relation to Alex Barrack's death?

4. Has Mr Simpson to your knowledge changed his name

5. If during the intervening years Mr Simpson has died please give details.

The reason for my asking question 3 was that it had been acknowledged by Simpson himself that he participated in bondage and sadomasochism, activities considered by the High Court and the European Court to be offences under the Sexual Offences Acts 1956 and 1967, and open to prosecution and conviction.

Following the usual letter of response I had my reply in the unusually short time of four weeks, from the DPP's 'Principal Private Secretary, Mrs J Rochetti:

> *"I can confirm that Mr Simpson is still employed by the Crown Prosecution Service and he is still known by that name. In confirming these details, I am also confirming that he has not passed away 'in the intervention years'.*

Mrs Rochetti was unable to give any answers to the location of Mr Simpson's office or whether any proceedings or disciplinary action had been taken against him because, under the FIO Act Section 42 (2) and (5) such information was exempt.

So there we have it. The sum total of all the many letters of requests for information made before and after the FIO Act, all invoking the right to justice, was only equal to the CPS conceding half a request. And what did I gain from that half?, only the bitter knowledge that the man I hold responsible for my son's death is still free, still fit and well, still employed by the CPS and probably still enjoying his 'gay' life. So, after leading my son into circumstances which deprived him of his life and his future, the person responsible for his death is allowed to escape any consequences of involvement in several nefarious deeds, and all because he remains under the protection of the law, or the protection of officers of the law.

Where is the justice in that?

# CHAPTER TWENTY SIX

*"Poetic Justice, with her lifted scales, when in nice balance, truth with gold she weighs,"*[142]
But
*"Justice is in one scale and self-preservation is in the other"*[143]

## Part one – The end is near

After all those years of sustained effort to try to achieve the truth for myself and justice for Alex, I had only succeeded in accessing the truth, well most of it anyway. As a result, I was more certain than ever that officials exercising their skills in the art of self-preservation and the manipulation of the justice system denied Alex justice.

In actual fact, although I had quite fiercely attacked the arguments put to me by officials of all the departments involved, not one of them has ever said openly that my data of the facts and circumstances was inaccurate, only my interpretations. Most of their arguments were directed at trying to convince me that there were other interpretations which better fitted the facts and the circumstances, finally resorting to using the FOI Act against me, and by the by use of excessive exemptions, and were able to refuse me information. Had those documents requested been released, they could have allowed me to appeal to the law courts for redress for the 'harm done to me.' This was indubitably a grave misuse of their powers, so with Mr Bennett's assistance I invoked my right to appeal against the MPS misconduct in both the original investigation and the denial of my rights. It is my right as a citizen of a UK, under Article 13 of the European Convention, to have an effective remedy from the British Government.

Such a remedy can at times mean monetary compensation, but when Mr Bennett, just after we had just started to use the FOI Act, suggested I apply to the Criminal Injuries Compensation Authority (CICA), I strongly objected to the idea, it was justice I wanted not money. When he explained that the motive behind such an application was not to obtain compensation

---

[142] The Dunclad
[143] Thomas Jefferson's writings. 1903

for me but a possible means of establishing my right to have information, as the CICA would require the MPS to open the case files for examination. Of course I agreed but I was taken aback though, to be told that if I was granted compensation, then Alex's father would, in accordance with the rules, receive the same amount even if he had not applied for it himself. It didn't seem fair when I had done all the work.

The guide I obtained with the application form gave a very simple explanation of the work of the CICA:

> *"The Criminal Injuries Compensation Authority Scheme allows financial awards to be made following the death of a close relative as the result of a violent crime".*

The application form itself, although detailed was not difficult, it was just a question of filling in the date and place of the incident, name of police station officers dealing with incident, the crime reference number and the name of the person who caused the injury. Unfortunately, there was the attached condition that the CICA did not deal with claims for injuries received after more than two years, and this snag had to be overcome as I was submitting a claim in November 2007, for an incident which happened in 1996.

Mr Bennett though, had means of getting round that obstacle, in his supporting letter to the IPCC dated 16 November 2007, he pointed out that I could not claim compensation until I had strong proof that Alex's death was due to a criminal act, and that was not available until the Police admitted that they had investigated a homicide. This admission was not made until the MPS refused to disclose information under the FOI Act on the grounds, stated openly in an official letter, that 'an emotive murder such as this one had to be conducted under strict secrecy', and from then on implicitly referred to Alex Barrack's death as a murder.

Mr Bennett therefore suggested to the IPCC, that the 20<sup>th</sup> April 2007 should be the correct date from which to start the two year restriction in my case, because it was then that I received positive proof that Alex had been unlawfully killed by a criminal action, and not as the result of a tragic accident, as previously claimed by the police. This suggestion was obviously accepted as the next letter indicated the case was progressing.

I feel it is not necessary to describe fully the details of the information requested as the reader is already well acquainted with all the facts of the case, passed to the CICA, therefore I will just outline the procedure which followed.

We had been advised that an application to the CICA was likely to be a prolonged process, and so it proved to be. Over the next year I received three requests for additional information, mainly relating to the documents in which I claimed indicated the grave mismanagement of investigations by the police, the CPS and the coroner.

It was not until $2^{nd}$ September 2008 that I had definite news of the progress being made. This was when that the Decision Maker, who had looked at my case, requested copies of the letters received by me from the police in April and October 2007. These letters dealt with the exemptions used for the refusing to disclose information, including the one referring to the emotive murder and my responses.

On November $28^{th}$ 2008, the final decision was made, and yes, it was another refusal:

> *"Having given careful consideration to all the information sent to the Authority and to the reports we have obtained from the police and other relevant authorities, I regret that I am unable to make an award under this scheme".*

The reason he gave was that the evidence did not show that Alex's death was directly attributable to a criminal injury, but rather the result of an unfortunate accidental injury. I was deeply upset by this decision, not because I had been refused compensation, but on what he had based his decision:

> *"This is based on the coroner's findings of accidental death and the police information which states that there was no evidence that William's death was the result of a criminal act".*

Every time the coroner's verdict was invoked to maintain there was no crime, a telling fact was completely ignored, which was, that a Justice of the High Court had considered that there was enough evidence of an unsafe inquest verdict, to allow me an appeal to the High Court for a second inquest.

Perhaps I could have accepted this failed claim more philosophically if the decision had been based on the more plausible reason, 'insufficient evidence' perhaps, because in 2008 there was so much of it missing, but to base it on the coroner's verdict which I tried for years to have overturned in a court of law, was a bitter pill to swallow. I felt insulted that the Decision Maker even considered that I would accept that decision, when he had totally ignored the fact, that the MPS had not only seriously delayed admitting that Alex's death was investigated as a murder, but also that the IPCC would have considered that it was against police ethics to have conducted their enquiries in strict secrecy, and that even in 1996, feeding false information to the family was not only misconduct, but also constituted a perversion of the course of justice.

I was just about at the end of my endurance, when once again my spirits were uplifted. Mr Bennett proposed I take yet another course of action, that I take my case to the Independent Police Complaints Commission (IPCC).

**Part two -** *"And differing judgements serve but to declare.*
*That truth lies somewhere, if we knew but where"[144].*

The Independent Police Complaints Commission is, reputedly, completely independent of the police when it is dealing with complaints about police behaviour, which do not conform to Police Standards of Professional Behaviour. I was about to find out for myself just how independent this Commission was.

Letters to the Public Access Office under the FOI Act had been applications for information, and of course, all had been refused. Therefore Mr Bennett considered that in this, I had sufficient grounds to complain to the IPCC about the misconduct and the breaching of procedures by the MPS. On the

---

[144] William Cowper – Hope (1782)

9th September 2008 I wrote a formal letter to Mr Bennett requesting his assistance in the preparation and presentation of the complaint which I intended to send to the IPCC.

Two days later the Mr Bennett sent a letter to the Director of the IPCC advising him that he was representing me in my complaint of police misconduct. What follows now is an account of what happened after sending the formal appeal to the IPCC. I have based this account mainly on my the correspondence with Inspector McKelvie, who was appointed the Investigating Officer by the IPCC, because it covers all the issues mentioned in my appeal, and avoids unnecessary repetition of the extraordinarily detailed reasons given for refusing my appeal.

Mr Bennett listed three areas of complaints which had adversely affected my FOI applications.

> *"Complaints of Mrs Doris Barrack re Metropolitan Police misconduct/breached procedures over the death of her son on May 4th 1996.*
>
> 1. *Loss of evidence (photos).*
> 2. *Failure to organise new DNA testing and failure to answer correspondence.*
> 3. *Continuing cover-up of vital evidence despite this being a case of murder or causing death by negligent manslaughter.*

This last point literally covered everything else in the investigations which gave me cause for complaint.

By the 19th of November Mr Bennett received acknowledgement letter which he forwarded to me. The letter advised me that the complaint had been forwarded to the Directorate of Professional Standards (DPS) of the Metropolitan Police for their consideration. This seemed very odd to me that I complain about the police to an independent body, who then, hand my complaint to the same police body for 'their consideration.' In my earlier agreement to the DPS being contacted, I was under the impression it was merely to inform them that a complaint had been made, I had not expected

311

that it would be the MPS who would be in control and decide whether or not I had a case.

Within a week I had a telephone from Inspector McKelvie of the MPS Directorate of Professional Standards. He was very charming and sympathetic when he questioned me about my son's 'tragic death'. But recalling that Mr Ensor of York CPS had been just as courteous and sympathetic, but because the results from that interview had proved to be so negative, I was guarded in my replies to Mr McKelvie. Mistrust certainly breeds more distrust.

Inspector McKelvie followed his phone call with an e-mail in which he requested Alex's date of birth, details of the police officers involved and the dates of the incidents. As further indication of the shallowness of all the police enquiries and research into my case, he informed me he had not managed to find any records in the system of any previous complaints. In addition he reminded me that there was a two year limit to making a complaint, and required me to explain why I had waited so long before taking action. I began to wonder if he had actually read Mr Bennett's official complaint in which he had stated quite clearly, that I had not known for certain that I had grounds for a complaint until 2007.

I lost no time in replying to, and in reminding Inspector McKelvie that I had sent numerous letters of complaint to, and had received replies from the MPS Police Commissioners Secretariat. I suggested that it would help him if he located the very long letter I had sent to Sir John Stevens, the then Commissioner of Police, which had resulted in the MRG Review being involved. I also referred him to Mr Bennett's letter and his explanation for the delay in my complaining officially to the IPCC.

Mr Bennett and I both had a very quick decision from Inspector Mc Kelvie, which was dated 10th of December 2008, but not received until the 22nd just before Christmas. It was to advise me that he would not allow the appeal and enclosed a long list of his findings on which he had based his decision, these I will leave for the moment. Altogether it was bad timing on his part to send such a letter during the season of good will, and certainly, a most unwelcome gift and one I was not prepared to accept submissively.

312

Nor was Mr Bennett who sent a very prompt letter to the Director of the IPCC appealing against Mr McKelvie's findings on the following grounds:

(a) I had not been given adequate information about the investigation now that it is complete
(b) I had good reasons to disagree with the findings of the investigation
(c) I had reason to disagree with the action proposed. (appeal refused).

On the 24th April I received the answer to this appeal from Erik Waitt, Casework Manager, who made it quite clear he was only dealing with the complaint against the inadequacy of Mr McKelvie's investigation and not of any other circumstances of the case:

*"I have upheld your appeal because the provision of information in relation to the finding was not sufficient.*

*However no further action is deemed necessary in respect of this complaint"*

Putting this in my more simple terms, I understood this to mean that although Mr McKelvie's research and findings were correct, he had not explained them adequately to me. However, there was nothing I could do about that particular appeal, because the letter ended, *"This decision is final."* There was little joy for me in that very minor success, I was no nearer getting the impartial inquiry I was seeking.

**Part 3 -** *The scales of justice are finally tipped against me.*

I return now to Inspector McKelvies appeal findings which were upheld by the IPCC, and although my appeal against his inadequate information was allowed on very limited grounds, the IPCC final decision was based on his entire account. I am not going attempt to cover the findings in full as they comprise nine pages of the details of the investigations made by the Directorate of Professional Standards all of which, apart from one item mentioned, were endorsed by the IPCC. Although the appeal deals with each of my complaints separately, each is accompanied by a mass of difficult and tedious detail. This, I feel, is not necessary to inflict on a reader; instead I will take a short cut.

The first of the IPCC appeal findings dealt with the question **'are the findings of the appeal appropriate?'** Quite obviously they were considered to be appropriate By Mr Waitt, in as much as the IO, Mr McKelvie covered just about every aspect of each complaint he could, constantly referring back to the various issues in my previous volume of correspondence, not really dealing with the points I was making, but agreeing with the negativity of the replies given by the MPS in repudiating my complaints. This included the investigations of the Serious Crime Group (ex-MRG). An excessive explanation was given for each complaint, but I cannot agree with their inadequate conclusions which were so obviously based on other officers' earlier opinions which I had already rejected. Also I noticed this lengthy document, was produced by the IPCC in a relatively short time. Relative that is, to the more extended time spent on each single complaint by various MPS Sections over the years.

The second finding concurred with the IO's excuse for the loss of the photo evidence. The IO claimed that following the CPS decision and the coroner's verdict, the police **could** no longer progress the matter as a murder investigation, and that policy dictated the return of photos and negatives to the owner. Also, in accordance with police policy and procedure, the negatives were not copied by the police, and if it had been necessary to show the photographs to me, the IO would have done so.

I disagree that that police could not continue the investigation, the police are not entirely bound by a coroner's verdict, it is not a rule of law, they can and often do, carry on with their enquiries, when in their opinion, the inquest verdict is not appropriate to the evidence. Mr Bennett can personally vouch for this occurring.

Most certainly, I can't accept that there were no copies made of the photos. Surely the CPS and other justice officials needed to have copies of the photos, and that includes the Director of Public Prosecutions, who ordered the CPS not to prosecute. Or does this mean that the originals were passed from department to department, if so, they must have been a bit dog-eared. Or is it the case that the police showed them only to selected officials, Dr

Heath for example, but apparently not the coroner? Therefore, it was not deemed necessary to make additional copies. Actually, my view is that it is more likely that if copies were not made, it was because they already knew, indeed must have known, the identity of the 'body'[145] in the photos. If it was not of Alex, then the authorities preferred as few people as possible to know the identity of the individual, but for their own ends and not for my good or that of the people and certainly not for the good of course of justice.

**The IPCC decision was that none of the above complaints could be substantiated.**

When the issue of **advanced DNA testing** was considered by Mr Mc Kelvie, the Investigating Officer, and Mr Waitt of the IPPC, it was decided that it was not a police conduct matter and therefore could not be considered by the DPS. Notwithstanding, the IO had discussed the matter in his report, and he maintained that even if new DNA testing did identify that Alex had worn the device, it would still not warrant a review of Alex's death with a view to new investigation.

Also, it would appear that the IO was attempting to manage my expectations of what my pursuit of further DNA testing might achieve, which to the IPCC, does not appear unreasonable in the circumstances. The IO had directed Mrs Barrack to more appropriate avenues to pursue about these matters. I am not sure what was meant by the term, the IO's continued management of my expectations, and why it was not unreasonable of him to do so, or why it was not unreasonable for me to continue my pursuit for further DNA analysis. I would have thought that it would be inconvenient for the MPS if in pursuing for new DNA testing and it proved positive the photo would provide real evidence that Alex had worn the mask. Because then Simpson's claim that he did not do so would be demolished, and show that the coroner's verdict of accidental death was badly flawed. This could result in a new inquest being granted and a more fitting verdict of an unlawful killing by murder or by negligent manslaughter. It would also give me grounds for requesting a new police inquiry and to challenge the CPS non-prosecution decision.

---

[145] Described so by Dr Heath

Furthermore, in my opinion the 'no further avenue for me to take' was nonsense I was not in apposition to seek a new independent source of testing without considerable funding. Only the MPS was in a position to order further analysis under the latest techniques but had refused. It did not seem feasible to me either, that improved DNA could only be scientifically applied to the limited elements of DNA found in the small tube. Especially so, because, it has been made quite clear to me that the main consideration of the MPS was its budget, but surely cost should not be allowed to impair the course of justice. Then perhaps here too, it was more convenient and possibly less embarrassing not to know whose DNA was actually present. I might add that I do not consider it feasible that the larger area of the inner surface of the head device had not been forensically examined as a matter of routine.

**The IPCC decided that there was no substantiated misconduct in my complaint.**

The next item on the list was with my complaint of a **continuing cover-up of vital evidence,** despite the fact that it was a crime of murder, or negligent manslaughter. Most of the findings constituted an exercise to excuse the police cover-up of a broad spectrum of the proceedings complained of, and well discussed by me throughout the book. The MRG Report was cited as upholding the police view that that there was no conspiracy. But that does not wash with me, no matter how many excuses the police come up with, I won't accept that their *modus operandi* was anything other than a cover-up for something detrimental to the reputation of some law enforcement officials, the evidence is there to prove my claim.

Interestingly, in the course of exonerating the police little snippets of information and misinformation were slipped in:

Although the IPCC agreed with Mr McKelvie's possible explanation that sensitive information was withheld to protect me from some of the more upsetting aspects Alex's death, nothing could be proved one way or the other. Very conveniently, **the age of the case meant** that there would not be a realistic prospect of achieving the standard of evidence needed to prove that there was misconduct on the part of the officers concerned.

It was also possible that the misinformation given was due to the initial confusion over the cause of the death, **however, this cannot be proved from the evidence available.** On the contrary, there was no confusion and there is evidence available to prove that, because I hold real evidence in a copy of the computer data sent to Gainsborough police by Limehouse Police ten days after Alex's death. It states that a post-mortem had been held and death was from natural causes. It is nonsense to claim that concern for my sensitivity was the reason the truth was kept from me when the Senior Investigating Officer had no compunction whatsoever in allowing me to face an inquest eight months later, ill-prepared to learn the shocking truth that Alex's death was due to a sadomasochistic ritual. It also begs the question what happened to the first autopsy report which was once in existence but is now missing. At the end of this two page unjustified exoneration of police conduct I was not surprised by the conclusion arrived at by Mr Waitt, that **The IPCC were satisfied that the investigation and findings were appropriate.** They were <u>conveniently</u> satisfied I would say, I certainly was not.

On the question **'Are the forces proposed actions following the IPCC investigation adequate?** The IPCC concurred with Mr McKelvie's finding that there was no case to answer against any officer or MPS staff within the complaint investigation and no further action was warranted. This left me wondering why I had wasted so much time and effect to prove that there was and why it was so necessary for the MPS to have spent so much time and expense in proving that there was not

When it came to the question- **was adequate information provided to me following the investigation of my complaint?** - it was considered by the IPCC that for the majority of my complaints there was, therefore - **no further information was required to be provided** especially when so much of the information provided was largely irrelevant.

The last question asked – **Are there any points raised by the complainant outside what the IPCC could consider?** Briefly the IPCC referred to two matters I had raised but had not made formal complaint and they were that the Senior Investigating officer was homosexual and that the police had failed to supply photographs to the coroner. I was very surprised that it was

317

suggested that if I wanted these two matters to be considered I should submit new complaints.

The result of these nine pages of convoluted explanation and exonerations was that on the basis of all their findings, **the IPCC decided to uphold Mr. McKelvies appeal, not mine**.

It took me some time to figure out where I actually stood, but eventually realised that although I had lost that case I had been offered an opportunity to make two further complaints. To be honest, I was rather reluctant to take up either point but it was one more step I felt I had to take.

So far, all the many complaints made by me had been dealt with piecemeal by the MPS in only considering the police role in Alex's case. The adverse effects of other departmental decisions had on police investigative processes, especially those of the Pathologist, the CPS and the coroner, had largely been ignored. In another attempt to have the whole case opened up to an in-depth investigation, Mr Bennett made two further complaints to the IPCC on my behalf. These were dealt with as a second appeal by the IPCC

1. Allowing a known homosexual to investigate my son's death
2. Failing to supply photographs to the coroner re the death of my son.

Number one complaint refers to DCI Baff but it cannot, for obvious reasons, be a criticism of his sexuality. It refers to the close profession association which he and other officers had with Mr Simpson. Mr Simpson was an admitted sadomasochist and I questioned if it was right for DCI Baff to investigate a suspicious death in the home of a fellow homosexual, who indulged in sadomasochistic practices with obvious risks to health and life. Practices which were crimes under the Offences against the Person Acts, and which had also been condemned by the High Court and the European Court and were open to prosecution and conviction.

Number two complaint was raised because I have never had it confirmed officially that the coroner had been issued with copies of Mr Simpson's photographs, when he had made no reference to this important evidence during the inquest. Indeed, he cut short Dr Heath's explanation of their importance to his autopsy findings.

In this new complaint I followed the usual procedure, of advising the Professional Standards Department of my intention and completing the official form of complaint to the IPCC, then receiving their usual acknowledgement, informing me that the complaint had been passed to the New Complaints Team on the 20th May 2009. I was outraged to read a sentence that was really admonishing in tone:

> *"Our staff is directly involved in investigating the most serious matters such as police shootings and deaths in custody .Other cases that do not meet the threshold for independent investigation are investigated by the police force involved."*

Although I don't disagree with the policy of protecting the police in such difficult situations, it implied I was out of line because my son's death was in a lower category and not as important as one where the legal position of the police was involved, and a complaint such as mine, should have been referred to a lower level of the IPCC and not to this special team. I wondered if the team consider me a nuisance, and that thought was quite pleasing.

However on the 27th July I received a letter from the Directorate of Professional Standards assuring me that the Directorate take it very seriously when a member of the public complains about one of their officers, and do everything in their power to deal with the complaint. I was not at all reassured by this promise because I knew that in the end the IPCC would accept the advice of the DPS, and so it proved to be the case. Timed to arrive just before Christmas, on the 18th December 2009, I received the letter containing the IPCC ultimate judgement on my complaints

A Patricia Napier, Case Manager, wrote this letter. It started by reminding me that the police have a duty to investigate or resolve locally all complaints that they record. **But,** if the incident took place more that twelve months before "the police force may ask us to agree that they dispense with the complaint". If then the dispensation was granted, no further investigation would be necessary.

The police had indeed applied for such a dispensation on the grounds that my complaint was out of time. Even though I had been advised that the last

319

two matters raised constituted new complaints, that advice did not imply "that they would not be capable of investigation after such a long time."

In respect of my complaint against DCI Baff being allowed to investigate Alex's death, I was informed that it was a matter of police conduct and operational policing which were not covered by the guidelines of the IPCC. Even if the family had raised these concerns earlier, it would not have guaranteed that these complaints would have been passed to someone else to deal with.

In dealing with my complaint that DCI Baff had failed to a provide a list of the photographs to me, M/S. Napier offered |Mr Waitt explanation that the police were under no obligation to supply me with any of the photographs and therefore the it did not constitute a misconduct matter. I don't agree with the next statement that asking me to view the photos would not have helped with the investigation. Because I could have attested that they were or were not of Alex and then it would not have been necessary for me to ask to see copies later. Viewing the photos would have settled a very disturbing question constantly worrying me - were they of Alex?

One of the snippets of useful information I mentioned before, was given as the result of my querying why the police did not appear to have provided the coroner with an itemized list of photographs for the inquest. From M/s Napier I learned that that it was the Crown Prosecution Service who decided what evidence the coroner should have and it was rather a matter for the coroner to decide what documents he should use at the inquest.

Now that was news to me, because all along I have assumed that the police decided on what evidence the coroner received. After all it was the coroner who ordered the inquest and decided from the autopsy report and the report made to him by the police, that further investigations were to be made, and that would be <u>before</u> the CPS would normally be involved. This was how I referred to the matter in my correspondence concerning the coroner's evidence and verdict, but no one corrected me.

In winding up the decision M/s Napier told me that no obvious cases of misconduct had been identified and in the face of that my complaints did not come under the definition of a complaint as defined in s12 of the Police

Reform Act 2002. Yet my complaints referred to misconduct in 1996/7. I wonder what the ruling was before the Police Reform Act 2002.

M/s Napier then said that in normal practice the complaint would have been recorded and investigated. *"However this task would be difficult at best, given that most of the paperwork and evidence of the decision would by now have been destroyed."* Further, she stated, that because of the length of time, and particularly since the case was reviewed by the MRG in 2005, it would be disproportionate to expect the police to carry out a reinvestigation now. I wonder just when did all this paper work disappeared, before or after the MRG Review, and why was so much of the paperwork destroyed when the case was not closed but was filed as an unsolved case? I would have thought that it was more in keeping with procedure, as has been followed in much earlier unsolved cases, that all documentary evidence should have been retained, including the photographs, pending new evidence coming to light and the case being reopened.

Nevertheless the above were the reasons why the IPCC, my last chance to appeal, decided to grant the dispensation and the police did not have to investigate the matter further as, **"This decision is final."**

And this is where justice fell flat on its face.

# CONCLUSIONS

*Justice is not blind, she is very clear sighted,*
*but men can apply a blindfold when it suits them*

**All doors to the High Court are locked against me - I close my file and wait for the adjudication of the people.**

That last chapter brings to and end my account of the death of my son Alex and my interpretations of the events, which lead me into a long frustrating search to have truth for myself and more importantly justice for Alex. I realise that in one way I have failed, but in another way I have been successful, because I have ensured that his case and his name did not slide into the obscurity that the Metropolitan Police and the Crown Prosecution Service, ably assisted by the coroner, would have preferred.

I very much hope that I have shown how the Justice System can fail the ordinary citizen, when its officials who are engaged to administer the law on behalf of the Crown, with fairness and impartiality, ignore or mismanage that responsibility.

I was once asked, "Do you hate the man who robbed you of your son?" I thought about that very carefully before deciding that I did not, but replied "No I don't hate him, but I despise him for his lack of moral courage in failing to accept his responsibility for Alex's death – but – I despise even more, those officials of the justice system who allowed him to do so."

Having said that, I would not like to think that I have given the impression that I am totally anti- police, because that is not the case. In my nursing career I had very good relations with the police in Shropshire for many years. Later in Lincolnshire, following my son's death, and especially Gainsborough Police, who showed me great kindness when confirming Alex's death, and as did the Lincoln Coroners Officer, who willingly provided me with very useful information to use in my research.

I truest too, that I **have** succeeded in my original intention to alert the public to situations where officials engaged in law enforcement, for their own ends, can enmesh ordinary citizens in a net of subterfuge and

322

conspiracy, interfering in the course of justice and denying relatives and victims of violence, their right to a just, fair and impartial hearing in a court of law.

It has been for me a long, harrowing experience, and after writing this book, I am wondering where on earth I found the stamina and tenacity to stand up, almost entirely alone and without funding, against a legion of trained lawyers backed by Treasury funding and the full powers of the law.

It would be most rewarding for me, if any family, who in future may have to face the ordeal of a police investigation and a coroners inquest, will profit from my experience, and make quite certain that they are fully informed on coroner's court procedures and have qualified legal representation. To do this, well before the date when they may have to undergo the shattering experience of an inquest, to be held over a loved one's sudden death. Whether that inquest arises from criminal action, or an accident from any cause, they should bear in mind, that a coroner's verdict can make all the difference to the police continuing their investigations into a case, or closing it. In some types of accident, a coroner's verdict can also affect the level of compensation awarded.

If my experience can help those engaged in persuading the Government to alter the law on legal aid for families facing the ordeal of an inquest, and make it possible for every victim's family, irrespective of status and income, to have qualified legal representation in a coroner's court. And if this will make certain that the coroner respects the rights of both victim and family, then, I will consider that it was worthwhile sacrificing my best retirement years for such a cause.

I now close my file on the Alex Barrack case, and leave it to the readers to make their own judgement on the merit of my arguments. . One last word though; many fine phrases have been written about justice, but there is one very inspiring quotation which in my younger days greatly moved me, but today, I view it with justifiable cynicism:

*"It is of fundamental importance that justice should not only be done, but should manifestly and undoubtedly be seen to be done."*[146]

---

[146] Hewart - Rex v Sussex Justices 9 11.23

Unfortunately, I was never allowed to see justice being done, the justice authorities themselves made sure of that.

Justice

A Can of Worms

# CLOSURE – FOR ALEX
## Alex RIP

1968 - 1996

*'...Move along these shades. In gentleness of heart;*
*with gentle hand touch - for there is spirit in the woods...'[147]*

When Alex died so suddenly it is so hard to describe the grief of having a son, so much younger than myself, leave this world before me. That was hard enough to bear, but learning of the unseemly circumstances of his death, supposedly from heart failure, so graphically described by DS Bathie, was doubly wounding. It seemed so unfair to me that having such a troubled life, he should loose it with so little dignity. He really deserved to be remembered for the person he was, for the courage, he has shown in facing and overcoming the problems in his short life. I wanted him to be remembered for that, and I resolved in those early days, that somehow I would restore his dignity.

This resolution become stronger when I learned the truth about his death, and that it was not an act of nature, but a cruel act of a man that had robbed him of his life and his future. But, how I was to restore his dignity and obliterate the memory of his lying alone and still in a cold chamber of a mortuary for seven months, I had no real idea. Not until I heard about the Woodland Trust, an organisation dedicated to the purchase and preservation of the country's diminishing woodland. At first I thought of a tree, a tall slim birch I thought would suit Alex best, so visited the Trust's Head Quarters near Grantham to arrange to dedicate one tree. I soon changed my mind when I learned that I could have an acre of woodland dedicated in perpetuity to Alex's memory, for a much larger donation. I decided at once, Alex should have an acre of woodland, and rest among trees where, in times when he was downhearted, he had been soothed and

---

[147] William Wordsworth – used by the Woodland Trust

comforted by their tranquillity. I immediately arranged for the Trust to start the quite lengthy process of selecting suitable areas.

This arrangement took place shortly before Alex's quiet, family funeral and cremation, on the 13th of December 1996; it was a Catholic service, not a mass, which I knew Alex would have preferred. When we left the crematorium it was some comfort to me to know that all the scarring of his life and death was being removed. On 20th December I collected his ashes, but I was devastated to find that the container they were in was a dreadful purple colour, roughly sarcophagus in shape, and so ugly. I had arranged with my parish priest to have Alex's ashes in church until the Woodland Trust completed the arrangements. Father Kevin took one look at the casket and exclaimed "Oh my dear Doris this won't do at all. Leave it with me." I left the church in tears as I thought he meant the casket was too ugly to have in the Sacristy.

I went early to Church for the Christmas Eve Virgil Mass, to avoid the later crowd. I felt so alone and miserable because Alex had gone, and there was no sign of the container. Father Kevin aroused me from my misery, saying "Come with me" and I followed him to the foot of the altar and he pointed to beautiful wooden casket placed near the altar and said, "Alex's ashes are in there now." It was a moment of grace for Alex and me, and a wonderful gesture on Father Kevin's part, and it made Christmas more bearable. My special thanks went to Cliff Bradley, a town undertaker, to whom Father Kevin had taken Alex's ashes in that ugly container. Mr Bradley knew how such dreadful object would add to a parent's grief and transferred Alex's ashes into the polished wooden casket.

Alex's ashes lay near the altar throughout the Christmas and the Easter festivals until Pentecost was over. Then when the acre of land I had selected was ready for the dedication, I took Alex home to spend a last night in his own room before taking him to his final resting place that I had chosen for him.

This was an area in Wormley Wood in Hertfordshire, because it was in a county where Alex had spent so many happy days with Maureen and Ken. It was also an area of native trees and plants, and of Special Scientific Interest, with a history going back to Roman times, yet not too far from modern civilisation. There was a footpath running along the edge of his grove and aircraft flying overhead, so it was ideally suitable for Alex's memorial.

In early June, Alex's father and a small group of friends joined me in a little
ceremony to pay tribute to Alex's life and to listen to music which Alex had known and loved in his young years, while Bill, his father, and I scattered his ashes and paid our own tribute to our son. We completed the day with a picnic nearby, where his friends reminisced about Alex's life in London and his friendship. It was so good to hear how they valued his friendship and support, and especially his 'wicked sense of humour.' I could see Bill was deeply moved by the expressions of affections for his son and so was I.

When Bill and the friends had departed I went back to what had been officially designated as Barrack Grove, but which I call Alex's little acre'. There I stood on a quiet June evening and felt that I had given Alex the memorial he deserved. I said to him "There you are Alex, your spirit is now with its creator and your body is a part of his creation, you can rest in peace my son". Then I turned away and left Alex to the peaceful tranquillity which had eluded him in life. As I walked to my car I felt a deep sense of contentment, knowing that I had restored his dignity. That sense of contentment stayed with me and was to support me through the long crusade I was to undertake.

William Alexander Barrack
Son of Doris and Bill
Rest in peace.